THE SHAMAN'S GENESIS
BOOK 4 OF THE SHAMANIC MYSTERIES

Norman W. Wilson PhD

THE SHAMAN'S GENESIS
BOOK 4 OF THE SHAMANIC MYSTERIES

A ZADKIEL PUBLISHING PAPERBACK

© Copyright 2019
Norman W. Wilson PhD

The right of Norman W. Wilson to be identified as author and channel of this work has been asserted by him in accordance with the Copyright, Designs and Patents Act 1988.

All Rights Reserved

No reproduction, copy or transmission of the publication may be made without written permission.

No paragraph of this publication may be reproduced, copied or transmitted save with the written permission of the publisher, or in accordance with the provisions of the Copyright Act 1956 (as amended).

Any person who does any unauthorised act in relation to this publication may be liable to criminal prosecution and civil claims for damages.

ISBN: 978-1-78695-209-7

Zadkiel Publishing
An Imprint of Fiction4All
www.fiction4all.com

This Edition
Published 2019

Cover Design:

PUBLISHER'S NOTE

FOOTNOTES – references [1] etc are included at the end of the relevant chapter where they occur.

CHAPTER ONE

She'd been sent by the Network to cover something ordinarily done by a film crew. She resented being told to take this assignment—an assignment for an underling. It was painfully clear they had found her replacement. She would show them! She was not through by a long shot.

A crowd had gathered at the Union, a massive *Ecole des Beaux-Arts* style complex. They had come to get a look at the panoplied behemoth with its underbelly illuminated with glowing blue lights. Those who came to see this mystery train viewed it with whispered awe. Those on the train did not see the Union's huge pillared front entrance nor its Great Hall with its high vaulted ceiling and two-toned marble floors. Nor did they stare at the city names carved around the perimeter of the upper walls that provided the throngs of visitors a Canadian geography lesson. The CN Tower that surpasses the Seattle Space Needle in height did not reflect down upon any personage from the train.

Some of those present speculated about the meaning of the seal of the great bald eagle on each car. They spoke in hushed whispers, afraid that someone on board would hear them. She directed her cameraman to pan the crowd. She quizzed some of those there, asking them what they thought. Giving them their few minutes of fame. Some thought the blue-white moon through which the eagle was flying held the key to the meaning. Several expressed concern that it was an evil thing especially since all the windows were blackened. Many thought it was a doom's day weapon. They waited. Finally tiring, the crowd and the media dispersed. However, the ever-persistent darling of Toronto TV, anchor, and reporter, Patricia Livingston did not. The darling of the nightly news? Ha! She had heard the rumors. The station had hired a much younger woman—a kid really, just out of college—a blond with big breasts and a toothy smile. The word that the Station was grooming this kid as an anchor was a warning. Not so subtle either. The evening news was her slot. "Well, girl! Get your butt in motion. The evening news still belongs to me."

Her presence had nearly created a story. She was the only anchor there. Knowingly, probably more by instinct, she had her cameraman drop her off around a corner of the massive railroad station. No need to tip the others that she thought there might be a story here. She cut through the Union and ducked out a side door to the loading area.

She dismissed the idea that this left-over relic of the Cold War was a prop for a movie. There would have been a media promo for that and that she would have known. She discounted the idea that it was a doom's day weapon because someone in government always leaked such things. And yesterday hadn't she lunched with the Under Secretary? Surely he would have said something, at least hinted that something was going on. The notion that the train belonged to a rock star didn't equate either. With all the blogs available someone would have written about it and that would have brought out a different crowd. There was someone who could generate this much mystery—the shaman. He'd made all the papers and news broadcasts a few months back. She had done a piece on him for the evening news. She would wait. And see!

The train had departed from Montreal. All tracks had been cleared for its speedy trip to Toronto. That much she knew. That meant the Canadian Railroad and most likely someone high up in government had to be involved. Patricia Livingston knew the when and the where. What she wanted to know was the who and the why. She intended to find out the answer to both.

She told her cameraman to bring back some food, a small digital camcorder, and a camera with a good telephoto lens. She hoped he did what he was told. He could be such a dip at times. It was going to be a long night. Once he had returned she dismissed him for the night. Nestled among some shipping crates, she settled in for the duration, grateful that she had remembered to bring her backpack from the van. A cough a couple of crates away reminded her that she was not in the safest of places. Quietly she opened her backpack and retrieved the Taser she always carried, a leftover memento from an affair with a private investigator. She watched as several large eighteen wheelers pulled up along the loading dock. She was impressed by the men's ant-like precision as they unloaded the trucks. This went on most of the night. Several times she caught herself dozing. The thought of the blond bimbo giving the nightly news brought her into sharp focus. They didn't fool her with their "Patricia is on assignment" crap.

Morning sunlight was welcome. Quickly leaving her hiding place, Patricia Livingston went into the Union, found a restroom, relieved herself, freshened her makeup, wiped her teeth with a tissue, popped a mint, and returned to her watch. The cameraman had returned with a Danish and hot coffee. She dismissed him without even saying thank you. "What a bitch," he thought as he walked away. "Maybe the rumors are true. Might not be so bad working with someone else."

Sipping black coffee from a Styrofoam, she watched as a stretch limo rolled up to the loading dock. Like the train, it had a bald eagle flying through a bluish moon painted on its side. "Now I'll see who's who," Patricia Livingston thought as she nibbled the Danish.

A large man, dressed in a light blue chauffeur's uniform stepped out of the limo and opened its side doors. She thought she recognized him. His name was Samuel, a member of a group called *The Brothers*. If her hunch was correct she now knew who was involved. Nine men, all dressed in light blue blazers and gray slacks, and a woman emerged. Samuel slid back in behind the wheel and drove off. "Something's not quite right. Maybe I'm wrong," Patricia Livingston thought. "The woman seems so out of place. I don't remember seeing her at Karuna House."

The woman's long blond hair was disheveled. Piled on top of her head, it appeared to be ready to tumble down at any minute. Her décolletage revealed the absence of a bra. She took her time walking across the cement dock to the train. Her stiletto heels clicked a syncopated rhythmic beat with the sway of her hips. She wasn't old. But even from where Patricia Livingston watched, you could tell she had been around the block more than a few times. The nine men walked a respectful distance, behind her, their hands folded in front of them, and their head slightly bowed, monk-like. "Wonder if they keep their heads lowered so they get a better view of the woman's swaying hips," Patricia Livingston thought, "Wonder where the limo went? Maybe to pick *him* up."

Totally alert. Tense! She waited. And waited. "I sure could use a scotch and soda." She'd taken to having a drink during the day, and especially before show time. It seemed to ease her pain, calm her. The coffee and Danish hadn't agreed with her. She fished around in her purse, found a package of Tums. Ate three. "Where is he? I'm sure those men are The Brothers and where they are *he* is not far behind." She knew that two of their number was in prison for murder. Her heart raced as she waited for the stretch limo to return. "Shit! Maybe he's already on that damn train," she muttered. "Need to get —,"

She stopped her thought. She spotted it, moving slowly toward the loading dock. Seeing the limo brought her to rapt attention. It eased to a stop. "Ha! There's the Indian. *He* must be in the limo. You don't see one without the other," Patricia Livingston mused. She caught the flash of light reflected from the guns he always wore. He leaned into an open window of the limo. "Always the protector," she thought as she snapped more pictures.

Isha stepped out of the limo, briefly spoke to the Indian, and waited. Her long blue-black hair is radiant. Patricia Livingston recognized her as the mystery woman at a lecture she had attended at Karuna House. Then *he* came out.

"My god!" Patricia Livingston exhaled. She hadn't realized she had been holding her breath. "He's more handsome than ever. Hmm. What I wouldn't give to—," Their movement cut her thought short.

Because they were in the open, Running-water hurriedly ushered the woman and man onto the train. At the top step, Running-water turned. Looked out over the area, slowly surveying the shadows along the large crates. He thought he had caught a glimpse of something shiny. He boarded the train. His hesitation did not escape the ever watchful and curious Patricia Livingston. "Man! He is so good. Nearly caught me. Must remember to use a non-reflective lens."

She watched the stretch limo drive off. Since she wasn't sure how she would get on that train, she waited. She was good at waiting. An armed guard stepped from around the corner of the dock. She needed a diversion to get by him.

CHAPTER TWO

Once he had Adam settled in his private car, Running-water took Isha to their compartment. It took up a full third of the next car. Space was left for an open sitting area, and then another large compartment which had been assigned to Samuel and Julie. The next two cars were Pullmans and that's where he assigned the remaining nine men of the group called The Brothers. Next came the dining car and lounge. In front of that was the cook's car and passenger only car. It was there that he met Jarrod, a Canadian Railroad official.

Jarrod had boarded the train at Montreal and he was to assist in facilitating the inspection of the freight cars. Because he was in uniform, Running-water didn't request identification. Jarrod, a stocky man in his early fifties, was provided a copy of the lading and manifest. He noted that car seven was located at the end of Adam's private car. There were hundreds of pages listing thousands of items. Each page was identified by car number, and each contained a numbered list of the contents and a diagram of where each box was placed on any given car. He had to hand it to them for their efficiency. Made his job easier, much easier to locate what he was looking for. The contents of car seven held his attention. Quickly he scanned down the list. His hands quivered causing the manifest to shake. "Shit!" he thought, "nearly a thousand boxes." He looked for numbered boxes marked family *and personal*. He was told there would be a hundred such boxes. He was to find out exactly where in car seven they were stacked.

Sensing Running-water looking at him, Jarrod quickly shuffled the ream of papers. Several pages fell to the floor. As he scooped them up he cleared his throat. "Looks like you've really got everything in great shape. The inspection boys should be happy the way you got things set up. Good job." He placed the manifest on the seat next to him. His hands felt clammy. Consciously he wiped his sweaty palms down his sides trousers before extending a handshake to Running-water. He hoped his close attention to the contents of car seven hadn't aroused Running-water's suspicions. "ZZ would be really pissed. Damn! Got to be more careful," Jarrod thought.

Patricia Livingston watched Running-water and Jarrod exit the train. The security guard joined them. Within minutes an official-looking government car drove up. Three men exited the federal vehicle. Recognizing their uniforms she wondered why they would be boarding the train. One man was dressed in the standard railroad black jacket, matching slacks, and cap. One was from Canadian Customs, and the third was a US Customs and Border Protection Agent. "Why here at Toronto? Why is the American involved? What is on the train that requires this amount of attention? The murder of Esaugetuh, Adam's father? That would involve the RCMP? Oh, hell! Just walk over there and begin asking questions," Patricia Livingston thought.

She didn't. Once again her wait and see instinct kicked in. More than once her patience had paid off in a getting a story.

The thought of Esaugetuh brought back a flood of memories. As hard-boiled and tough as she thought she was, she nearly lost it when she photographed what was left of him. Even now the visual memory made her queasy. Adam had discovered his father's decaying body behind a bricked-up wall in the basement garage of Karuna House, the Toronto Victorian mansion that housed The Brothers. They were a disparate group of twelve men, randomly picked up from the streets of Toronto. Broken, homeless derelicts. It had been a benevolent gesture on the part of Esaugetuh— A gesture that cost him his life. There wasn't much left but some decayed flesh and bones but the coroner's report had indicated he had been drugged. Using a telescopic lens she'd gotten a look into the three by three-foot room. She had also taken some photos of The Brother, Thomas, as he sat handcuffed in the back seat of a police cruiser. "What a whimpering, sniveling bastard!" she thought. The arrival of the stretch limo caught her attention. "Wonder who's arriving?" She readied her camera.

Unlike before, Samuel did not get out and open the door. Running-water had bolted from the train at a fast run toward the limo; its motor remained running. The back window rolled down. Bending his six-foot frame down to the open window, his long hair, the color of a raven's blue-black feathers tumbled down around his handsome face. Before speaking to whoever was inside, he turned his head. Patricia Livingston caught the ever-present sensual pout on his lips. He spoke to those inside. The door opened and light flashed off his gun as he stepped back. A man, medium build, and sporting short-cropped sandy hair stepped out. "Hmm. Not bad in the looks department. Wonder who he is?" Patricia Livingston thought. Unlike the Indian, he was dressed in whites and didn't seem to be armed. He extended his hand to someone still inside. A woman slowly emerged. Her face and head were covered with a long black scarf.

From her hiding place, Patricia Livingston couldn't tell who it was. Whoever she was, she was very pregnant. The man in white reached back into the limo and extracted a leather satchel. Patricia Livingston with her Jobian patience waited and watched. Even with the help of the two men, it took a while for the woman to negotiate the steps of the train. Patricia Livingston busied herself with taking more photos. She ran her tongue along her painted lips seeking an imaginary taste of scotch. Her preference was a thirty year Glenfiddich Single Malt. She could almost taste its seductively woody flavor. She reminded herself to tuck a bottle into her backpack next time.

Finally, the three of them were on board. The chauffeur turned the limo around and began to drive it on to a flatbed. The armed guard remained on the platform. Now was the time for a much-needed diversion. She remembered hearing someone a few boxes from where she was hiding. She found a street bum inside. He smelled badly of booze and urine. She offered him fifty if he'd go over to the guard and urinate on him. He did. The guard decked him. Once the guard had left his post to clean up, Patricia Livingston, backpack slung over her shoulder, camera in hand, ran for the train, and in a single leap landed on the top step. She grabbed the handrail and pulled herself into the vestibule.

The excitement brought a rush. She felt energized by the possibility of a scoop. She needed a good story; a story to boost her image as well as her ratings. Both had been doing poorly. "Well, I'll show them. This broad ain't done yet. What a girl's gotta do; a girl's gotta do. Right now I need a place to hide."

She knew the important persons would be housed toward the rear of the train. Security would dictate that in the event of a derailment. Others would be closer to the front of the train. Turning to the right and toward the front of the train, she was surprised to find that she was in a Pullman. Quickly she ducked into a restroom. Using her cell phone she called her office, rattled off a whispered report, told her cameraman where he could find the flash card from her camera, and then settled herself until she could make her next move. "What's on this train that has attracted the attention of the authorities?" That question nagged her.

While she waited, others on the train waited for their evening meal. The chefs had prepared a gourmet dinner of vodka pea soup, spiced pear salad with creamy Saga cheese, herb-infused pheasants, wild rice seasoned with just a touch of Garam Masala, and garlic green legumes. The wine of choice was Côtes du Rhone. Dessert was a mound of chocolate mousse floated on a sea of imported Godiva White Chocolate Liqueur. The tantalizing smells nourished her own growing hunger. As she fished around in her backpack, she wished she had a drink. "Damn! I've missed the cocktail hour at

Chartreuse." She found a high protein bar and nibbled on that, chewing each bite slowly. It lasted longer that way. She didn't know she was not the only one who waited.

CHAPTER THREE

As Adam waited for the train to pull out, he smelled the food; yet it held no interest to him. He was glad to be on board, away from Karuna House, and headed to the United States. He'd been gone too long. He wanted to go home. Home? He didn't have a home! Neither the 20,000 acre Quebec ranch nor Karuna House in Toronto was home. The mansion, where his father had been betrayed and brutally murdered, offended his senses. The ranch and its spring-fed lake reeked with lingering memories of death; the result of a shoot-out with a group of would-be terrorists. He couldn't stay at either one. Sitting at his desk, Adam fiddled with the obsidian that hung around his neck. It had been given to him by Howakhan, the Wisdom Keeper. At times he was sure it burned into his soul, a stark reminder of the powers from the Other Side. Even though he wanted to return to the States, a dark foreboding hung over him, sullying his disposition. He worried about Daphne and their unborn child. He felt she was safer in New Mexico with her mother.

He wondered if he dared to hope to be free of the ogre that hunted him. He'd lost count of the number of attempts upon his life and upon the life of his soul-mate, Running-water. Their life's ink had been scrawled upon the same page much in the same manner as letters are connected to form words. Remove a letter, and the word is no longer the same. That's the way they were. Remove one and the other changed.

He had the train retrofitted in Montreal; had it loaded with the ranch's furnishings; paintings by the great Romantic artists, rare books, objects des art in marble and brass, a vast treasure in precious gems, rare coins, millions in American dollars. And then there was the ancient deerskin with its strange markings. When the shaman had this panoplied behemoth brought to Toronto it had caused a national sensation as it sped across the Canadian countryside. And now he waited for it to move out. And it would as soon as Running-water and those agents had everything ironed out.

Adam's phone vibrated. It was Running-water. He had reached an agreement with the Customs' agents. The train would stop at Blaine, Washington. Be side-tracked there and be inspected. Since it carried passengers as well as freight other legal issues had to be addressed. He would be coming back shortly.

Hearing a light tap on his door, Adam, thinking it was his dinner being brought to him, said, "Come in," and continued his occupation with papers on his desk. He wasn't sure if he smelled her first or felt her presence. Whichever it was, it caused a flush to come over him, a warmth he had not felt in a long time.

As he turned, she was in his arms, kissing him, hugging him with her whole being. Too much time apart had passed between them. Something she would never allow again. In their hungered embrace they forgot she was in her ninth month and she let out a yelp. A loud knock and the door opening stopped Adam's concerned response.

"Glad to see you found him," Running-water said to his sister. Daphne was glowing in her pregnancy and he took delight in his twin's radiance. She got up from Adam's lap and embraced him. Her long blue-black hair hung down over full breasts and stopped at the top of her very large abdomen. Her eyes, reflecting endless happiness, spilled their joy in tears, something she had always done when she was very happy. Even as a child she would cry when she was especially happy. As with many twins they seemed to communicate without words. Adam tuned into this but said nothing.

"The agents seemed satisfied with the way we have things set up. I don't think we'll have any problems crossing the border," Running-water said.

"Why was it necessary for these additional agents to board my train, especially here?" Adam said. "Did you receive any communication from the Canadian government or from the railroad that additional people were coming on board?"

"No. I thought you had," Running-water replied.

"And the guy, what's his name, who was on the train when it arrived?"

"Jarrod. He's an agent of the railroad. I went over the manifests with him. He seemed to think we had everything we'd need for the Border crossing. What's bothering you, Adam?"

"I just think it's odd that they are on board now. We've got several hours before we reach the border. They could have boarded us there. Are you sure we have no one else on board?"

Had he but known. And he should have known; he was the shaman. News anchor and reporter Patricia Livingston was on board. Death, sequestered on board, waited hungrily with his scythe. But then, Adam was only tuned into the vibrations going on in front of him. He noticed Daphne look at her brother. He was now sure that they were communicating.

"How long have you two telecommunicated?" Adam asked.

"Forever, I guess. Thought you knew that," Running-water said.

"Is that important Adam? We only seem to know what each other is thinking when we are close," Daphne said.

"It seems to run in the family," Adam said.

"What does that mean? Goodness Adam, you are acting strange," Daphne said. She was holding her stomach. A slight frown crossed her brow. "I need to sit down. My feet and back are killing me."

They moved into the parlor the private car. Daphne eased herself down into a red leather chair; one Adam had brought from the ranch. It supported her back and felt good. "Better. Now, what about this business of knowing what each other says? About it running in the family?"

"Just before we learned the truth about my father, I had sent a telepathic message to Running-water. His twin sons answered me. At first, I thought it was Running-water playing head games with me. In visualization, I saw that the twins were indeed talking to me. Remarkable and so young."

"You hadn't mentioned that before. You sure it was my sons?" Running-water asked.

"Did I hear you say you were talking to my sons? That's not possible, Adam. They are just now beginning to talk. I'm sure my mother-in-law didn't put them on the phone," Isha said as she closed the door to Adam's private car. After giving her sister-in-law a hung, Isha again asked. "How is that possible? Explain."

"Telepathically. It surprised me. Obviously, you have no idea that they can telecommunicate."

"You're positive?" Isha said.

"Absolutely. You ought to tune into them. I can help you with that. In fact, now is as good a time as any to begin their training," Adam said.

"Training? For what?" Running-water said.

"Come. Sit down. You can start now," Adam said, ignoring Running-water's question.

"Wait one minute. Before you start training *my* babies, I have a question," Isha said.

"Which is?" Running-water said. He was taken back by his wife's sudden possessiveness.

"The boys have a pale blue cclorization about them," Isha replied. The worry showed in her dark eyes.

"An aura?" Adam asked.

"No. Not really. It's more of a skin tone, a bluish undertone. [1] A couple of times I thought they actually glowed, especially after I turned off their bedroom light," Isha replied.

"And so it has begun. The prophecy rings true." Adam said. He seemed to be elsewhere.

"Prophecy? What in the world are you talking about?" Isha said.

The train jerked, nearly toppling the red leather chair in which Daphne was sitting. She gasped. A contraction? She had hoped to make it to the United States before giving birth. Now she wasn't so sure! It would take them three days to get to Blaine. The train moved on to the main tracks and began its push northward toward Sudbury and then it would travel west to then turn south to the US Border. No stops were planned.

[1] Persons who ingest colloidal silver have a blue skin color. This condition is called argyra. That is not the case with Running-water and Isha's twins.

CHAPTER FOUR

Daphne was not the only one nearly upset by the sudden jerk of the train. Patricia Livingston nearly fell off the edge of the sink upon which she had perched. She was trying to decide where she should relocate. "Maybe the cook's quarters? Pretend I'm doing a piece on food on board trains. It might work." To ease the tension she did a series of isometrics. Feeling better despite her gnawing hunger. The high protein bar had not diminished her need for food. "Damn. wish I had stuck a couple of nips in my backpack. Must remember to do that next time." She fumbled around in her backpack and found the sandwiches her cameraman had gotten for her. Despite their squashed condition, she woofed one down.

She wondered if her cameraman had found the flash card and had done what she had told him. At times he's such a dumb bastard. Not bad in bed. "You really are such a tramp aren't you old girl? Old? My god! I'm really squirrelly. Come on, get game, girl. Just because the station has brought in a twenty-year-old doesn't mean a thing. Oh, shit! Who am I kidding? That's why I'm where I am. I'm here to prove I still got what it takes. Damn! Sure wish I had a drink."

The train had picked up speed and the ride smoothed. Cautiously she opened the restroom door, peered out. No one in sight. Before exiting, Patricia Livingston paused in front of the mirror, loosened a button on her light green blouse, and then tucked in it so that it stretched over her firm breasts. Next, she adjusted a dangling gold earring.

Rummaging around in her backpack, she found a lipstick and repainted her lips, accentuating the slight pout. "Not bad at all for a forty-year-old. Oops, I mean a thirty-something. Well, hell, I don't look forty," she said exiting from the restroom.

Fluffing her dark brown hair and adjusting her short skirt Patricia Livingston, television anchor and reporter, shook her tight butt and cautiously headed toward the front of the train. She let her nose be her guide to the cook's kitchen. The train's speed had increased and the swaying of the cars made it difficult for her to walk in a straight line. She put a hand along the wall of the Pullman to steady herself. The lack of security surprised her. She wondered where Adam's personal pilot and navigator were. She made a mental note to check on Dutch Masters and Brett Montana. They had not been in Toronto at Karuna House when she went there to do the story on Esaugetuh's murder. The image of the messy scene still made her shudder. "What the hell was that guy's name that was charged with his murder? I did research on him. Thomas? Thomas Ataman. He and his brother Joseph had been involved in a swindle of an old couple. Joseph had been indicted on the suspicion of murdering them. He'd gotten off on a technicality."

Heavy breathing and soft giggling caught her attention. She stopped and listened. She knew that sound and a smile parted her collagen lips. There was a note stuck on the door that read do not disturb. It was signed Samuel and Julie. "Must be the blond I saw with The Brothers," Patricia Livingston thought as she slipped off her shoes. She scooted on down the corridor toward the next car. A loud thud on the roof of the car brought her to a standstill. She listened. Sounded like someone running. "Must be my imagination. No one could jump on top of this train let alone be running on it. We must be moving over a hundred miles an hour." Quickly she slipped on her shoes and pushed open the door to the vestibule. A blast of chilly air slapped her.

CHAPTER FIVE

On the roof of Adam's private car there was a loud banging it wasn't that they actually heard it as it was having felt it. It vibrated along the roof line and traveled down the side of the car. Running-water with guns drawn went to the end of the car. He stopped. Listened. Metal striking against metal! Adam quickly ushered Daphne and Isha to the bedroom. As he helped her lay down, Adam sensed that the stress of traveling was taking its toll. It still puzzled him why she had decided to join him. He'd ask her later. He returned to the parlor and on into the office where Running-water was talking on his cell phone. The one area they had not covered with security cameras was the roof.

"It's Brett. He's on the roof," Running-water said as he cranked open the emergency hatch.

"What's going on? Did he say?" Adam said.

The hatch was fully open and Brett Montana jumped down; landing cat-like on his feet. His muscles bulged beneath the skin-tight black micro skin long-sleeved tee. As he stood up the matching black micro skin pants stretched a firm outline of his masculine parts. The black balaclavas covered his head and most of his blackened face. "Trouble ahead," Brett said as he pulled off the balaclavas revealing cropped black hair, a tad longer than the usual military cut.

"What kind of trouble?" Adam asked.

"Dutch and I have been flying a few miles ahead of the train. The tracks are blocked. When I checked with the engineer he knew nothing about it. Thought it best I drop in."

There was a knock on the door. Running-water opened it. It was Samuel, still trying to get his pants on. He was armed with an Uzi. Dutch had called him from the chopper. Right behind him was Dr. Allan Bach. Nodding to Adam, he said, "I came on board with your wife? Where is she?"

"She and Isha are at the end of the car in the bedroom," Adam said stepping aside so Dr. Bach could get by.

Brett unstrapped his Uzi and dropped his backpack. His muscles rippled as he brought out two additional clips, checked them, and then attached them to his belt. Next, he whipped open his cell phone and punched in a number. "Slow the train and gradually bring it to a complete stop." He hadn't waited for approval. He simply acted. He was trained as a Navy Seal. Once you know the score you act; you don't discuss the action.

Immediately the train began to slow. They were on a desolate stretch of rail. The train stopped and then there was a loud clang up and down its length as armored steel plates slid into place adding additional cover to the darkened windows. The engineer's window was enclosed with a heavy wrap-around shield and the steel door sealed the cab to prevent entrance from the outside. The massive light on the train went out and night vision cameras took its place. The blue lights along the underside of the cars changed to infrared sensors. If by chance any of the cars were penetrated from below, those on board would be warned. All the vestibules connecting the twenty cars were sealed with heavy gauge steel plates thus preventing anyone from boarding or leaving the train. As a leftover relic of the Cold War, it was originally designed to withstand an atomic blast. It had been retrofitted to accommodate modern technology.

The door to Adam's private car opened. The agent found an Uzi stock in his face. Startled, he stepped back. "Whoa. I just came back to tell you the authorities have been notified that the tracks are blocked. Probably put there by a bunch of dang kids thinking it would be fun to stop a train. They—uh—will send someone out. May take a while for him to get here." The guns made him very nervous.

"Someone?" Running-water said.

"Uh, yeah. That's all I can tell ya."

"We'll take care of it. You go back up front and stay there," Adam said dismissing the agent with a quick thrust of his chin.

"Uh, sure. Sure. I'll do that."

Once the door had closed, Running-water pushed a button on the console and the door electronically locked. He then slid a two-inch thick steel bar into place. "You know something I don't?" he asked Adam.

"I said before I don't know why we have these agents on board. That bothers me. How did he know about the blockade? Check with the engineer to see if any of them had been in touch with him."

Running-waters mind swirled with minutia as he punched the number for the engineer. Had he missed something? Something he should not have. "If I could just remember." He shook his head to quell the rumblings going on in his mind. His blue-black hair swirled around his worried face.

"Adam, this train can take a good hit; even survive the destruction of the rails. The blockade may be rigged with explosives. It might be better if we didn't try to ram it. Let's wait and see what happens," Running-water said still struggling to find some long piece of memory information.

"Any idea of what it's like?" Adam asked Brett.

"Not a whole lot. From what I could tell from the air, I don't believe this was a kids' stunt."

"Why's that?" Running-water asked.

"The railroad ties are laced with what looks like steel poles. Whoever did this, meant to stop this train," Brett said.

"And Dutch? Is he armed?" Adam asked.

"Just his personal weapon. The chopper isn't," Brett said.

"Hmm. Contact him and have him leave the area. Might be good to keep him low keyed. And tell him thanks for flying Daphne here. I had wondered where you and he had gotten off to," Adam said.

"No problem. I'll give him a head's up once I get to the engineer's cab," Brett said. The heavy door slammed behind him. Samuel pushed the button to electronically lock it and then slid the steel bar across.

Adam went to Daphne. Dr. Bach and Isha were still with her. Sensing her discomfort, Adam gently placed his finger on the tip of her slightly upturned nose, drew a line down it, and then blew into her eyes. At that moment he was sure they were the most beautiful eyes in the world. She sensed his love. He began to hum, low at first, gradually increasing in pitch. Daphne was under.

"How long will she remain hypnotized?" Dr. Bach said.

"She'll remain that way until I call her name. Probably not more than a couple of hours. She is distressed. I think her time is nearly upon her. I had hoped that our son would be born in the United States," Adam said.

"Son? Don't you know? You knew about Isha's twins. How is it you do not know about your own wife?" Dr. Bach said.

"You're saying Daphne is carrying more than one child?" Adam ignored the subtle challenge of Dr. Bach.

"Yes. She's carrying triplets." And not willing to let his question go, Dr. Bach again asked, "How is it you didn't know that?"

"She didn't tell me and since we have not been together for eight of those nine months there was no way for me to know," Adam said. He sat down on the edge of the bed.

Slowly he passed his hands over her swollen abdomen. He looked up, his mouth open in disbelief. "You're wrong, Allan. She's carrying quadruplets. My god! Four boys!"

A loud knock at the door brought Samuel to full attention. He released the safety on his Uzi. He nodded to Running-water that he was ready. The door was released and Samuel removed the steel bar. Slowly he opened the door, the Uzi pointed out in front of him. A man identified himself as Customs' Agent Zeek Zero. Lowering his weapon, Samuel stepped aside so he could enter.

"I came back to see if everything was okay. Sorry about the blockade. Damn kids. They don't realize the damage they could do." His wide eyes darted everywhere, taking in everything, making a computerized list. His lower lip quivered as he checked the number of weapons Samuel and Running-water had.

The slight movement jarred loose the sought memory—the memory he had so desperately wanted—causing Running-water to color. "Damn! How could I have missed so obvious a thing?"

Jarrod and the other agent, both of them, had taken too long checking the manifest for car seven. That should have set up an alarm. "Adam had caused to be concerned. Damn it!" Running-water thought. "We're okay here, Mr. Zero. Return to your assigned area and remain there."

Running-water's cold tone surprised Adam as he entered the office. He was about to question Running-water but was silenced by a telepathic thought. *Danger!*

CHAPTER SIX

Zeek Zero was beside himself. Runningwater's demeanor told him that they were suspicious, that the kids blocking the rails was not swallowed. They couldn't afford any screw-ups. Great care had gone into the planning. Every detail had been worked out. Every step had been mapped out. One little mistake. That's all it would take. And a mistake had been made. His face flushed. "Just one god-damned little mistake. Somehow Jarrod has tipped them off. That stupid dumb bastard. I knew it was a mistake to let him make the first contact."

The more his anger mounted the quicker he walked toward the passengers' only car. He was so pissed he didn't notice the woman chatting with one of the chefs. He didn't go unnoticed. By the time he got to the first ca, he was running. There the others waited for the dynamite charges to explode. The explosion they got was not expected.

The metal door of the car slammed shut. ZZ raced up the aisle and stopped directly behind Jarrod, leaned over, whispered into his ear, and then slit his throat. Blood poured out of the gaping wound. The others, stunned by this violence against one of their own, sat and watched as Jarrod's heart pumped his life away. Jarrod never made a sound except for a single stinking fart. The fetid smell seemed to fill the car, suffocating those who sat too numb to move.

"Pick him up and get him out of here. Get ready for a firefight," ZZ growled.

"Jesus! Why in the hell did you go and do that? Why'd you have to go and kill him?" Pierre said snapping out of his shocked stupor.

"Somehow that jackass tipped our hand. They know something's afoot and they are very well armed. I've come too far now to not get what I came for," ZZ said.

"You sure about that? Maybe you just decided you want a bigger share of all those millions stashed in car seven. Maybe you've decided to keep it all? We'll keep our eyes on you from now on," Pierre said. He pulled a Lugar from his pocket.

"Go ahead you asshole. Pull the trigger. Don't you think they'll hear a shot and flying up here? That what are you going to do?" ZZ said.

A shot rang out. ZZ fell to the floor holding his stomach, mouth open in disbelief. Before he could say anything, Pierre fired a second shot, ending it.

Patricia Livingston thought she heard something go pop. She remembered the man hurrying by as she chatted with the chef. She hurried to the passenger car.

Pierre looked down at ZZ. "I don't think they heard anything at the back of the train. If they did, I'll tell them you killed Jarrod. That's what I'll tell them. Nobody calls me an asshole and gets away with it."

Turning to Al he said, "You got any problems with any of this?"

"Uh, no. No. Should the others have blown up the tracks by now? Why aren't they here? They should have been here by now."

"Don't go wetting your pants. The train didn't hit the barricade now, did it? So there wasn't an explosion. Somehow they learned of the barricade. Damn that Jarrod! Well did it?"

"No," Al said.

"Well, that explains why there wasn't an explosion. Got to notify the boss so he can notify the others. They'll be waiting for our signal."

Pierre took out his phone, punched in the numbers. No signal. "Damn! The metal shields. I'll go outside. Be back." He couldn't open the door to the vestibule. The doors were locked.

"Shit! Check ZZ's pockets to see if he has a key to fit this door," Pierre said.

Al didn't move. He couldn't. He was a big man, strong, but murder was a part of his life's plan. He had been promised there would be no gunplay, no one getting hurt. It was supposed to be simple. Just empty car seven and be off. His head was spinning. He felt sick to his stomach. He ran down the corridor toward the back of the car. As he got to the end of the car the last image he had was a woman taking his picture through the window of the door. It came up and gushed out of his mouth and nose. It was read. He thought he was dying. He was! Pierre had fired one shot. Al's brains splattered against the window. Patricia Livingston stifled a scream and dropped to the floor. Her hands shook as she sucked in air, gasping, gulping air as she struggled to breathe. She forced herself to think of why she was on this train. That calmed her. "My god, maybe he saw me?"

CHAPTER SEVEN

Pierre rifled through the dead Zeek Zero's pockets. No keys. He turned to go back down the corridor to check Al's pockets. It was then that he noticed it. He should have known. All of them should have known. The awful realization of what he had just done struck him. Jarrod hadn't tipped them off. They had been had from the beginning. In the corner was a small security camera. Looking directly into the camera Pierre shot the watchers a bird and then fired one shot. The little camera exploded. That shot sent Patricia Livingston cowering in a corner. Frantically, she fished around for the Taser in her backpack.

Because of Adam's concern, Running-water had engaged the security cameras just as Pierre gave them the bird. "You want me to go up there and take him out?" Running-water said.

"No. Brett's closer. Take him alive. I want to find out more about who's involved," Adam said. He reached over and punched another button giving them a wide view from the cook's car.

"Who's that?" Running-water said

"How in the hell did she get on the train? Damn!" Adam's face reddened. He pushed a number on the console. "Brett, we have Patricia Livingston on board. She crouched on the platform just outside of the passengers' car. Get her and bring her back here."

Samuel with Julie in tow arrived. Adam had sent him to bring his bride to his private car. Seeing the doctor and Isha at the end of the car, Julie went to them. Samuel had told her about Daphne.

"She under hypnosis," Isha said responding to Julie's concerned face.

"You ever delivered a baby?" Dr. Bach asked Julie.

"No. Had one though."

"I've had Red Cross medical training. I can help," Isha said. "You think things are going to pop?"

"Anytime now," Dr. Bach replied.

CHAPTER EIGHT

Dr. Allan Bach, young and handsome as handsome is, had been the bright and up-coming surgeon at a prominent New York hospital. His patients adored him; the nurses took bets on who would get into his pants first. He, for his part, encouraged such betting. The result being numerous sexual trysts. Female interns offered themselves as offerings to a god.

He had entered college at age fourteen, completed a four-year degree in liberal arts by sixteen. At eighteen he had finished a degree in biological sciences and was at twenty well on his way through med school. As a young teenager in college where the females were older than he, he found they had no interest in his sexual fantasies. By twenty-five, he had completed his meds, his internship, and his specializations. He'd also added twenty-five sexual exploits to his repertoire.

As many young men do, he looked forward to a long and brilliant career, eventual marriage, and children. Then a patient in his care went into shock. He couldn't be found. He was in a supply closet banging a nurse's aide. The patient died. The whole thing most likely would have blown over had it been anybody but a prominent person. The hospital and then the manufacturer of the failed monitor made a deal. To head off investigations by the state's health department and the attorney-general they chose to make Dr. Allan Bach their scapegoat. He was fired. His once brilliant career was over. He was crucified in the local press and media. He could still see the ugly headline, *Sex Crazed Doctor Lets Patient Die*

How Adam learned about him remains a mystery. He had gathered enough evidence to know that it was a malfunctioning machine that caused the patient's death. Further, the duty nurse, who just happened to be the wife of the hospital director, hadn't followed emergency procedures. However it was, Adam owned a private sanitarium in a Toronto suburb. He hired Dr. Bach to be its medical director. It was there that he had delivered via cesarean section, Running-water and Isha's twin boys. And now here he was, a traveling private physician to a very pregnant Indian woman.

Adam had come down on him really hard, demanding a strict regimen, and long hours. Yet, at the same time, he had shown him compassion. As Dr. Bach reviewed his situation he admitted that he had no room for complaint.

" Thanks to Adam I've got a license to practice even if it is restricted. I'm paid very well. He treats me with respect—He said I had to reopen a trust account," Dr. Bach thought as he sat in a chair next to Daphne's bed. " I didn't understand at first. Then I realized he was talking about human trust. He gave me his trust. And now I have another opportunity to make another deposit in that account."

Daphne stirred in her bed. She groaned with the onslaught of contractions.

CHAPTER NINE

Daphne's groans brought Adam to her side. He could see the small beads of sweat forming along her forehead. He moved his hands over her abdomen. They hovered there, taking on a life of their own. Gradually they began to move in circles over her very large stomach. A pale blue glow emanated from his hands. Keeping his voice even-toned he spoke his wife's name.

Daphne's eyes fluttered open and then a little smile of recognition appeared at the corner of her lips.

"Her water break?" Julie asked.

"Yes. Better get ready," Dr. Bach replied as he handed a list to Isha. "Can you put her under again, Adam? It'll make things easier for her."

Adam looked at his wife. More perspiration had formed along her hairline. Looking into her eyes he saw the pain building and yet he knew she would not scream. Even though she was a modern woman she took pride in being an Indian woman. She grimaced as the contractions increased.

"No. Don't, Adam," Daphne said to Adam as he prepared to hypnotize her. "Help me up. Please. I need to squat in the birthing position. I need a stool or a box. I want to do this the old way. I can do this."

Isha brought warm moist towels and gently laid them across Daphne's protruding abdomen. Next, she brought clean sheets and piled them close by. She had a large clear plastic sheet which she gently slid under Daphne. Adam created a smudge of sage, sweet grass, and cedar. It was lit and with

Adam's instructions, Julie began to fan it over Daphne. Dr. Bach then got into the act. If Adam was right about the number of babies, this was going to take some time. He removed the warm towels from her abdomen. To ease the birthing he massaged Daphne's stomach with baby oil. In the old days bear grease would have been used. He had learned to respect the ways of the First People as well as Native Americans. "The old ones didn't have it all wrong," he thought.

Samuel, beside himself, turned away in embarrassment. He had just lost his virginity and wasn't sure about all this female business. Running-water began to play his flute. A soft melody filled the car. It had an inner lilting timbre.

Adam squatted down behind Daphne, gently pulled her into his raised spread legs to give her needed support. It allowed her to keep her own knees apart. He extended his cupped hands along her sides for her to push against. He would be her birthing stool. Then in rhythm with Running-water's flute, Adam began to hum, softly, gradually increasing the pitch until its sound filled the entire car. Flute sounds had been lost to the dominant hum and Running-water silenced his playing.

Adam felt Daphne's body relax as her breathing steadied. But not for long. He felt the pressure on his hands with each new contraction.

"Pant. Don't push until I tell you to," Dr. Bach said. "Okay. We have crowning. Push."

The head slowly emerged and then Dr. Bach eased out one shoulder and then the other. He palmed him off to Isha who suctioned the boy's mouth and then his nose to prevent fluid buildup in his lungs. She wrapped him in a warmed soft blanket.

An explosion rocked the train. Adam did not move, nor did he stop humming. He was creating a harmonic resonance in tune with his wife's body. She controlled its pitch.

Running-water turned his attention to the television console to see what had happened. Nothing at the front of the train. Punching up another camera he saw billowing smoke rising up into the air. The tracks at the rear of the train had been blown up, making escape impossible. A second explosion announced the arrival of number two son. The blockade at the front of the train had been blown up. Pieces of broken railroad ties hit the front of the train.

"Damn! Where's Brett? He should have been back by now? Maybe we better get in touch with Dutch and have him return to the train," Running-water muttered as he turned from watching the monitor to watching the birthing process. The speed with which the next two babies were born fascinated him. He had missed the birth of his own twins.

The umbilical cords were cut, and the placentas were carefully wrapped and put aside. Later, when they had a place they could call home, they would be placed in the ground on top of which a tree would be planted. In that way, the boys would be given a direct link to their spiritual mother, earth. The four identical boys were bathed and wrapped in warm blankets. Adam gently stroked Daphne's head, kissed her as he gently eased her down onto the mattress. As he got up, Dr. Bach examined

Daphne, wiped her face with a damp cloth, and gave her a small amount of water. He was amazed by the small amount of blood loss and at how well she was doing. Julie and Isha stepped in to bathe her and dress her in a clean gown.

Adam took one son at a time, held him up toward one of the four corners, whispered something into each ear, and then gently blew into its mouth. The quadruplets gave off a pale blue light as Adam passed his hands over them. Isha noticed this but kept it to herself. She would watch and when the time came, she would demand an explanation.

The formula was warmed and Adam fed each of his sons and then passed each to Daphne. She wondered if this was the way it was going to be. Was she to be viewed only as the carrier of his seed, that their babies would be HIS sons. Just for an instant, the resentment swelled in her as she cradled her children. A fuzzy image of a trial from long ago slowly formed in her mind. In it, the accused was acquitted of killing his mother because she was not really his mother; she was just the receptacle of his father's seed. She struggled to clear her mind of the image of Apollo defending Orestes, son of the great warrior king, Agamemnon.

"You named them?" Daphne whispered trying to hide the hurt she felt.

"No. I loaned them names in honor of your father, grandfather, your uncle, and your brother," Adam said, bending down and kissing her. "I have not sung their names. All in good time they will have names of their own. Then we'll sing them together."

Daphne wrapped her arms around Adam's neck and returned his kiss as Dr. Bach gave her an injection. Her resentment faded. She could now drift into a comfortable sleep.

CHAPTER TEN

Loud banging at the door brought everyone to rapt attention. Guns drawn, Running-water released the electronic lock and Samuel shoved the steel bar forward, and opened the door. It was Brett with a very angry Patricia Livingston. She was flaying her arms and legs as Brett dragged her into the car. He had her in a choker-hold and when he released her, obscenities filled the air.

"You bastard. I'll get you for this."

Patricia Livingston didn't have a chance to defend herself. From across the room, Isha appeared and slapped her across her open mouth. And then again with a forceful backhand. Patricia Livingston dropped to the floor in disbelief and shock. No one had ever slapped her. "Keep your filthy mouth shut. Open it and I'll slit your throat," Isha whispered. As he bent down she flashed a long thin-bladed knife ever so close to Patricia Livingston's nose. "I don't know how you got on this train, but I do know you were not invited. How dare you raise your voice! There are newborn babies present and they don't need to hear your filth."

Rapid pinging vibrated along the length of the train as bullets from automatic weapons ricocheted off the armored cars. Daphne moaned in her sleep. Patricia Livingston remained crouched on the floor patting her face where she had been slapped. She was sure it was going to swell and be black and blue. Her anger mounted. Pissed because she got caught, pissed because her battered face wouldn't be seen on the nightly news, yet how grateful she was at least with people she knew. She shook her head in an effort to erase the image of splattered brains from her mind. The quadruplets' crying broke into her thoughts. Isha and Julie each picked up two and began humming to them. The pinging intensified. Still, Adam did nothing.

"Why doesn't he do something?" Patricia Livingston thought. "Surely with his powers he can do something?"

There was loud whoosh. The car rocked back and forth. She felt the vibrations and decided to get up from the floor. She sought the comfort of the other two women. She was surprised when Isha offered her one of the quads. She was more surprised that holding such a small life could feel so wonderful. Because she had been given one of the quads Patricia Livingston knew she had been accepted into the women's inner circle. During a time of danger, some inner quality of their make-up brings women together. They drop all pretenses and unite. She had seen it in other countries in time of disaster. Women together. For that she was grateful.

The lights flickered and then went to emergency power. The red lights created an eerie outline of the darkened figures. Julie and Isha still had three of the babies. It was then that both women noticed a bluish glow about them.

"Explain this and do it now," Isha demanded as she held two of the quads out to their father.

"Yeah, Adam. What the hell's going on with your sons?" Running-water asked.

"I don't have time to explain," Adam said.

"Yes, you do. We can wipe out these guys any time you want. They are no real threat," Running-water said, looking back at the monitors.

Patricia Livingston adjusted her backpack she still had in her hand. The adjustment, she hoped, brought the hidden camera into the correct position. She hoped it was working.

"Your sons and mine, Daphne's and mine," Adam said, correcting himself, "are very special children. They possess gifts that set them apart from others. It's part of the prophecy. That's all I will say about it. Despite what you think, Running-water, we are in grave danger. If the armament is penetrated we can lose it. There is no place for us to go."

Isha began to say something but a look from Running-water stopped her. He was bleached-flour-white. And she grew afraid. Never had she seen her husband look like this. And her concern quickly spread to Julie and Patricia Livingston.

"They have inside information. I believe there are still some of them on the train. I counted at least four. The engineer may be one of them," Adam said, breaking the silence.

"One," Patricia Livingston said.

"One what?" Adam snapped.

"One man left on the train."

"How do you know this?" Adam asked.

"I saw one man get his throat slit and saw two shot," Patricia Livingston replied.

"You're absolutely sure of this?" Running-water asked.

"Yes. I watched two of them sit there and let one guy bleed to death. One of them then killed the other two. My god, one guy's brains splattered all over the door window right in front of me. There were only four uniformed men in that car. The Canadian Railroad Agent is the one left. He was trying to call out on his cell phone."

Running-water remained very quiet. He knew that Adam was right. If their armament was penetrated it would be all over for them. His lawyer-mind raced through pages of scenarios as he searched for a solution. Solutions, he knew had to be possible, all he had to do was find them.

Brett's fertile imagination took him to the act of creation. That caused him to blush. Even in a crisis he always felt horny. He said it always gave him an edge. And his horniness took him to Patricia Livingston. "She's sure a looker," he thought.

"Miss Livingston, I—,"

"Don't even go there. I've put up with that sh— , I mean, that nonsense all my life. *Livingston I presume* has haunted me."

"What I was about to ask was if you would be willing to take a stroll with me," Brett answered.

"A stroll? Are you out of your ever—,"

"Adam, you got a bottle of wine? This sweet little *thang* and I are going for a stroll toward the front of the train," Brett, said, dropping his Uzi and two side arms. "I think between Miss Livingston and me, we can take this guy out. What do you say, Miss Livingston? You game?" Brett asked, flashing his best smile. There was just a touch of a boyish rogue. She liked that.

"Of course. Give me a bottle, opened, please," Patricia Livingston said as she moved over to Brett and putting her arms around his waist. "What-evah you say "darlin'." Their attempt at Southern drawl relieved the tension. She liked the way he felt, solid.

"Don't worry; we'll bring him back alive unless he's got an arsenal stashed up there," Brett said. He hoped there was an arsenal. If there was it could get ugly.

CHAPTER ELEVEN

On their way to the front of the train, Brett and Patricia Livingston splashed wine on themselves and as they drew closer to the passenger car they grew louder, even staggering their walk. With a quick jerk, Brett pulled on the door handle. Nothing. He could see the blood and bits of brain matter on the window. He pulled on the door again. Runningwater had electronically released it. With a swoosh, it gave way and opened. The remains of the carnage were everywhere. The coppery smell of the blood assaulted their noses. The three bodies lay where they died. Patricia Livingston closed her eyes and forced a loud giggle.

"Just stop. You *are* such a naughty man," Patricia Livingston said, staggering down the aisle ahead of Brett. The shooter had to be hiding behind a row of seats. To continue the tease to get him to show himself she artfully staggered from one side to the other, taking pains to look behind each row of seats. "Where is he? He's got to be here. Maybe he had been able to get off the train after all," Patricia thought.

Her instincts told her otherwise. She faked a fall, rolled over on her back and called out, "Come here you gorgeous hunk. Whew! What a stud you are," she said to Brett. "And he is!" She thought.

"Don't worry, baby. What you need is a real man, not some drunken jerk. I'll show you hot." Pierre said, coming up from behind one of the rows of seats. He ambled over to Patricia and stood over her. He was so busy trying to get his pants open he didn't see her knee come up. He doubled up in agony. "Too bad I didn't get this on film," Patricia thought.

"Bitch, you'll pay for that. Oh, how you'll pay. I'm gonna enjoy hurting you," Pierre said still clutching his testicles.

Patricia Livingston slammed into him, feet first. Her stiletto heels cutting deep into his gut. He reeled backward and fell to the floor. As he struggled to get up, he clenched his fists ready to pummel her. He didn't get the chance. There was a sharp snap as Brett's fist slammed into Pierre's face, breaking his jaw and nose. Pierre hit the floor, rolled around groaning. Using Pierre's belt and shoelaces, Brett tied him up. The shoelaces cut deep into Pierre's wrists.

"You're good. Damn good!" Brett said to Patricia Livingston.

"Thank you, kind sir." She looked at him, letting him know she was deliberating assessing him, and liking what she saw. "Umm, not bad. Not bad at all," she thought.

"You still up to some more adventure?" Brett asked.

"Why not? What you got in mind?"

"Since we've gone this far, let's check on the engineers. Seems to me one of them should have called in that blockade as soon as Dutch and I notified them," Brett said.

That wasn't exactly what she had hoped he had in mind but she decided to go along. "Whew! That micro whatever-it's-called that he's dressed in. What a hunk!" At the engineer's cab, Brett pushed the intercom to talk with the engineer on duty. When the train was refurbished they had not placed a two-way video cam in the engineer's cab. He refused to open the door to them. Brett finally convinced the engineer that they were not the enemy. After much hesitation, he finally admitted he had notified the CN Railroad of the problem. After getting his assurance that he would stay put, Brett and Patricia Livingston went back into the passengers' coach, picked up the very angry Pierre and headed back to Adam's private car.

CHAPTER TWELVE

At the first sleeper car, Brett and Patricia Livingston were greeted by nine very scared and upset men. The Brothers had roused themselves from their stupor of fear and had ventured out of their compartments. Charles, the young man who had castrated himself in the belief it would make him pure, assumed the role as spokesman for the group.

"We know there's trouble. There's always trouble when Adam's around. Our question—No, *my* question is what kind of trouble?"

"People have been killed," Patricia Livingston said.

Charles stepped back as the smell of wine assaulted his nose. It reminded him of his drunken mother, Julie. The look of total disdain was all the very unkempt Miss Livingston needed. She clobbered him with a left hook. The force rocked him on his heels. Blood spurted from his nose.

"Nobody looks down their nose at me," Patricia said, "especially some two-bit punk from the streets." She immediately regretted saying that.

Brett was again surprised by the strength of this petite woman. A smile crept across his face.

"What's so damn funny, jackass?"

"Nothing. Nothing at all, Miss Livingston," Brett said, tucking his chin in to avoid getting clobbered.

Pierre groaned. Patricia Livingston kicked him and he cried out in pain. "Call me a bitch, will you."

She was definitely feeling better. Being discovered, dragged to Adam's private care, and then slapped, not once, but twice had built up some real resentments.

Another round of rapid pinging hit the car. In a panic, The Brothers fell to the floor. They continued to lay there as three rapid loud explosions rocked the train.

"Grenades. They're using grenades," Brett said. "Come on. We need to get back to Adam and quick."

Their prisoner was not cooperative and that was a mistake. Brett slung him over his shoulder, head facing down his backside. As they rushed down the aisles of the cars Pierre's head took a number of severe bumps. The fact that the lights weren't flickering told Brett that they had not been compromised. Once inside Adam's private car, Brett slammed Pierre into a chair. "Remember, we didn't guarantee that he wouldn't get bruised," Brett said in reply to Adam's quizzical looks.

"You scum. You ain't nothin' but a bunch of weirdoes. If you think I'm tellin' you anything you're full of shit," Pierre said, spitting blood on the floor.

"Wrong!" Adam said, passing his finger down the bridge of Pierre's bloody nose. Then he gently blew into Pierre's dark eyes.

A high pitched humming filled the area. Adam made a PSI ball [1] in the palm of his hand and then tossed it on the floor. An orange fiery ball circled Pierre's feet. He squirmed in his chair, lifted his feet, and then tried to stand on top of the chair. As he did, the flames he saw grew larger, higher, and hotter. His screaming woke Daphne and the quads.

Daphne looked around her; her dazed eyes didn't want to focus. She thought she was dreaming. The thud of human flesh on the floor told her she was not dreaming. The sound of her sons crying roused her further. She struggled to get up. Her body, lead-like, was too heavy for her to move. She was sure she was strapped down. Isha, whispering to her, was trying to help her sit up. Then she brought the four babies to their mother. Daphne felt their warmth and began to hum to them. Once they quieted she turned her attention to what was going on around her. She watched with continued amazement at the wonder that was her husband. Yet, she was unsure of what it was she was seeing as she floated in and out of sleep. Isha quietly removed the quads.

Within minutes Pierre was babbling. Sometimes child-like he gushed past memories; other times he spewed anger from his swollen lips. Choked by tears, he told Adam everything. There had been nine of them including a Montreal dispatcher who provided inside information and the four motorcyclists who were continuing their attack on the blockaded train. They raced up one side and then down the other side of the train, firing high powered weaponry and lobbing an occasional grenade.

"We need a subterfuge that would draw those motorcyclists into one spot. It would have to be just long enough for us to take them down. Any suggestions?" Adam asked. He face was drawn and pale.

Noticing that Pierre was seated by a window, Patricia Livingston went over, opened the curtain, pulled up the blinds. Turning to Adam she asked, "Can you pull back the metal shield? If you can, I think I can give you the distraction you want."

There was a clanking up and down the train as the window shields were lowered.

Patricia Livingston jumped on Pierre, her knees in his protruding gut, grabbed him by the hair, shoved his head back, and pretended to kiss him. The dimly lighted interior of the train car created a believable silhouette. The first cyclist pulled up, ready to fire another round, stopped, and began watching the feigned activity—a voyeur on a Harley. Wondering why he wasn't firing his weapon, the other three cyclists pulled up. That's exactly what Adam wanted.

"Damn! Look at that old fart getting it on. Jesus! Some guys have all the luck. Wonder who she is?"

That pause was all that was needed; they were cut down by a barrage of bullets from the top of the train where Brett and Running-water had secreted themselves. Dutch, who had been called to come back, flew over the area, flood lighting it. As he flew in over the stranded train he counted four dead bodies, and then set the chopper down for an easy landing. He made a dash for the train guns drawn. As he ran up the lowered steps two UH-1 Huey helicopters did a fly by, came back, and landed. He wondered if the choppers had been bought from the U.S. Army. Even back when he was still in the Seals the military had begun to replace them. Several Canadian Royal Mounted Police and railroad detectives jumped out of the choppers. Running-water met them, exchanged a few words, and then escorted Captain Alex Steward of the CRMP into Adam's private car. The Captain informed Adam that armed guards would be posted along the train and would remain in place until the tracks were repaired and the train was able to proceed. A repair crew had been sent out and would be arriving by early morning. Adam thanked the Captain and had Samuel escort him to the passenger car to inspect its bloody mess. There would be many questions. Running-water's legal mind was grateful for the videos taken by the surveillance cameras. They would provide answers to many of the questions.

Dutch took his chopper airborne, landed it on the roof of Adam's private car, tied it down, and then joined the guards. His appearance startled the Mounties. He was dressed in blue fatigues, blue gloves, and blue painted face. He matched the color of the train perfectly. When he stood by one of the cars, he became invisible. Some of the Mounties thought it was a bit Hollywoodish, but then none of them had been in a firefight, fought hand to hand in steaming jungles, or crawled on their bellies through a barrage of enemy fire.

---

[1] A PSI ball is psychic energy drawn from within an individual, or from the universe. It can be programmed, directed. It is a powerful spurt of energy. There are various techniques available for generating and creating PSI-energy.

CHAPTER THIRTEEN

Patricia Livingston thought about Brett, the cut of his chin, even the flair of his nostrils. Bulges in all the right places. "What a stallion!" she thought. "Damn good looking." She flushed as she thought of what it would be like to bed him down. Her desire to reclaim her position at her station, to remain the diva of Canadian television overcame her sex urge. "I'll be damned if I'll let some young snip take my place."

She stepped out onto the vestibule, exited from the train. Pulled her cell phone from her backpack, punched in a number and waited. After a few minutes, she had given her report. Next, she sought out the pilot of one of the helicopters that had brought the Mounties. Speaking in hushed tones she got him to agree to take her secreted videotape to the nearest television affiliate. To help ensure its delivery she slipped him a couple hundred bucks and implied that she would meet up with him later. "What a jerk," she thought as she watched him take off. "I'm sure as hell not going to jump into bed with him." She did have some standards. At the moment she just couldn't think what they were.

The country would be electrified by what it saw and she would be propelled into national attention. She was sure some of the American feeds would pick it up and BBC would play it. The possibilities made her giddy with anticipation. "I'll show that young bitch," she thought. "Go ahead, honey, just try to take my place!"

Having lived from suitcase to suitcase for years she had learned to pack just the right clothes, jeans, and a couple of blouses, underwear, and a skirt. Personals were always a hassle for her. By necessity, she limited herself to the minimum of facial paint and creams. Her Eau de Parfum was always the exquisitely classic, *Chanel*. One thing she never overlooked was an outfit for after hours. This time she had packed a soft pink velour après ski outfit. She sniffed it to make sure it did not smell of the sandwich that had been stuffed into her backpack. She slid into it with ease. It clung to her curves in all the right places. Not one to bother with bras, she pulled the zipper of the top down far enough to reveal considerable cleavage. She left the compartment Adam had graciously assigned to her and went to the dining car to meet Brett for drinks. As she neared the car, the tantalizing flush returned. "Easy girl," she thought.

As she entered the car she was greeted with laughter and music. Newlyweds, Samuel and Julie, Dr. Bach, Dutch, and Brett were celebrating. Even the staid Brothers were there. The lively conversation stopped, the music stopped, and everyone turned and looked at her. She felt self-conscious. Something she hadn't felt since she was a teenager. Before she could speak, the group broke out in spontaneous applause. Brett went to her, handed her a drink and introduced her as the new hero to the group. She was embarrassed. Shocked. Pleased. Actually stunned. These feelings were not on her emotional-menu. She was used to the professional accolades and the phony cheesy smiles that everyone gave. And the pretend applause. This spontaneous stuff was different.

Brett pulled her to him, kissed her on the mouth and just as he was about to release her, she returned his kiss and wrapped one of her long legs around him. Dutch filled the air with whistles and cat calls. She let go of the kiss, took a long look at the odd collection of people in the room and then burst into tears. For the first time in her life, Patricia Livingston felt she was really accepted. Whatever this group of odd-balls had going for it, she wanted to be part of it. She sat down at one of the tables and continued to cry. Her crying finally dried up. The emotional outburst surprised her. She downed her drink. "It's so unlike me to bawl like some stupid little girl," she thought as she indicated she was ready for a second drink. Had she known there was a bar she would have come sooner. She was ready for her third drink. Thought better. Decided against it.

While this group kicked back, enjoying the much-needed release, Adam had his hands full with four very hungry boys. Daphne watched as her husband deftly change diapers and prepared four bottles of formula. She wondered how he knew how to change diapers and put them on. She wondered how he was going to feed them. She thought she should help but before she could decide she dozed off again. As soon as Adam had one quad fed, he carefully snuggled him in a drawer of the desk just below the bank of television monitors. Once the last one was fed and all had fallen to sleep, Adam knelt down beside his wife and gently kissed her and whispered, "I love you."

She heard him with her soul and was content.

Sitting by his wife, Adam marveled at the miracle he had witnessed. Somehow he had to create a home where they would be safe; a place where his sons could grow into manhood without the fear of being murdered. A single tear welled up as his sense of concern deepened. Death, always patient— waited. So many deaths. If it's my wealth that is wanted they can have it. Just leave me alone. Running-water thinks it's my powers. I have no control over that. I am what I am," Adam thought.

A tap at the door brought him to his feet. He grabbed an Uzi, took it off safety and went to the door. He realized the mistake of not having a video camera there or at least a call box. He released the electronic lock, shoved the steel bar back, and cautiously opened it. It was Dr. Bach, Running-water and Isha.

"Thought you might need some help," Isha said, looking around, "Where are they, the babies?"

Adam pointed toward the desk with four open drawers. The visitors stifled a laugh. Dr. Bach checked Daphne and then each baby. Satisfied, he went back to the door, opened it, and with an exaggerated grunt, dragged in a cart full of hot food. Its smell brought Daphne around. She was ready to eat. Dr. Bach had seen to the menu, making sure she got easily digestible foods and a small quantity. He even provided a glass of rich red wine Before retiring Adam constructed a sling over their bed, big enough to hold the quads, close to Daphne. She could reach up and touch them and they could smell her, hear her heartbeat. [1]

Morning brought the end of a night without incident—a welcome reprieve. Two full work crews from the railroad had arrived. The clanking of metal against metal woke the sleepers. Several sections of track had to be laid once the damaged rails and ties were removed. The windows of the train were uncovered and the morning sunlight brought a sense of renewal to those on board. Adam exited from the train, met each worker, and thanked them as he shook their hands. Into each he laid a hundred dollar bill. Patricia Livingston was there, filming and recording every word, every movement that Adam made. For a couple of minutes, she focused on the faces of the men, framing the expressions as they realized they had been given a hundred dollar bill. During those few minutes, the supervisor of the work crew handed Adam a small package. Patricia Livingston did not catch that. The sincerity in his voice struck a chord. She remembered attending his lecture at Karuna House back in Toronto. It seemed like years ago, yet it was not.

She remembered being seated just to the left of center in what had been an elegant ballroom. From there she watched every move he made. So caught up in watching his crotch, she nearly forgot to turn on her tape recorder. She remembered thinking how absolutely breathtaking he was. His words came back to her: 'Trust engenders harmony and peace; it engenders love. When that trust is betrayed, love flies out the window.' *Betrayal* leaped back at her, caught in her throat, strangling her. "That's

Adam's secret. He gives trust, as well as love, unconditionally. My god! I've betrayed all of that!" A shudder wracked her body and it wasn't caused by the cold.

She realized she was alone! The men were working, Adam had disappeared and as she turned to go back to the train, she came face to face with Brett. His look told her everything.

"Miss Livingston, Adam wants to see you."

"I'll be right there," Patricia Livingston, said, struggling to maintain her composure.

"Now, Miss Livingston," Brett said, reaching for her arm. She knew better than to resist. She had been that route before.

[1] This approach has been suggested by Gaston Lavoie, Maniwaki, Quebec, CA.

CHAPTER FOURTEEN

She felt a tremor deep within her as she stepped through the open door into Adam's private car. The all too frequent nausea forced her to repeatedly swallow. She nodded her head in appreciation to Brett for holding the door open for her. Steeling herself for the worst, she forced her professional smile, adjusted her skirt, and sucked in her gut. She jumped when the door slammed behind her. Its metallic clang reminded her of a closing cell door in a prison, a sound she had heard all too often when she had covered the crime beat.

"Have a seat," Running-water said, looking up from one of the monitors.

"I'll stand. Thanks anyway. By the way, I meant to ask you earlier if you have another name." She hoped it would take her mind off the growing anxiety she felt.

"Paul Dakota," Running-water replied, "Adam will see you shortly."

"Well, Paul, why does Adam want to see me?"

"I'll tell you," Adam said as he entered from the rear of the car. "Your presence on this train is a disruption. You put yourself on my train and inserted yourself into our private lives. I did not ask you here. It's not that I am not grateful for the help you gave in ending the crisis on board this train. I am and for that I thank you. Now, however, your presence is an effrontery. Airing of the deaths of four people on this train and the deaths of those outside on national television is reprehensible. Showing pictures of my sons, and the very private moments between my wife and me is an unforgivable transgression. I've arranged for my pilot to fly you to the nearest town and you can make your own way from there."

"In the meantime, Miss Livingston," Running-water said, "I am bringing legal suit against you and your television station for the invasion of our privacy."

"Go ahead you as—." Catching herself and remembering the slap in the face for swearing, Patricia Livingston rephrased her words.

"Go ahead you big ape. That will simply generate more publicity. It seems to me that with all the deaths surrounding your little entourage there will be a significant investigation. And that will tie you up for months."

"Threats do not bother me," Running-water replied.

"Let's get one thing straight. First of all, I don't threat. Second, I am a reporter. I go where the news is. That's my job. That's how I earn my living. I didn't create the interest in your doings even though there was a time and not that long ago when Adam wanted my help. Or have you forgotten he contacted me? How many deaths that night, Adam? You created national interest with this fancy tomb you call a train. You had it painted luminous black, lit up with blue neon lights, fancy insignia, blackened windows, and moved at high speeds during the night. Don't talk to me about creating a story that you didn't want. You did that! You're the one who didn't do personnel checks and let murderers on board. All I did was report it, and I might add, factually. And frankly, I don't give a damn if you think it was in good taste or not. You've a few things in that area to learn."

"She's right, Adam. We created the story. You can't fault her there," Brett said.

"No one asked for your opinion," Running-water shot back.

"Tough! All of us know you and Adam are tight-assed buddies, but that doesn't give you the right to be disrespectful toward the rest of us. Ever since Dutch and I had the jet blown up under us you've been a real pain in the ass. Well, we sure as hell have carried our weight and then some. And that, *my brother* entitles me to have my say," Brett said.

"You better remember who pays you," Running-water snapped.

"Stop! Just listen to yourselves. Where's the love and compassion you supposedly support? What a joke! I'll hitch a ride back with the track crew," Patricia Livingston said.

"No way. Dressed the way you are. You wouldn't last an hour before they raped you. I'll fly you back myself," Brett said.

"Not in our plane," Running-water said.

"Screw you! You don't own that chopper. Dutch and I paid for its rental. Come on, Patricia, we're getting the hell out of here," Brett said.

Patricia Livingston was pleasantly surprised by Brett's defense. She liked that. She was about to say something but was interrupted by Adam.

"She's right. I created the interest. I am responsible. The damage has been done. We have to live with it. When we come to the next stop you can exit then."

Daphne came out from their bedroom, dressed in a long flowing pink robe; her hair brushed back, showed her high cheek bones that platformed exquisite dark eyes. Pale from birthing four babies, she was still incredibly beautiful.

"Damage? What damage? Damage to what?" Daphne asked.

"Our sons. The world now knows of their existence," Adam replied, "There are so few quadruplets in the world, the publicity will be unmerciful. Are you supposed to be up?"

"Yes! So? Now we don't have to send out birth announcements," Daphne said as she went to Patricia Livingston's side and taking her by the hand, said, "Do you mind helping me? The four of them are quite a handful and I'm still weak from their birthing."

As the two women left to care for the babies, Daphne looked at Adam and he understood that this was a time for him to defer to her. Patricia Livingston would remain.

Adam turned to Brett and Running-water and said, "I don't know the cause of your differences but I want it to end and end now. No more bickering. Have we not seen enough ugliness? We certainly don't need to create it among ourselves. If you have complaints, bring them out in the open so they may be dealt with. Understood?"

CHAPTER FIFTEEN

Slowly the train eased its way across the repaired track. Brett heard the whir and vibration of helicopter blades. He scrambled up the escape hatch. In his rush, he forgot his backpack and weapons and started back down to get them. Running-water met him. He handed up the gear and then extended his hand. It was a firm handshake.

"Fly safe, my friend," Running-water said as Brett's body disappeared through the hatch.

Leaning back into the hatch, a broad smile on his face, Brett gave a thumbs-up and then disappeared.

Running-water secured the hatch and turned to speak to Adam. He wasn't there. Shrugging his shoulders, he went back to the monitors. He watched the landscape slip by at an ever faster pace as the train picked up speed and the click-clack of the cars rolling along the rails smoothed out into a steady hypnotic rhythm. A sudden gust of air broadsided him. He swung around in his chair; his gun at his side.

A giant of a man peered down on him. His dark eyes and thick black eyebrows accentuated his grim face. An unlit cigar hung at the corner of his curled lip. He tongued it from one side of his mouth to the other.

Running-water leaned back in his chair; cocked his head back. "How'd you get in here? Who are you? What do you want?

"I'll ask the questions," the man said, his voice as huge as he was.

"Uh-uh. Move and you're dead." Running-water brought his automatic into full view. "You answer my questions."

The huge man hesitated just long enough to size up the person in front of him. Slowly and calmly he looked directly at Running-water's eyes. In their coldness, he saw death.

"I'm Jonathan O'Banyon, an investigator for the Canadian Railroad. I was told I'd find a guy called Running-water back here. You him?"

"You found him. When did you come on board?"

"Just before the train moved out. Adam told me you were here. Now then, can I get to my questions?" Jonathan said, easing himself into a chair, spread his long legs out in front of him, leaned back and said, "Now that introductions are over, you ready to answer my questions?"

"Fire away."

"There seems to be some confusion over the contents of car number seven. Mind going over the contents of that box car?"

Running-water stood up. "Adam should answer that question. It's his stuff. I'll call him and have him join us."

"No need. You probably have a good idea of what's stored there and we can just go on from there," O'Banyon replied, trying to be casual.

"Adam will join us," Running-water said. He put his automatic to O'Banyon's head. "Move and you're history."

Running-water got real quiet. O'Banyon couldn't hear him breathing. He knew from experience that you automatically hold your breath just before you pull the trigger. He could feel the trigger on the Glock 25 being slowly tightened. He waited for the explosion. He closed his eyes.

The connecting door to the car opened and shut with a bang. O'Banyon sank lower into his chair.

"You didn't wet your pants, now did you?" Running-water said.

O'Banyon face reddened.

"Got your message. Who's this?" Adam asked.

Before Running-water could explain, Daphne and Patricia Livingston entered from the sleeping compartment, each carrying two babies.

"I heard you say you wanted to know the contents of car seven? Here's our treasure," Daphne said as she held up two of her sons. "Car seven contains diapers, formula, clothes, medicines, and baby furniture. When you have four it takes a lot. That's why the boxes are marked Family/Personal."

"What's your interest in the seventh car?" Patricia Livingston said, cradling two of the quads.

Jonathan O'Banyon mouth dropped open. Shit. Just wait till I get my hands on the bastard who planned this. I'll kill the son-of-a-bitch.

"You were asked a question," Running-water said. He jabbed his Glock 25 into the back of O'Banyon's neck.

"Word had it there was millions in cash and jewels stashed in a bunch of boxes in car seven. It was supposed to be easy pickings. No one was to get hurt. What a mess." O'Banyon shook his head.

"You're saying you had information from someone who is on this train?" Patricia Livingston said.

"Yes, ma'am. Funny dude," O'Banyon replied.

"Funny dude? How so?" Running-water asked, giving O'Banyon another jab with his Glock- 25.

"He was wearing a uniform of some kind. Not a military or police uniform. More like some uppity boarding school. Had a fancy logo on the breast pocket."

"What did he look like?" Adam said.

"He was tall, not as tall as me though; skinny, boney kind of skinny. You know what I mean? He wore a ski cap. Covered up most of his face. He had red hair. That much I know."

"Red hair? How do you know that if his head was covered?" Running-water asked.

"One of his eyebrows wasn't completely covered. It was reddish color and his eyes were green so I just assumed he had red hair."

"Charles," Adam said.

CHAPTER SIXTEEN

Premonition? Charles couldn't get a handle on it. Whatever it was, he felt the need to look his best.

After showering down he scrubbed his teeth and applied a generous amount of whitener. Waited the required amount of time, rinsed, and spat it out. He splashed extra aftershave on his face, slicked back his hair. Slipped on his gray slacks and light blue blazer, the uniform, as he called it. He looked at his image in the full-length mirror. Struck a couple of different poses. Not bad. Not bad at all.

He stepped in closer to the mirror; looked at the golden logo of The Esaugetuh Benevolent Society. Fussed with the jacket's breast pocket trying to make the logo straight. Can't tell me that it wasn't deliberately sown on crooked. With a flick of his wrist, he undid the second button of his collarless light blue shirt. He looked down at his spit-polished black shoes. The left one had a spot. Damn. Must a splashed some aftershave on it. He rubbed it up and down on the back of his leg. The shine returned. He hiked up his pants to make sure his very full crotch was prominent and humped the air.

He was ready to hit the streets. He knew how to strut.

What a joke. No streets here.

The mirror didn't answer.

Charles opened the door of his compartment. Adam, Running-water, and O'Banyon were standing there.

He sucked air. Waited for something to happen. What will Adam do with me? Prison doesn't frighten me. Hell, I've been beaten and raped too many times to be afraid of that.

"You betrayed a trust, as well as the memory of my father, the man who took you off the streets and gave you a home," Adam said. "I'd like to know why."

Charles had expected a screaming lecture, but there was no yelling, no hatred in Adam's voice, no pious pitying for a wayward child. He stood there a couple of minutes. He opened his mouth to speak. Nothing came out. Nothing. His hatred froze in his throat, strangled him, and suffocated him until he came totally undone and collapsed in complete silent hysteria.

Running-water stepped over the quivering heap on the floor, entered Charles' compartment, and began a systematic search. And like the youth he was, Charles had kept a detailed account of his plot to pull off the *Great Train Robbery*. [1] Running-water shook his head in disbelief. Hate filled delusional ranting. Sick. A real psycho. He stopped reading and tuned into what Adam was saying.

"My father, Esaugetuh, must have seen something of value in you to have pulled you from the gutter. In my ignorance, I credited your personal self-castration to misguided youth. Unwittingly, I left you in the corruption that had snaked its way throughout Karuna House. At that time I didn't know Joseph had murdered my father and that Thomas was his brother. I realized you needed to come to terms with what you perceived as a despicable act—sex with your mother, Julie. I sought her out and brought her to Karuna House."

Finally getting his voice, Charles blurted, "Why? Why? My god. The sight of her made me sick. You knew how I felt, yet you brought her there. You did it to torture me. It's always the same with you do-gooders. Your way or no way. Yeah, that's your motto. It was the same on the streets. You get a mark and as soon as you don't deliver the way he wants, the promise is withdrawn. The only difference? You didn't beat me. You might just as well have. What you did is—is worse. Unforgivable."

"No. It was to help you realize you did not have sex with your mother. At that moment in time, she was not your mother. She was a doped up drunk who didn't even know where she was. And you are not even sure, by your own admission back at Karuna House, that you actually had intercourse. All you remembered was waking up and finding your naked mother in bed with you," Adam said.

"It don't matter. It's too late."

" You *can* redeem yourself. You violated the trust given to you. Earn it back," Adam said.

"Earn it back? How? Seven men are dead because of me. Shit. There wasn't supposed to be any killing. My god it was—,"

"Accept what is. Work to change what is not," Adam said.

---

[1] 1903 film photographed and directed by Edwin S. Porter; a milestone in film history.

CHAPTER SEVENTEEN

Samuel and Julie, on their way to the dining car, had to walk through the Pullman occupied by The Brothers. At Charles' compartment, they saw Charles on the floor in a fetal position. Julie clutched Samuel's arm. "Oh no! What? What has happened?"

"He's alright. Just putting on a show. He's the one behind the attempted robbery," Running-water said.

"Is that true? Answer me. Are you responsible for all those deaths?"

Julie bent down. Looked directly at Charles. Slapped him.

"I can't believe that you hate me so much that you were willing to hurt the one person in this world who befriended you. Who wanted nothing in return. At least I never pretended to be other than I am—a whore. But you, you have pretended to be other than what you are." She stopped, sucked in her breath. "You are a liar, a cheat, a thief, and a murderer. Yes, a murderer!

She slapped him again. Turning to Samuel she said, "Let's go. I can't stand the sight of him."

Tears filled her eyes as Samuel gently put his arm around her, held her to him.

"Wait, please—mother."

"Please, he says. Did you hear that? Mother, he calls me. Yesterday he wouldn't even speak to me. Wait? Why should I wait? What more can you possibly say?"

"You can come to my trial"

The calmness in Charles' voice surprised all of them.

That registered surprise set well with him. Got'em again. He wiped his mouth to hide the smirk. Once again the great Charles has seized the day. Carpe diem or whatever the phrase is.

"Ay and maybe you'll stay for mine, too?" O'Banyon said. What a mess I've gotten myself into."

"Don't count on it. Either of you," Julie said. She walked away.

Running-water took Charles and O'Banyon to the baggage car and locked them in. He notified the engineer call ahead to have the local authorities meet them.

Using the train's intercom, Adam called The Brothers to a meeting in the train's dining car. And like Charles, they knew they were in trouble. And like a bunch of little schoolboys who had been caught doing some mischief, they filed into the dining car, one behind the other.

Adam said nothing. He was staring out the window. The train zipped by the beautiful Canadian countryside. He did not see it. The dreaded longing in his heart had festered. His father's last words had come to him through time; uttered as he died, came back to him now, haunted him: "What is it you desire?" I'm not sure I know anymore.

Turning to The Brothers who had seated themselves at various tables, Adam said, "You have failed your obligations. Oh, not to me. In that respect you have none. I'm talking about your obligations as human beings. And you may have a need to ask what those are since you failed them.

77

My question is did you fail your obligations out of ignorance, out of disregard or out of irresponsibility? If it was out of ignorance then that failure is mine for not giving you the proper instruction. If it is out of disregard or irresponsibility then I have failed you by not teaching you to be aware of the sanctity of human value and to be responsible for that value. Either way, the responsibility for your situation is mine. For that, I apologize and ask that you forgive me."

The Brothers remained in their seats; stunned by what they had just heard. It was difficult for them to adjust to this man. Their former Master, Joseph, had been a screaming banshee, often unnecessarily crude, and frequently violent toward them. They knew this man was capable of killing, that he held great shamanistic powers, that he was one of the wealthiest men in the world, and that he had survived many attempts on his life. But none of that told them what he was. And it was this *what* that had kept them in a mental state of disarray and emotional upheaval. And like zombies, they continued sitting there saying nothing.

Adam left them.

The Brothers were not the only ones who heard Adam's words. Patricia Livingston caught every word and recorded it. As Adam approached the end of the dining car she spoke to him. "Can we talk? I mean really talk?"

"Off the record?" Adam said.

"No. For the record. What I have to say needs to be on the record," Patricia Livingston said.

"You're recording this conversation?"

"Every word. May I begin?"

"Okay," Adam said, indicating they should sit down.

"First, I'm sorry for invading your privacy. Second, I'm sorry for releasing the video of the killing of those men. True, it was a great story and my ratings soared to a new high, but that doesn't really justify the very poor taste, the effrontery to their families, and to you. It was worse than when an embedded newsperson filmed an American soldier killing an Iraqi insurgent during the second Iraqi war. It's hard for me to explain but it's so easy to get caught up, to let the swell of the emotional moment carry you away. All reason leaves you except one: Get the story! Sometimes we in the media forget we have a higher ethic and we violate that in the name of the 'news.' Adam, I am ashamed. And like you asked The Brothers to forgive you, I ask you to forgive me. Will you?"

"Will you, Adam?" Daphne asked, entering the dining car. "I have."

"Of course. We'll not bring this up again. Understood?"

"Understood," Patricia Livingston said, reaching across the table and taking Adam's hand.

As she held his hand, a pale blue light surrounded it. Its radiance encompassed her hand, hovered there, and then left.

"How long have you been ill?" Adam said.

"I—I don't know what you're talking about," Patricia Livingston said.

Immediately she knew that was a mistake. She turned her head to hide the quiver on her slightly parted lips. No one knew of her physical problem. She had concealed it from her producers, even her doctor. Admittedly the pain had grown worse but then after her third drink, she didn't feel it anymore. The fact was, by the fourth, she felt very little.

"About three months. Sometimes the pain really gets to me."

"May I do a scan?" He nodded his head toward the floor.

Patricia Livingston hesitated for a moment, then got down on the floor and lay on her back. Lately, I've been spending a lot of time on my back. And hasn't been for sex. Adam passed his hands over her. They stopped, hovered near the duodenum, changed from the light blue to a pink and then to a bright red. They trembled.

"I'd like Dr. Bach to take a look at you. He'll want to order some tests once we reach the States. I want you to lie really still for the next few minutes. You'll feel heat and you will feel it build. Don't be alarmed. It won't burn you," Adam said.

Adam's hands again moved over Patricia Livingston's abdomen, and again stopped at the duodenum. The heat in his hands began to build and she felt a low vibration. At first, she thought it was just the humming of the train but when it seemed to fill the dining car she realized it was coming from Adam. His whole body was glowing. A blue aura engulfed him.

Good god, I can see right through him.

The humming stopped the blue light that surrounded Adam's body disappeared.

And all was quiet.

She lay there for a moment, sat up, looked at Adam and then at Daphne.

"Thank you. Thank you. Even a double scotch never made me feel this good. Whatever it is you do, it's fantastic," Patricia Livingston said, getting up.

CHAPTER EIGHTEEN

Arm in arm, Daphne and Patricia Livingston left Adam sitting in the dining car. Their bonding bewildered him. What is it that Daphne senses that I haven't? Okay. So I had initiated contact with Patricia Livingston for publicity for my lecture series. What was it about her then that attracted me? Integrity! There was integrity in her reporting of the news. That was why I had invited her to hear my lecture. She would report without editorializing.

As the darkened train sped along, Adam looked out and watched the waning moon. It raced along with the speeding train and its presence reminded him of the short stay he had at Esaugetuh's ranch. There, in spite of the deaths that had surrounded him, he had watched another moon and marveled at it. When reflected in the lake, the moon lost its stationary golden shape, changing according to the movements of the water. The human soul is not dissimilar. The material body in which the soul is housed determines its shape, that is, its nature, outlook, and behavior. Too bad Narcissus didn't realize the shape he saw reflected back at him was illusional and would be the cause of his downfall. The obvious lesson for all soul keepers is not to mistake the illusion of mortality for reality.

Surely the heavens must be rift with such delusional souls—souls that fell for the all too prevalent notion that this present, this now, is all there is. Somehow, in some way, people have got to believe again. If all one does is set aside a Sunday, a Saturday as a holy day, or goes down on bended knee in prayer seven times a day, or makes an offering at the base of a statue, what happens to the rest of the time? Is spirituality gone?

It's not going to church beliefs, not the brimstone and hell-fire kind of thing, not the promise of rewards and punishments for following or not following established dogma, but in a genuine compassionate existence made possible by—by what? God? No, that denies human free will. What then?

The reemergence of a lost thought nearly made itself known. It always seemed right at the tip of his tongue and yet, it always evaded him. Even as a young kid answers never quite came into existence. The man whom he had called father, believing him to be his real father, was not into answering questions. Actually, that man had never legally adopted him. That revelation had come after both he and his biological mother had been murdered. Strangely, it was not nearly the shock as when he learned that Esaugetuh, who had adopted him, was his real father. And he felt sure that within all of that there should have been an answer.

What? What is it? Adam said out loud.

"What?" Daphne said, returning from feeding their sons and setting down in a chair next to her husband. Gently she slipped her hand over his.

Then he knew, knew for sure. It wasn't the subject of a lecture, intellectualized and released in unbelieving monotones. It was here—now—and at last, he knew it, understood it. He pulled Daphne closer to him, smelling her freshness. Then softly he whispered, "I know the secrets of secrets."

CHAPTER NINETEEN

The train rumbled on and the two of them sat there, quiet for a moment, thinking of what was and maybe what was hoped for. She was the first to speak.

"Which is?" She looked into Adam's azure blue eyes, eyes that belied his heritage. Searching for understanding. She waited for his reply.

"Love!" Adam said. "We've got to learn how to love again. That's Charles' problem. He never learned to love; that's why he rejects it when it is given; rejects it because he doesn't know what it is. And don't we reject as a matter of course, those things we don't know, don't understand. And isn't that the basis of bigotry, prejudice, and malice?"

"But surely, Adam, Charles must have known his mother's love?" Daphne said.

"No. He was just an object. When we objectify, all emotion flies out the window. Love is emotion. It is emotional and is emotion driven. Remember when you came to my bed, mounted me, and we spent the night in orgiastic ecstasy. It was then that I filled you with my seed and you conceived our sons. We were not known to each other. We had not courted. There was no love there even though there was much emotion. Love embodies a different kind of emotion. When my first son came into the world and I held him in my arms, I knew at that moment what love was. And when your birthing was finished, I looked at you and understood its complexity and saw its beauty in your soul. Then I knew that which Esaugetuh had known all those years he had to live without being by the side of my mother. Such is the strength of love and its wonderment. In the beginning, you were the object of my physical release. And I yours. Objectification does not allow for love. I've not been able to express it, to get it out into the open."

"And you want to know if I *really* love you?" Daphne said.

"I know you do," Adam said, placing a finger on her lips, tracing their outline, and then kissing her.

"Somehow," he continued, "Charles must know love as the ultimate reason for all life." Adam said.

"What will you do about them? We'll soon arrive at a town. Are you having them arrested?" Daphne said.

"There are no witnesses that they tried to rob this train. Anyone who could connect them to the attempted robbery is dead. In court, it would be their word against ours especially if Charles' diary disappeared. And since we did not see either of them attempt to rob us, or kills anyone, what we can say?"

On their return to their car, Adam and Daphne stopped at Samuel and Julie's compartment to tell them Charles would not be arrested Julie grabbed Adam around the neck, hugged him, and began to cry.

"How can I make him understand?" Julie said, wiping away her tears, and smearing her mascara. She now had two blackened eyes.

"Make him realize that you chose to keep him. You could have aborted him, given him up for adoption, or thrown him into a dumpster. Ask him to withhold judgment about the way you earned your living. One more thing, Julie, if you two really did have sex, make him understand it was not personal," Daphne said.

"I just don't think I can face him. He's so full of hatred," Julie said.

"Look, why don't you join us? Adam and Samuel will bring Charles and that Mr. O'Banyon there," Daphne said, giving Adam a nod indicating that he should go along.

CHAPTER TWENTY

Charles and O'Banyon nearly knocked one another down dancing along the narrow aisles. Charles twirled around O'Banyon, unable to control his delight in his sudden good fortune. He clapped his hands and stomped his feet pretending to do an Irish jig.

All is not lost. I still might be able to grab some of the money stashed in car seven. Who gives a raps ass that seven is a special number to these half-breeds. They're not fooling me with this baby furniture crap. I ought to know. I helped pack it.

Adam shook his head as he and Samuel tried to hurry the dancing maelstroms toward his private car. The giant and the beanpole brought laughter. It filled the train and it felt good. So engrossed in the shenanigans no one noticed the train had slowed and had come to a complete stop.

A thud on the roof brought Running-water to rapt attention. With guns drawn he listened. When he heard the tap-tap on the escape hatch, he cautiously opened it. Brett jumped down.

"Since the train didn't stop at that last town I thought I better drop in and see what was happening."

"Why don't you just tell the truth?" Running-water said, winking at Adam who had just walked in.

"What do you mean truth?" Brett said.

"Well, we all know you have a special interest in Patricia Livingston and that's the real reason you dropped in," Adam said, picking up the cue from

Running-water. And he knew because he had read Brett's thought.

"Did I hear my name mentioned?"

Running-water began to play his flute. *Love Is a Many Splendored Thing* filled the car. Brett's face reddened. Without warning, he got down on his knees.

"Patricia, will you marry me?"

The flute quieted. They waited to hear a reply. None came. A loud sob slashed through the silence as Patricia Livingston cried out, "You're cruel! All of you! And mean spirited! How could you?"

"Hold on there just one damn minute," Brett said. "I'm serious. I don't go around asking women to marry me. Now answer my question. Will you or won't you marry me?"

Stunned, Patricia Livingston stood perfectly still. Not one word came from her open mouth. She was in his arms, covering his handsome face with kisses. Crying all the while.

"I take it you've said yes," Brett said, laughing and swinging her around in the air.

"Yes!"

"This calls for a toast," Adam said.

And they toasted the couple, forgetting the ugliness they had experienced.

"Almost forgot. Got a DVD for you, Adam. And a copy of the Toronto paper. Thought you'd find them interesting," Brett said. "Our in house reporter is up for a CNMA."

"What's that?" Adam said.

"The Canadian National Media Award. The DVD is a copy of her broadcast. Be sure you watch it. She's quite the woman, Adam."

"Uh huh," Adam said, slapping Brett on the butt.

The train had barely picked up speed when it again slowed and then stopped. There was no railroad station, no passenger, or loading dock. They were at a crossing. Red lights atop a car flashed as it raced alongside of the train. Whoever was driving slammed on the brakes and the little car dove-tailed. The clank of the train's steps being lowered echoed throughout the train.
"What's happening?
The door to Adam's car was jerked open. A stream of cold air rushed into the car. A man wrapped in a long black cape with a black wool beret on his head entered. He was followed by two others covered with hooded ponchos With a gesture out of a Barrymore silent movie, the cloaked figure flung back his cape revealing the white rounded collar of a priest.
"Forgive me, but I was told there was to be a wedding here. Has someone played a very bad joke?"
"Put your weapons down. No mistake padre," Dutch Masters said, pulling back his hood. "You going to make a liar out of me, Brett?"
"He most certainly is not," Patricia Livingston said.
Everything had become almost surreal. She had not imagined herself married. *What do I know about this guy? Actually, beyond the facts that he is handsome, obviously well-endowed in all the right places, and a fighter, I know absolutely nothing*

about him. My god, I can't believe I'm not craving a drink.

The ceremony, though brief, was capped with a champagne toast to the newlyweds. From a traditional perspective, the wedding was unusual in that there weren't a best man or bride's maids, and there wasn't an exchange of rings. The nuptials were sealed by a kiss. But then, who needed all the trapping? The memory should be that of commitment rather than ceremonial display. The priest left and Dutch left. Others returned to their compartments. Brett and Patricia Livingston went to her compartment.

CHAPTER TWENTY-ONE

Daphne and Adam put their sons to bed. Daphne, still recouping from the birthing process, retired. Admitting that she had overdone she felt grateful that Adam had decided to give her the whole bed. Pulling the covers around her, she snuggled in their warmth and was soon asleep. He went back into his office.

Adam checked the monitors, punching up each car one at a time. A couple of the Brothers were still in the dining car, playing cards. The security camera in the passenger car had been replaced. Adam checked it. No one was there. Even though everything seemed normal, he felt he wasn't alone. The hair on his arms stood up. The obsidian pulsed against his naked skin.

Turning from the monitors Adam said, "Who are you?"

"I am aham brachmasi—pure spirit—pure soul as your people call it."

"My people?"

"Yes, the white man."

"Ah, but am I not your son and if I am how is it you say 'my people? You sound belligerent."

"You have all the trappings of a white man. Look around you. You haven't learned much have you?"

"I live in a white man's world despite the fact that the vast majority of the world's population is not white. Besides you know very well I am a half-breed; a bastard child from —," He stopped. His anger surprised him.

"So you do; so you are."

"Well then, should I not operate within the rules of that governance?"

"To do so forsakes your own people and their ways. Denies who you are."

"Those ways are gone. I cannot be as they once were. I cannot be what I am not."

"And what are you?"

"I'm not an Indian from the old days who walks around in leather and moccasins and braided hair. I do not attach another name such as American Indian or Native American to my identity as some ethnic groups do. I am a modern man, alive in a modern world. I am an American!"

"And so you are."

"And what's that supposed to mean?"

"You are what you say you are, Modern Man. So, what will you do with that identification?"

"I will speak to the modern mind not of our heritage as Indians native to the Americas or First Nation People wronged. Such a posture produces negativism, instills prejudice, and promotes separation as do the other ethnic modifiers so popular these days. Modifiers such as Italian-American, Asian-American, African-American, or Mexican-American. I speak of a broader vision."

"And that is?"

"I will speak of the wonder of all humanity, of being benevolent, compassionate, of loving no matter the color of one's skin or the origin of one's ancestry."

"And how does that differ from other bringers of *Words of Life*?"

"Educate through example."

"And is that not what Christ did? Look at what it got Him—crucified!"

"Were you?"

"Was I what?"

"Like Him, prepared for your death?"

"Humph!"

"That won't do. Surely you have some wisdom for me to share with my sons, your grandsons? Some wisdom to ease this dying business."

"Did I not tell you that I am pure spirit, pure soul? Death is not an end product. It's more of a transmigration—an evolving into a different realm of existence. Death is not to be feared. It's simply another form of birth. Your woman just gave birth to four of your sons. In one sense that was death. They lost the warmth and security of their mother's womb, a place where there was no fear. They were forced into a new and strange place. That was transmigration for them. Death is a birthing. I'm surprised you don't have questions about living. Got that all figured out do you?"

"Of course not! I've figured out one thing, though."

"And that is?"

"The ground of all being."

"And does this ground of all being have a name?"

"Love!"

"Hmm. Might be hope for you after all. Love certainly is the ground of all being: love of Self, love of the Great Spirits, love of all creations, love of one's mate, and children. I've got to go. I can't keep coming back for these little chats just because you have a question."

"I didn't call you back. For whatever reason you are here, I am glad. You say you can't keep coming back. I say why not? You once told me that you would always be with me. And if you are always with me, then there is the expectation of communication. After all, am I not part of you?"

"That you are; you are that."

Daphne walked into the office and said, "Adam who are you talking to?"

"My father," Adam replied.

"It's nice that you pray. It will set a good example for our sons," Daphne said.

"I wasn't praying."

CHAPTER TWENTY-TWO

Daphne leaned and kissed Adam on his forehead and returned to their bed. Adam remained where he was. The hum of the train told him they were traveling at a very high speed. Yet he felt no sense of danger. He leaned back and let his thoughts wander.

Strange things have been taking place throughout the world. Actually the whole universe. A meteor turned the night sky into morning in the northwestern part of the United States. Tornadoes ripped through parts of the country causing great damage and death. Volcanoes have sprung to life spewing forth their steam and fire. Large ice balls have fallen on a city in Spain; a giant wave came up out of the bowels of the ocean and created havoc in Indonesia. A hurricane destroyed much of an American city. Venus, our sister planet, transected the sun. White clouds filled with lightning. New planets have been discovered. Light itself has been frozen.

And that's not all. Something is still happening to me. Maybe I should say in me. The mark on my arm of an eagle's feather with its bolt of lightning is more pronounced. The lightning bolt seems to glow. Just beneath its surface, I feel a vibration whenever I touch it. I wonder if it's part of my continued transformation or another sign.

The vibration just beneath the eagle feather hemangioma held his attention as did its deepening shades of color. Its changing rhythmic pattern held a special fascination for him. With concentration, he separated its rhythmic pattern from the clickety-clack of the train and from his heartbeat. It's more distinct. Unique. Not quite a ping.

When I wear the Wisdom Keeper's obsidian amulet it pulses a blue light. More a blue glow than a light. It's subtle. I think its pulsing is affected by the blue planets themselves; Neptune, Uranus, and of course Earth. I feel another influence but I can't identify its source. Nor can I say exactly what it is.

And for a time, he continued his fascination with the mark on his arm pulsing in perfect synchronization with the obsidian amulet that hung around his neck. Adam knew that everything vibrates and oscillates through the broad stretches of infinity. Motion produces changes, everything in nature passes through perpetual change. And all of this he understood, but not the change in the shamanistic symbol that burned into his arm. Besides pulsing and glowing in the dark the bolt of lightning that passed through the eagle's feather seemed to flash in a distinct complimentary beat of its own. Adam didn't draw a connection between that and his azure blue eyes. He didn't know both glowed.

If Daphne has noticed the glowing mark she hasn't mentioned it. I'm grateful for that. What could I tell her? Somewhere, somehow, at some time, the question of my being has to be answered. And when it is, all will be known.

Is it possible that I am a soul-bearer and not a user of a soul-catcher? Of course. It's so obvious. Damn! It's been there all along. Why haven't I seen it? As a soul-bearer, I carry the soul of my father, the great shaman— Esaugetuh. My god! That's why he told me there could only be one. I am as my father, reincarnate!

But also different. My powers seem so much stronger than my father's. And I seem to have several he did not. I feel that I'm still developing. These powers are so strange to me. I don't know if they're psychic, paranormal, or extraterrestrial. Good god! What if I'm an alien experiment? Science has been making inroads into the nature and power of the mind. Some people have been able to control electronic devices by simply thinking. Others move objects. The mind's total energy capacity has not yet been measured. As yet, its power and potential are not fully realized. I wonder if that old saw, 'mind over matter' is really true.

Maybe by some strange quirk in my genetic code, I'm able to tap into the mind powers of the informed universe. There's a word for it. Ah! Got it! The Akasha. Maybe I can access the Akasha Field more than others can. Maybe I'm just more sensitive than others. An Intuitive? Maybe that's it and nothing more. And surely that should be enough?

He leaned back in his chair. Sleep claimed him.

CHAPTER TWENTY-THREE

And the train rolled on through the night. Most on board were asleep. However, two were not. They whispered of lost dreams, dreams of wealth, and dreams of fame. Two other men lost themselves in the communion of their bodies with those of their wives. Another asleep in his chair waited for his time. The two whisperers slowly inched their way along the dimly lit corridor headed for the now infamous car number seven and the promise of their dreams.

They were an odd couple: The older one was a mammoth from some other age—perhaps a descendant of the giants that had at one time inhabited the earth. His height prevented him from standing erect. Inching his way along with his head bowed irritated his neck. His disposition was anything but pleasant. The beanpole had convinced him that car seven really did hold a vast fortune by revealing he was present when it was packed for shipment. As proof, he showed pictures he had taken with his cell phone.

Because of the giant's constant grumblings, the young beanpole wondered if he had made yet another mistake. He'd have to be very careful with this man. Unconsciously he felt for the knife beneath the blue blazer, strapped to his chest, just to the left of his open shirt. It comforted him in a strange way. A wry smile parted his thin lips as he remembered its previous use. He had used it to castrate himself. Forgotten pain, now remembered, brought little beads of perspiration along the space between his bent nose and upper lip. His breathing became labored.

"Be quiet! Jesus, you sound like a damn dog in heat," O'Banyon said.

Charles was sure everyone on the train heard his gravely hoarse whispering. Instinct brought a menu of explanations for being where he was. He was good at quick explanations.

Hadn't I been totally convincing with Adam and that oaf my mother married? The thought of the two of them having sex sobered him and he concentrated on his movements. Soon they would have to exit and either crawl along the top of the speeding train to car seven or inch their way along the outside of the cars.

The big man, the railroad detective, opted to inch his way along the outside of the car, clinging precariously to the wafer-thin overhang; his feet flopped around searching for a foothold. Finding one, he held on, sucking in his breath. The train was moving at top speed and the dust flying up from its wheels stung his eyes.

Jesus, that engineer must be pushing well over a hundred.

O'Banyon's fingers dug deeper into the overhang as he adjusted his weight. Slowly he turned his head back to see if Charles was following. He was. He continued to inch his way along. Already his hands and fingers ached.

Jesus! I just too old for this crap. I'm sure I correctly calculated the number of feet we had to go before we could climb to the top of car seven. Adam's private car should be eighty-five feet long. Sure seems longer.

O'Banyon knew how to open the hatch. All he had to do was pop a spring under the lid. He had brought a small steel rod for that. It would be an easy drop down into the loaded car and the fabulous wealth it contained.

Not sure if I should let the bean pole go down first. I don't trust him. Seems to me he should have tipped us off that Adam was wise to our plans.

I want cash. No in jewelry or coins for me. I understand there's some kind of a jeweled golden box. No one knew what was in it. That would be awkward to carry. The gold bars that are supposedly stored in car seven would be too heavy. Besides, how would I dispose of such things? Now paper money I can handle.

So enamored with what he'd look for, O'Banyon relaxed his grip. No one on board heard him yell, "Oh shit!" No one heard his body hit the ground. No one saw it bounce down a slope into a gully. No one saw it jerk its last moments of life.

Stupid idiot. I don't need him anyway. Once I get inside I take what I can and wait for the train to make a stop. Then I'll jump off and disappear. No one will know until I'm long gone.

Slowly he inched his way concentrating with his whole being on the placement of hands and feet. Beads of sweat soaked his shirt and his blue blazer. He felt it run down his sides. He shivered.

Damn. This is the pits. Thank god I'm almost there. Then it's easy does it.

The train swayed as it rounded a curve and began to cross a long trestle bridge. Charles' head flew back, slammed into one of the girders. The rest of his body plummeted hundreds of feet below landing at the edge of the river's bank.

CHAPTER TWENTY-FOUR

The Brothers gathered themselves up and headed for the dining car. As was now their custom, they walked in single file, one behind the other. And part of that custom was to eat as a group. The morning sun was coming up and it was time for their breakfast. In the dining car, they realized that Charles was missing.

Goliath, the name they had assigned to O'Banyon, didn't show up either. He made them feel uncomfortable, particularly with his attachment to Charles. Both he and Charles seem to have vanished. Being a suspicious lot they wondered who among them would be next. From the original twelve, they now numbered only eight. Samuel was married and couldn't be counted. For all they knew, their former leader, Joseph and his brother Thomas would die in prison.

Adam and his immediate circle no longer ate with them furthering their sense of isolation. And they did feel isolated! They hadn't even told of the birth of the quadruplets; nor had they been invited to see them. And they were ignored during the recent marriage of that nosy reporter. With reluctance, they gave her a kudos for popping snippy Charles in the nose.

And they hadn't been told where they were going. At least back at Karuna House, they functioned as a *brotherhood*. Now they wondered if they had made a mistake following Adam. What were they? What did they believe in? What did they do? Why did they exist? The answer to this last question they concluded was 'for no apparent reason. They may not have sensed a reason for their existence, but someone else did. And she would make her presence known in good time. Her price for knowing was death.

Their growing depression and these nagging questions were attributed to their restless nights, nights filled with wakened dreams, nightmarish things. Sometimes they felt a terrible suffocating presence in their compartments.

Running-water found gloomy group seated at two tables. He ignored their dark silence.

"We're not far from the American Border. Have your papers ready, compartments open, and suitcases open. If you are asked questions, answer them truthfully. Any questions?" Running-water said.

No one responded. No one looked at him. But one among them became extremely agitated. He stood up and quickly left; his unfinished breakfast left on his plate. No one commented as he left. No one asked where he was going. No one mentioned that Charles was missing. No one mentioned the Jonathan O'Banyon was missing. Why should they? Were they ever included in any of the discussions? No. Always just told—an afterthought. And that's exactly how they had just been treated.

After a long wait, the train was allowed to ease its way onto a side track. Its massive engine now a mere rumble. The occupants waited. Minutes crawled into unsettled hours. Running-water, pacing the floor in Adam's private car, continually checked the monitors. He saw a team of inspectors slowly approaching the train. A two-man team had dogs with them. Others had various pieces of electronic equipment. None made any effort to board the train.

"Don't fret so, my brother. I'm sure everything going to be okay," Adam said.

"Maybe not," Samuel said, entering the private car. "Charles and O'Banyon are missing."

"Are you sure?" Running-water said.

"Yeah. I've checked all the compartments as well as the other passenger areas."

"Damn! The Brothers are already wired. I'm not sure about the stability of any of them. One took off once I went over the protocol for their entrance into the United States," Running-water said.

"You're sure Charles and O'Banyon aren't around?" Adam said. "Could they have stepped off the train while we were waiting to be moved to a side track?"

"I don't know about that. I'm also concerned that those inspectors may find a stash of pot or some other illegal drugs. We just don't know what The Brothers have with them. Charles is a known drug user as well as his mother," Running-water said.

"Not so. Julie doesn't use drugs. She's straight," Samuel said.

"Sorry, Samuel. I meant she used to use and it's possible she still has an illegal substance stashed in her belongings. She could have forgotten it. Something left over from another time," Running-water said. He again looked at the monitors.

He noticed that the members of the Canadian Border Service Agency were looking up at the sky. Even the man from the Customs Excise Union Douanes Accise was occupied by something in the sky. The sound of a helicopter approaching was picked up by the train's external microphones.

With more grace than a bird, Dutch landed the chopper on the roof of the train.

With one continuous motion, Dutch secured the chopper and had eased himself down over the side of the train. He had his Uzi slung over his shoulder and his side arms were very visible. A second person eased himself down the side of the train to the ground. Unlike Dutch, this man had an Uzi slung over each shoulder and one in hand. Both men positioned themselves near the entrance to Adam's car. Running-water opened the door and lowered the steps.

"Nice entrance. Who's your friend?" Running-water said, extending his hand to Dutch.

"Will Rexford's my name. You must be Running-water."

"He's a former Seal. A buddy of mine. Thought some extra security would come in handy. That okay with you?" Dutch said.

"No problem. Glad to you have you aboard, Will."

CHAPTER TWENTY-FIVE

The three men continued to speak to one another in hushed tones. Slowly they looked over the crowd that had gathered.

"Nothing unusual," Running-water said. Then spoke into his radio phone. Clanking up and down the line announced the steps were being lowered all along the train.

Samuel and Brett stepped off the train. And they, like those already on the ground, were heavily armed. The new man was quickly introduced. Brett shook Will Rexford's extended hand.

Odd that Dutch brought in another man. He's not been mentioned him before. Even during our time in the Seals together he had never mentioned a Will Rexford.

The five took up a military position, legs spread slightly apart, at ease, but ever alert and ready. Running-water again spoke into his radio phone.

Seven of The Brothers, each dressed in a blue blazer, gray slacks, and a banded light blue shirt, slowly stepped off the train and walked in single file to where Adam's security team waited. They didn't speak, and like a bunch of little boys waiting for a dose of bad tasting medicine, they kept their heads down.

Nex, the train's professional staff exited the train and lined up. These were followed by two chefs, four waiters, a barman, and three housekeepers. They too, lined up and waited. Each carried their legal documentation.

Standing there in public view made them uncomfortable. They shifted from one foot to the other and back again. The Brothers waited. Their guardians waited. Finally, four women emerged from the train; each carried one of the quadruplets. People watching assumed each child belonged to the woman carrying it.

"Got to be some kind of a religious cult," said a woman.

The armed men stepped in front of the women as a shield against the curious lookers.

Running-water re-boarded the train. Shortly he returned, followed by Adam who stepped across the tracks and introduced himself to the Customs officials. Awed by his commanding stature, the agents barely spoke above a whisper as each, in turn, introduced himself. As they shook Adam's hand they felt euphoric warmth engulf them, a renewed sense of well-being.

"Gentlemen if you will follow me you can begin your inspection," Adam said.

"Excellent," Michael Lane, the group's supervisor, said.

Adam stopped, turned, and faced Michael Lane. "I'm sorry. We seem to be missing some people. We'll need to locate them.

"What? Missing people? Yes, of course."

Lane was watching one of the women. He was sure it was Patricia Livingston. He had seen her news report and knew she was on this train.

Damn! Wonder if she recognized me. It couldn't have been that long ago. I guess it must be. I had just turned twenty-one and had gone into Toronto to tie one on and to get laid. I was in a bar at an upscale hotel. No flea-bag joint for me on that night. When she walked in, every man turned his head. Man. I nearly fell off my bar stool when she sat on one next to me. She could have picked anyone. The rest is history.

"History. Yeah man, history," Michael said.

"History?" Adam asked.

Realizing he had spoken out loud Michael Lane made a quick reply he hoped would cover him.

"History. Yes. This train has created quite a history for itself. So you have people missing?"

"Yes. We'll have to delay the inspection until we locate them. I apologize for any inconvenience. Perhaps you'd join me as I look for them?"

Reluctantly Michael Lane agreed. His body build belied his true size. Broad shoulders, bulging biceps, and narrow waist created an impression of a much larger man. Beneath his cool polite demeanor, he nurtured his growing resentment at being assigned the task of inspecting this phantom train—this death train—and its group of weirdoes. He had another private assignment that waited for his attention—one that paid him handsomely.

Michael Lane took a good look at the man speaking to him. An automatic smile parted his lips as he recognized Adam as the very man he had been hired to kill. *Lady Luck is with me after all. I thought I was to wipe this guy in Toronto and here he is. All mine for the taking. Just to pissed to have noticed. Can't have that. Stay focused.*

A slight flush flowed along his square jaw. Realizing he had been spoken to, Michael cleared his throat. "People missing?"

"Yes, as I said we have some people missing. Will you join me in searching the train for them?" Adam said.

"Of course. Of course," Lane replied. Man. How lucky can I get? I can whack this guy and be off the train before anyone notices. He felt for the dragon that hung on his neck. One quick slice with this and he's dead.

Adam and Michael Lane boarded the train. Running-water broke ranks and came up behind them.

"No, you don't! Not without me."

The commanding tone of Running-water's voice caught Michael Lane's attention. Wonder who really called the shouts in this weird group? Damn weird is right. Just look at that long hair. A Jesus freak. Shit! What hell kind of a mess have I gotten into? Should've checked it out better? Would have except I needed some quick cash. Careless on my part. Better take care.

They began with passenger's coach where the killings had taken place. Lane looked at the blood stains still on the carpeted floor. His nostrils flared at the coppery smell of blood and urine.

"Heard you had a blood bath. Evidently, the RCMP found no cause to detain you or any member of your group. By the looks of the outside of the cars, it must have been some shoot out. Just like in the old Western movies. Man, the cars are riddled with bullets. One seems to have been targeted more than the others. That one, your private car?" Michael Lane asked.

"Yes," Adam said.

"Rumor has it you are carrying a huge treasure on this train. Is that true?"

"Perhaps I can explain," Daphne said as she and Isha came up behind them.

"Please do," Michael said, making no effort to hide his appreciation of the two beautiful women standing before him. He liked tall women.

"I gave birth on board," Daphne said.

"And did the other women also give birth?"

"No," Daphne laughed, "I had quadruplets. I would like to get them back on board as soon as possible. They're only two days old. Do you think you could arrange for that?"

"I'm sure we can accommodate that," Michael Lane said.

"Wonderful! I need a fresh supply of diapers, more formula, and some additional blankets, and baby powder. Could you send someone along with my husband to get them and while there take care of your necessary inspection?"

"No problem. Where are they stored?"

"Car seven," Daphne said.

You didn't answer my question about the rumored treasure, Adam. Any truth to that?"

"Right in front of you. Aren't they absolutely beautiful? Adam doesn't like me to call them beautiful. Says it's not manly to call boys beautiful. I told him all babies are beautiful to their mothers," Daphne said. Her deep dark eyes sparkled.

"And who is this lovely lady?" Michael asked, giving Isha his best smile.

"I'm Isha Dakota. My husband, Paul, is right behind you."

"Ah, a family," Michael said.

"Yes. Running-water, as we call him, is my twin brother," Daphne said." Adam, you said people are missing. I haven't seen Dr. Bach. What's going on?"

"And who is this Dr. Bach?" Michael Lane said.

"He's my personal physician and travels with me," Daphne said.

"I see. Of course. Shall we get on with it?" Michael Lane said. His voice had returned to its official tone. He had to remind himself to do that.

Man, when I agreed to pop this guy for twenty grand I didn't know there'd be all these others. I don't like surprises. No complications. Neat and tidy is the way I like things. It's going to cost the man. I'll have to be careful with this Running-water. I wasn't told about him either.

He waited for Running-water to stop talking on his cell phone.

Immediately Dutch Masters entered the car. With him was a member of the inspection team. Once they had joined Adam they headed for car seven. Michael Lane remained with Running-water to continue the search for the missing people.

Shit! How'd I end up saddled with this guy? I wonder if they suspect something. They sure never leave Adam alone. And that really complicates things.

CHAPTER TWENTY-SIX

Running-water and Michael completed their search of the passenger's car and found no one. The same held true for the cooks' car and the dining car. Entering the first sleeper car, they found Dr. Bach on his knees and covered in blood.

"What the hell is this?" Running-water said.

"He's sliced the veins in his arms," Dr. Bach said.

"How'd you find him?" Michael Lane asked.

"On my way to exit the train, I heard him fall. Opened the door and found him.

"Who are you?" Dr. Bach said.

"Michael Lane, Customs."

"Damn! He's gone. He sure knew how to do it," Dr. Bach said.

"He got a name? What can you tell me about him?" Lane said.

"His name is Julius. I don't know his last name. Perhaps Running-water can tell you something more than that," Dr. Bach said.

"Damn! You'll have to excuse me while I notify the local police on both sides of the Border. The Canadian Railroad will most likely send in more people. They'll send in their own investigators and there's the question of jurisdiction. Both our governments will get in involved. What a damn mess! Sure hope you have ample food supply on board. There's going to be one hell of a long delay," Michael Lane said.

He was pissed. Jesus. Suicide! Another complication. Always the damn complications. My man said I had an easy target. Lying bastard.

"You're right of course. Perhaps the personnel inspection process could be speeded up? Least get that out of the way?" Running-water asked.

"Suppose we begin with the doc here. Your papers." Michael snapped.

Realizing he might be here for days fueled his building anger. That lying bastard will be pissed because the job still hasn't been done. Maybe even demand the ten grand advance back. Screw that. One thing is for sure. Michael Lane doesn't leave a job unfinished. It's just going to take a little longer.

Running-water gave his papers to Lane. Because of the continued threat of terrorism, a computer check on an international data bank was a common procedure. This time, however, they were asked to provide fingerprints as well as DNA samples. Agents would be along to do that. Clutching their papers in his hand, Michael Lane turned to exit the train.

"I'll go with you. Want to make sure—,"

"What did you say?" Michael said.

"I said I'll go with you to see that we get our papers back," Running-water said.

"Excuse me! What are you implying?" Lane said.

"As an attorney, I want to make sure our rights are protected. I'll go along to make sure they are," Running-water said, swinging his Uzi from his shoulder. He didn't like Lane's tone of.

"Just great. And I suppose all of these people are your clients?"

'No, Just the passengers. Each should have his papers in order. Shall we get on with it?" Running-water said.

"Yeah. Let's," Michael said, struggling to keep his tone civil.

By nightfall, the inspection was still going on. Most of the passengers had had their papers checked, had been fingerprinted, and their DNA samples were taken. The Pullmans had been checked. Some of the freight cars still had to be inspected. Passengers were allowed to re-board the train under a lockdown. A new contingency of law enforcement and investigators had arrived. Michael Lane was beside himself. Shit! They'll just get in my way.

Brett and Dutch, joined the new contingency, providing the necessary information, directions, and quiet supervision. Michael Lane joined Adam and Running-water in the dining car. They informed him of Julius' suicide.

"Any idea as to why Julius took his own life?"

"I didn't search his compartment. Thought it best to leave it to Mr. Lane and his team," Running-water said.

"I've assigned an inspector to look into it," Michael Lane said.

Samuel with his Uzi standing in the vestibule made him nervous.

"If anything is found to indicate a cause for his suicide I'll let you know. As a courtesy, nothing official."

"Thank you," Adam said, offering coffee.

"What exactly are you? I mean, what is it that you are supposed to be? We've been told you're a VIP. Word has it that your Pentagon, as well as your Homeland Security, has taken a special interest in your doings," Michael Lane said.

"Let me try to answer your first question but before I do I know nothing about any communications from the United States Government regarding my activities or me."

Adam paused and then continued, "Seems I stand corrected. My attorney has had communications from both of those agencies. It seems they have contacted your Canadian officials."

"Now that's what I call a readjustment of memory, wouldn't you say?" Michael said.

"No. Running-water corrected me," Adam said.

"I didn't hear him say anything," Michael said.

"Ah! We communicate by telepathy," Adam said.

"Hmm. I was told you had certain powers. That one of them?"

"I don't view telepathic communication as a power. It's an ability. Just as some people have the ability to paint, design buildings, some have the ability to 'mind-talk.' Actually, many people have that ability but don't use it or don't realize what it is."

"You saying an ordinary person can telecommunicate," Michael said.

"Yes. To answer your original question, I'm a shaman, a medicine man or a healer, if you prefer. My father was a First Nation shaman."

"Yeah, I heard he was murdered in a mansion at Toronto," Michael said.

"And like him, I'm a healer," Adam said, ignoring the comment about his father's murder. "My hands are healing hands. In addition to that, I have certain abilities that help people heal themselves by using the powers of their own bodies, actually their belief systems. And there are certain psychic forces I do not fully understand."

"What about those guys who are dressed alike?" Who are they?"

"Men from the streets, rescued by my father, and for whom I now provide. Each man has suffered hardships, tough times, and personal tragedies. They dress alike because they wish to do so. They had thought they were going to be a religious group and had dressed in long robes. I had to put a stop to that and their current attire is a compromise. They are not part of a religious group or cult. Nor am I a leader of any such group. My father believed that each of us should be a fisher of men like another who has gone before us," Adam said.

"And this Julius, he was one of those derelicts?" Michael Lane said.

"Yes. I understand he was one of the last few he had pulled off the streets."

"And your father was a 'fisher of men'?"

"You could say that. His name, Esaugetuh, means 'master of breath'. In this case, a master of life. He was highly respected and at the same time feared by Native people on both sides of the Border. I think he really tried to emulate Jesus Christ in many ways. And like Christ, he was concerned about the unfortunate. His kindness got him murdered," Adam said. His tone emphasized his uncertainty of such behavior.

"Adam, there's a guy out here who says he needs to see Mr. Lane. Should I let him in?" Samuel said.

"I'll go out," Michael said.

Within minutes Michael Lane returned to the dining car. He had a legal sized envelope in his hand. "Looks like we have a suicide note. I'll read it to you."

He carefully removed the single sheet of paper from the envelope. He had surgical gloves on.

I'm so sorry but I can't. I just can't do what is wanted. Maybe others can, but not me. I may be a bum but whatever else I am, I'm not a—, I can't do it. Please try to understand.

"Any idea what he's talking about?"

"None. I've not asked him to do something he didn't want to do."

Michael Lane carefully folded the note, re-inserted it into its envelope, and then slid it into the larger envelope.

Still interested in Adam's life and doings, looking for any weakness he could use, Michael Lane, said, "How did your father's kindness get him killed?"

"He took in twelve men whom he found living desperate lives on the city streets. Two of them betrayed him. The same two attempted to kill me," Adam said.

"So you do know who the murderers are?"

"Yes. Justice has been served."

"Ah! They've been killed?" Michael asked.

"No. They are in prison."

Running-water's phone vibrated. He listened to the voice and then, excusing himself, went to the vestibule of the dining car. Samuel spoke to him and then he returned to the dining car.

"Inspector Lane, your men want to see you. It seems they have found human remains on the side of one of the cars," Running-water said.

CHAPTER TWENTY-SEVEN

The discovery of human remains splattered along the side of one of the train's cars resulted in a media frenzy. Patricia Livingston asked Adam about continuing her story. His immediate agreement was a pleasant surprise. She was not the only one who was surprised.

Michael Lane's feelings were hurt when she walked past him, did not recognize him, and didn't even give him a second look. I couldn't have been that bad. What a bitch.

Patricia Livingston was all business. She had a cell phone tucked under her chin, a video camera in one hand. Slowly she paned the investigation team, and then did a long shot along the train. She took care not to actually film the pieces of a human head and arm stuck on the side of car six. Even her voice was subdued, not quite a whisper nor was it like the announcer at a golf tournament; her tone suggested she was letting the world in on a secret.

The inspection was getting more and more complicated. Michael Lane shook his head in disgust. He wanted to be done with this. He wanted to be done with his contract. The suicide was definitely an American case; the human remains splattered on one of the cars were a Canadian case. The question of jurisdiction had now taken center stage. The Canadian Integrated Border Enforcement Team would now get very involved. Canadian Railroad's detectives would have miles of railroad track to swarm over as they looked for the rest of body parts. Forensic teams from both countries converged at the Border. The vital question was how the groups should be coordinated. Both governments agreed that one person should head-up both incidents: the suicide and the human remains.

How in hell am I going to whack this guy with all these people around?

Michael Lane was told he would be the coordinator. *They didn't even ask me. The least they could have done was give me some time to think about it. Now I've got to concentrate on this mess. No time for my target. What a piece of rotten luck.*

He liked to make sure things were neat and that involved planning time. Normally he arranged these extra-curricular activities, as he liked to call them, to take place during his vacation time. His vacation had been canceled. The one saving grace was that his victim was right here. One of the things he took pride in was his ability to organize, to handle minute details. He could sift through vast amounts of minutia and see patterns, a skill he used as he studied his targets. Within a couple of hours, he had the forensic team well in place.

The discovery of human remains necessitated further questioning of the entire group in an effort to get a time frame of when the missing were last seen. Despite Michael's organizational skills, the investigation was delayed by two hours as he waited for a coroner show up.

Another goddamned complication.

He briefed the coroner, a snip of a man who seemed to delight in being painfully slow. A high pitched scream penetrated his building anger.

Holly shit! What the hell's that?

CHAPTER TWENTY-EIGHT

Julie had spotted the frontal part of what had been her son's head.

Patricia Livingston caught the anguish on Julie's face; the total loss of a hoped-for new beginning. The destruction was complete.

Charles' open eyes bore into her, an ogre condemning her for conceiving him. She would never forget those eyes and the sense of total disgust they held. Samuel rushed to his screaming wife and tried to get her to move away from the gruesome sight. She lashed at him, kicking and screaming. He slapped her hard across the face. She went limp. Samuel picked her up and carried back onto the train. After placing her limp body on the bed in their compartment, he held his face in his hands and sobbed. He had not meant to hit her so hard. She was the only joy he had ever known in his life.

Oh my god! Oh my god! I've killed her.

Adam placed his hand on Samuel's shoulder. He looked up; face tear-streaked, and his chest heaving.

"I didn't mean to hit her so hard, Adam. Hones, I didn't. I just wanted her to get control."

"I know. May I?" Adam said, gently pulling Samuel away.

Slowly, Adam moved his hands over Julie's limp body. Gradually they began to glow as a low hum filled the compartment. At first, Samuel thought it was the train's engine but when he saw the pale blue light surrounding Adam grow brighter he remembered a past experience. Adam had done the same thing to Charles as he was now doing to

Julie. Charles had collapsed because of his self-castration. Yet, he thought he remembered Adam's hands being bright red back then. His struggle to remember was cut short by Julie calling his name.

"Oh, Samuel! Samuel! It's just so awful. Just when I thought there might a glimmer of a chance. Bingo! Charles ends up dead. I just knew he would end up dead. God only knows where the rest of his body is. Maybe wild animals have eaten it by now." She shuddered.

"He'll be found. Just a little time is needed. I'm so sorry I hit you. Forgive me. I will never strike you again. You've got to believe me, Julie," Samuel pleaded.

And she knew he meant it. She pulled his face to hers and kissed him.

"You're all I got now!" Julie whispered.

"Julie, any idea how Charles got out there or why he was out there?" Adam said.

"No, none."

"And you, Samuel. You have any ideas?" Adam said.

"O'Banyon is missing. They were in cahoots to rob you. Find O'Banyon and I'll bet you'll get some answers."

"I didn't know he was missing. When did you know this?"

"When the crew came out and lined up. He wasn't with them. Sorry, Adam. I thought he had left the train to report to one of the inspectors."

"She okay?" Michael Lane said, pointing to Julie. "I want to ask her some questions."

"I'm fine. What do you want to know?"

"You recognized the remains. Mind telling me who it was?" Michael Lane said.

"My son. He was just nineteen," Julie said, beginning to cry.

"I'm sorry for your loss, ma'am. I know this is difficult for you. I have just a couple of questions if you don't mind," Michael Lane said.

"It's okay. I know you are only trying to do your job."

"Any idea why your son would have been on the outside of the train?"

"Probably trying to rob it. Find that O'Banyon. Both of them had tried to rob this train and both are responsible for the deaths on this train," Julie said.

"O'Banyon, the railroad detective? Is this true, Adam? One of the CRR's own? Shit! Now there will be even more of a delay. With one of their own involved and missing, the railroad people will really get anal. You didn't say you held two of the robbers on the train. What were you doing with them?" Michael said.

Damn. More complications. His eyes narrowed as if he were taking aim through his high-powered rifle.

"Charles was the ringleader of the group. O'Banyon was the inside man. Once the others had been killed, O'Banyon confessed and that led us to Charles," Adam said.

"So you just decided to keep them! And they tried to escape; is that it? Why were you keeping them?" Michael said. "

Jesus, this guy is really a whacko.

"Charles and O'Banyon had agreed to turn themselves in. However, there was no direct evidence linking them to the attempted robbery of this train or to the deaths in the passenger car. In a court of law, it would have been their word against mine. And since there was no one who could corroborate my claim, I saw no point in pursuing prosecution. I gave them the option of remaining with the group or leaving. They chose to stay. *They were not* prisoners as you have implied," Adam said.

Adam's tone had a finality about it. The subject was closed. And that presented Michael with yet another problem. Should I report this information to my superiors or keep my mouth shut? If I keep quiet they find out. I could get fired or end up in jail. If I report this I'll never get out of here.

"Ethical issues are never easy. The real question is what good is served by reporting what I have told you? In my case, I answered that question by giving them both another chance," Adam said, watching Michael.

"Jesus! How'd you know what I was thinking? Never mind. It's one of your abilities, right?" Michael said, shaking his head in disbelief.

"Isn't the question, what good is being served?" Adam said, ignoring the questions about his ability to read other people's thought.

"Yeah, I guess you're right. Have you ever wondered that maybe you're not a very good 'fisher of men'? Have you ever considered the need to change your basis for making judgments?" Michael said, changing the focus in order to gain time to compose his thoughts.

"Yes. I've questioned not only my judgment but what I'm about. I do so all the time. Sometimes

I even wonder what my life would have been like had I not tracked down my father, gone on my vision quest, and had become a shaman," Adam said.

"Boring, probably and lost opportunities," Michael said, almost meaning it.

Adam wanted to like this man. He sensed a strange integrity about him, yet there was something, something that made him hesitate. He couldn't quite put his finger on what it was.

"Any idea how long we'll be here?" Running-water asked. It was the question nagging Adam. His anxiety increased as more delays were experienced.

"No, I don't. How in the hell do you expect me to know that?" Michael said.

"You're the man in charge. Seems to me you ought to have some idea as to how much longer you are going to hold this train and its passengers hostage. If this was just a freight train it would have been gone long ago," Running-water said.

"Unfortunately this is not a normal train. In addition to the shoot-out which resulted in eight deaths, you now have a suicide on board and body parts clinking to the side of one of the cars, and a missing person. And all of this is on top of the fact that you are a passenger-freight train. Is it possible Detective O'Banyon got off the train at your last stop?" Michael said.

"No. Everyone was accounted for. I suspect he and Charles had decided to take a crack at robbing the train, got into a fight, and Charles got eliminated. O'Banyon was a giant of a man and Charles was—well—,"

Adam interrupted, "Would the use of a helicopter help speed up the search back along the tracks? If so, you may use the one on the roof of my train," Adam said.

"That would sure speed things up. It would be nice if we had FLIR to detect body heat. Decaying bodies give off heat," Michael said.

"No problem. Just tell my pilot what you need and he'll get it," Adam said.

"You don't understand. Only governmental agencies have that kind of equipment. It might take a couple of days before we could get—,"

"I'll see what can be arranged anyway," Running-water said. He flipped open his cell phone to make a call.

"We can get a U.S. Naval chopper here that has the kind of sensing equipment that you want. But there's a hitch. It would be flying in Canadian airspace and we do not have a mutual agreement for such use except in a national disaster. It'll take some time before all the concerned parties can be contacted."

"Well that's that," Michael Lane said, turning to go outside, he stopped. "Thanks."

CHAPTER TWENTY-NINE

Outside Michael Lane was greeted by pandemonium. Everywhere he turned there were reporters with their cameramen, yelling out pesky questions. They jabbed their microphones into his face as he tried to make his way through the crowd. Helicopters from various TV and radio stations hovered above. Lookers from the cars waiting to cross the border milled around, taking pictures, and getting in the way. One woman nearly knocked him down trying to get closer to the 'death train.' The back-up at the Border crossing was unimaginable. People began honking their car horns, shouting obscenities, gunning their vehicle engines. Some tried to back up and turn around which caused a further auto-log-jam. Tempers flared. The truckers couldn't get through. Semi after semi soon lined the roadway. A couple of fist fights broke out, and name calling plagued the unarmed Canadian Customs Agents. They walked off the job. No one blamed them for that. Michael Lane very much wanted to do the same, but instead, ordered the Border closed. That created further havoc. Several fender-benders created more hostilities. Local police from both sides intermingled, each trying to clear the area and to re-establish order. Michael Lane was beside himself. Always the complications. Man, when shit happens; it really happens. I don't need all this crap.

Disgusted by the display, Adam called Patricia Livingston to meet with him. Pleased that he had asked for her help, she kissed him on his cheek. She really had been forgiven. Things in her world were finally going her way.

"Keep the media people away from the staff, the authorities, and away from our group. Have them stay back. If they violate that they will get nothing. All information regarding the investigations will come from you," Adam said.

"No problem, just give me five minutes to fix my face. A girl has got to look her best," Patricia Livingston said, giving him a wink.

Totally energized; animated, the darling of the Canadian news was at her best. She could have just as easily been an actress. Her performance won her applause. It was a mix of officiousness, sarcasm, and good-natured humor. The plunging neckline and the sexy broad stance was perfect. The pandemonium calmed. Her reputation as a master of repartee was not lost on her fellow reporters. Making sure her local affiliate was in place, she gave the necessary details.

"Hey Patricia, how'd you get on this train?"

"Climbed on board with my own two feet," Patricia Livingston replied, dancing a little jig, twirled around, and shook her butt at the crowd.

The reporters responded with catcalls. Some yelling for more.

"So, what else is new?" A reporter yelled.

"I got married two days ago and this business is messing up my honeymoon."

"Well, I'll be damned," someone said. "Never thought you'd take the plunge."

"So who's the lucky guy? He got a name?" Asked another.

"Brett. Brett Montana. He's one of those with the Uzis."

"Great job. You are one impressive lady, you know that?" Brett said, walking over to her.

"It did go well didn't it?"

"I'm taking up the chopper. Running-water is going with me. There's a railroad trestle we crossed a couple of hundred miles back. That's most likely the place where Charles bought it. Figure it might speed up the investigation. Running-water is concerned about Adam. Sooner we get this settled, the better it will be all the way around."

Why? Why must the two of you go? Let the governments take care of it," Patricia Livingston said.

"If we don't get involved we may be here for days, maybe weeks. You just talked to Adam. Didn't you check him out? It's like he's not even here. He senses something." Brett said. His boyish smile spread across his handsome face. "You got an extra camera? If you do, I'll shoot some footage for you."

Reluctantly she gave him her camera. She could cop one from one of the other cameramen. She kissed him, held it as she tried to ward off the apprehension she felt. January can be tricky in northern Washington, particularly along the Canadian Border. The day had grayed; the temperature had dropped, and the wind had picked up. She watched her husband and Running-water take off in the small helicopter. The wind buffeted it like the bird in a badminton game. Patricia Livingston hugged herself. She shivered. Hot coffee laced with bourbon would not have stopped this shiver. It came from deep within her, foreboding, gnawing at her gut.

The Fraser River Valley of British Columbia has a reputation for its high winds and storms that roared down into the state of Washington. Today was no exception. Seventy miles per hour wind gusts buffeted the region. Frigid air shot through the valley as far south as Mount Vernon in Washington State. The ominous gray skies darkened. Snow caught by the winds swirled like miniature tornadoes. Their vortexes visible. The snow began to accumulate and by midday six inches had turned into a foot and a half. Unlike the Northeast, Washington is not equipped to handle heavy snow. Traffic snarled as cars slammed into one another; some ending up in ditches while others slid into guardrails. A multi-car pile-up stopped all traffic on I-5. The Highway Patrol closed all the mountain passes. Those that got caught in the mountains had to sit and wait it out.

Fortunately, the helicopters from the television stations had returned to their home bases before the storm hit. Only a few of the ground crews were left to suffer the storm—one that would be called the storm of the century. Adam opened the passenger car and dining car to the reporters as well as the teams of inspectors and investigators. Hot coffee, soup, and sandwiches were provided. Once they were warmed and fed, they went about their business.

Patricia Livingston phoned in further details to her station returned to her compartment. The congratulatory kudos from station management did not abate her growing unease. She paced back and forth. Cat nervous. I need a drink. Calm me down.

She headed forward to the dining car and its bar. At Running-water's compartment, she heard Isha crying. She tapped on the door. Isha, her eyes red from crying, opened the door. Her face pale.

"Your crying. What's wrong?" Patricia asked. "

"I have such a dreadful feeling. Something's wrong. I know it. I've not heard from Running-water. He promised he'd check in."

"The weather may be causing problems and he can't call in. I'm sure that's it," Patricia Livingston said, trying to convince herself.

"I just know something has happened. I feel it," Isha said, blowing her nose. "You ever just get a feeling and it won't go away?"

"You bet. I'm on edge myself. I was going for a drink. Want to come?"

The storm's building intensity increased their anxiety. Driven by fierce winds the snow swirled around the train. Powerful gusts, hitting the train broadside, rocked the cars. Several times they had to brace themselves.

CHAPTER THIRTY

The mark on Adam's arm bothered him; the obsidian hung around his neck irritated his skin. The more he paced the more agitated he became. In mid-step he stopped; tried to quiet himself. He listened with his mind. It came through. Faint at first; grew stronger and clearer. Running-water was yelling. "We're going down."

Adam sat down at his desk. Closed his eyes. Concentrated. He tried to visualize where they were. Slowly an image formed, dark, unyielding in detail. Damn. I don't know what I saw. A rock? The chopper? Too dark to see.

He got up, began his pacing all over again. I'm absolutely sure I heard Running-water's voice. Got to do something.

Daphne watched her husband, seeing his anguish. Uncertain as to what she should do, she occupied herself with their sons. They had not lived together long enough for her to know if he would be pleased or annoyed if she went to him. A knock at their door changed their focus. Cautiously Daphne opened the door. It was Julie. Her mascara-eyes were a darkened mess from her crying.

"May I come in? I don't want to be alone. God, I'm so alone!"

"Of course. But you are not alone. You are among friends. Besides, you have an adoring husband. Don't shut him out," Daphne said, closing the door and securing it.

"I can't stand it. My only child dead. Gone forever. You don't understand. You can't until,"

"Until what?" Daphne said.

"Oh God! I didn't mean—I'm so sorry. What a dumb thing to say."

"It's okay. You've got to understand that your son died a long time ago. The life Charles led, his bitterness, his lying, and his self-castration all were not done by the little boy you once knew. All that was done by someone else. Even he didn't know who he was. He came back into your life a stranger. He was someone you did not know, could not know. Be grateful he's no longer tortured by his demons. You have a man who desperately wants to build a life with you, a life filled with adoring love. Don't throw it away. Don't let assumed guilt drown you. Move on," Daphne said.

"How do you handle all of this?" Julie said.

"What do you mean?"

"Well, Adam and all that stuff he does; the attempts on his life, and now the quadruplets. Not to mention The Brothers, and the rest of us."

"Julie, would you excuse us, please. I need to speak with Daphne," Adam said.

Sensing her husband's urgency, Daphne said, "Julie, we'll talk later."

The door had barely closed when the train, without warning, lurched, nearly knocking Daphne down.

"The train's moving. Have we been released?" Daphne said.

"No. It's backing up. We're heading back. Running-water and Brett—,"

"Oh no! Don't say it. Please don't," Daphne said, breaking into tears. "Are you sure?"

"Yes. I heard Running-water yelling 'we're going down.''

"Do Isha and Patricia know?"

"Not yet. I'm going to go and get them. I thought perhaps you could—,"

"Of course. Have them come here."

"I want to make sure everyone is on board including Michael Lane. Get a hold of Samuel and tell him his wife needs him."

As soon as Isha saw Adam she immediately knew he had bad news. Tears flowed. Adam explained that the chopper had gone down, that he wasn't exactly sure where, and that he had ordered the train to back up and head east.

"Anything I can do to help?" Patricia Livingston said, biting her lower lip. Hard as she tried she couldn't stop her tears. They welled up, spilled over, and splashed down her ashen face.

There were just a few places where young Charles could have been decapitated. One of those was about two hundred miles east of Vancouver. There was a trestle bridge there and it was to that that Brett and Running-water were headed. It was somewhere along that route that two men if they were still alive, waited to die.

The trip was going to be long and tedious. The need for a second engine had not been anticipated so the current one would be pushing the cars rather than pulling them. This made it impossible for the engineer to see in front of the train. The storm had continued to grow in intensity, lashing out at the train, making it difficult for the engineer as he leaned out the cab's window trying to see. He thought of himself as Casey Jones, the engineer made famous by Wallace Saunders's ballad. The whirling snow stinging his face and eyes brought him back to reality. He remembered the remote cameras. With a flick of a couple of switches, he brought up an image on the monitor. The small stationary flood light was not strong enough to penetrate the swirling snow. He felt he could at least detect any large object on the tracks. Gradually he ratcheted the train's speed up to thirty-five miles per hour.

Adam called Dutch and asked him to bring Will Rexford and Michael Lane to his car. A Canadian Royal Mounted Policeman joined them. Adam again explained that the chopper with Brett and Running-water on board had crashed, that it had gone down somewhere between Vancouver and a railroad trestle, about two hundred miles out.

"This is insane. You can't see anything from a moving train. You certainly don't plan on a foot search, or do you?" Dutch said. "Man, even you can't see in this storm."

"How do you know that the chopper has gone down? Did they radio in? " Michael Lane said.

"No, they didn't call in."

"Well, then they probably just sat the bird down to wait out the storm," Lane said.

Adam caught a shift in Lane's tone. It wasn't quite sincere. He let it pass.

"Stop this train immediately. You've not been cleared. Nothing can be done until morning. Even then, it's doubtful if you'd see much," the CRMP said. "The way this storm is developing it may not end for several hours."

"At the speed, we're moving it'll be late tomorrow when we get there. If there are any survivors they'll be dead by then," Will Rexford said.

As if it had taken a cue from the conversation the train picked up speed. Soon it was hitting seventy miles per hour. Pushed to eighty and then hit a hundred. It roared along the snow-covered tracks. It's blue lights glowed along its underbelly and along its sides—a mental demon headed toward hell.

The engineer held the whistle at full blast. He knew he was moving at a dangerous speed. Even though the tracks were supposed to be clear, he knew there was always the danger of an animal or a landslide. Modern technology did fail sometimes and there would no advanced warning. He really felt like Casey Jones. He even remembered a line from the ballad: *Fireman, don't you fret, keep knockin' at the fire door, don't give up yet. I'm goin' to run her till she leaves the rail.*

And that's exactly what he'd do. He'd run her till she got where she was supposed to go or she left the rails. For once in his dull life, the engineer felt important. Why I'd be a hero.

Adam had everyone move to the passenger car near the engine despite its bloody mess. If there should be a problem there would be several cars in front of them. Give them a better chance of survival. He grabbed up the quads and hurried Daphne to the passenger car.

"Dutch come with me. We need to find out what the hell is going on. Where are Samuel and Julie? Will, go and find them and bring them here," Adam said.

Adam pulled the engineer's cab door open. The engineer was drunk, passed out and slumped over the console. Two empty bottles of whiskey lay on the cab floor.

"Son-of-a-bitch!" Dutch said, pulling the drunken engineer's head back, and giving him a quick hard slap across the face.

"Leaf me alone." His eyes were glazed, watery pools.

"How do you slow this train down?" Adam asked, examining the console.

The engineer slide off his seat hit his head on the corner of the console, and fell to the floor, unconscious.

"You know anything about trains? See if you can figure out how to slow this behemoth down," Adam said.

The cockpit, that's what it was in Dutch's mind, wasn't all that difficult. He soon had it figured out and the train began to slow down.

"What speed you want?" Dutch said.

"How far you think we are from that trestle?" Adam said.

"I'd guess we've got at least two more hours, maybe longer. I know what you're thinking. If Brett and Running-water are injured, unconscious, or trapped, they won't last long in this storm. Damn! I should have known better than to let Brett take the chopper up in this storm," Dutch said.

"Don't blame yourself. Try maintaining seventy and hope for the best. Stick his head out the window," Adam said nodding toward the drunken engineer. "And then throw him in a shower. I'll send up the reserve engineer as soon as I find him,"

Adam said, leaving the cab and heading back to the passenger car.

He didn't stop nor did he acknowledge any of those assembled there. Adam found the other engineer curled up in his bunk, sent him forward, and then on a fast run, headed for car seven.

CHAPTER THIRTY-ONE

Adam decided not to let the others know what he intended to do. Doing so would create problems. Samuel, he knew, would insist on going and that would mean Dutch and Will Rexford would want to go. Michael Lane and the Canadian Royal Mounted Police Officer would try to get involved. Michael Lane bothers me. I'll deal with that later. I'll try to telecommunicate with Running-water. If he's not badly hurt he may be able to tune into my thought waves.

Adam reached car seven and checked its lock and door to see if there had been any attempt to open it. There had been none. That added to the puzzle of why Charles was on the outside of the train. If he and O'Banyon were making another attempt at robbing the train, O'Banyon should have known there was a door into both ends of car seven. Wonder why he split? He knew I wasn't going to press charges.

He inserted the key and with a single click, the door was unlocked. Adam switched on a light, a single light bulb, a low wattage bulb which barely created sufficient light for him to read the manifest. He removed one of the emergency flashlights that were fastened to each side of the doorway. Carefully he read the numbers and their identification. Once he had the identifying numbers of the boxes he wanted he checked the locator map.

If the car had been loaded according to Running-water's instructions, boxes of like content would be grouped together. He found the first of several boxes he had wanted. Slowly he pried open its lid, removed the gold jewel-encrusted case, and took out its contents. Carefully he untied the leather thongs that held the rolled deerskin. Laying it out flat on top of a box, Adam moved his hand across the skin, seeking to sense its portent. Tears welled up and a desperate cry escaped from his soul as he sought comfort from this ancient document, the oldest extant document found in North America. His heart sought and wanted reassurance. He sought comfort from its aged message. Even though he could not read it, the Wisdom Keeper, Kowahkan, had revealed its essence to him just before he returned to the spirit world. The deerskin supported what had been thought to be rumors, made up stories by old shaman—the storytellers of the Ancient Ones. Most stories are forgotten now as well as the languages in which they were told.

He knew he was to care for his *brothers* and he had interpreted that to mean his fellow man. That was what his father had intended him to do. He was a healer—a healer of the body and soul. Kowahkan's amulet hanging around his neck glowed, warming itself by some unknown force. Feeling its warmth against his bare skin, Adam thumbed it, sensing its ever-present vibration. It comforted him.

With great care, he returned the ancient scroll to its jeweled container and then placed it into its wooden box, sealed its lid and put it back. He had hoped it would have brought a sense of his father to him. It did not.

Disappointed, he sat down; legs crossed Indian style, and began to meditate. He felt if he could calm his mind he might be able to once again communicate with his father, Esaugetuh. He also knew if he was going to find his two friends, he would need all of his senses and strength. A calm mind was essential and that in turn would allow him to build his energies. After fifteen minutes of meditation, Adam lit a bundle of sage and sweet grass. Slowly he smudged its aromatic smoke around him: first to his abdomen, then to his chest, and finally to his head. He sat there for another few minutes and then got up and went about searching for several other boxes. His muscles rippled tight against his shirt as he lifted box after box. His movements were smooth and continuous—synchronized.

He found what he was looking for. Stripping off his clothes, he put on the deerskins pants he had unpacked. They fit tight to his muscular thighs, accenting his firm butt. Next, he stepped into deerskin boots with the fur on the inside, and a parka made of Buffalo. Had there been a mirror, he would have seen a large wooly beast, a Sasquatch with a very human face. Quickly he opened the box containing emergency equipment. He found a receiver for a GPRS and hoped it would pick up a signal from the chopper. He stuffed a backpack with first aid materials, energy bars, water, and attached that to a folded stretcher and rolled blanket. Next, he fastened a loop of rope on his belt. He had his walkie-talkie, checked its frequency to make sure it was still set to the one he used to communicate with Dutch.

The radio squawked. It was Dutch calling from the engineer's cab. They had reached the railroad trestle. Adam instructed Dutch to have the train moved across the trestle and to stop, light up the entire train, and wait for further instructions. As soon as the train had stopped, Adam slipped out the door at the end of car seven, relocked it, and dropped to the ground. Deep snow softened his jump.

Adam immediately turned on the GPRS receiver, took his bearings, and started the long treacherous climb into total darkness. During his quiet time, Adam had used distant viewing to see if he could get a picture of the downed helicopter. A picture of an object, unclear, was all he could pick up. He wasn't sure what it was, but it gave him a direction. He kept that image fixed in his mind as he trudged along. The going was tedious. The storm's fierce winds lashed at him, screaming their defiance. He was soon covered with a hoary frost and became invisible on the terrain. Tree branches slapped him in the face as he pushed his way through the mounting snow. He knew that his tracks would soon be covered over and would be worthless as a guide back. The wind was creating large drifts, any one of which could send him cascading to his death. With his adze, he systematically cut a mark on the trees. An hour into his climb, Adam stopped and looked back. The snow reflected a faint glow from the lighted train. His Cobra squawked.

"What the hell do you think you're doing? Have you lost your frigging mind?' Dutch yelled.

"I'm fine. Hang tight. Keep this line open and keep the train's lights on. I can see the glow. I'll be in touch. Got to keep moving. Time's running out," Adam said.

After another forty-five minutes of pushing himself, Adam felt the strain. His breathing was labored. The muscles in his legs began to cramp. He wondered if this was déjà vu remembering another time he was wandering in deep woods. Not marking his way had been a hard-learned lesson. He stopped. Listened. The faint beeping of the GPRS receiver finally caught his attention. He continued due north as the signal grew stronger. Adam's heart raced with expectancy. Silently he prayed that he would find them alive.

A miscalculation sent him tumbling down an embankment. He rolled, slid, and fell head over heels through an eternity. His tumbling stopped. He lay still. Total blackness engulfed him. Slowly he moved his arms and then his legs. He felt no broken bones. His ankle hurt. He stood up and nearly fell down. It was impossible for him to put any weight on his left foot. Adam knew it would soon begin to swell and would give him problems. Quickly he opened the top of his boot and packed it with snow. That would help keep the swelling down. He didn't have time to do a self-healing. Time was running out. He made a walking stick by cutting a limb from a tree, stripping it of branches. Slowly and painfully he began the treacherous climb back up the slope. He was sure that for every step forward he slipped back two. The strain was getting to him. His back hurt. His legs hurt. He stopped, moved upward, stopped, and moved upward. As he neared the top he heard, sensed, felt it. Running-water was sending him a mind-thought. Adam replied.

I am here! Are you hurt?

We are both hurt; not sure how bad off Brett is, but I think it's pretty bad. I think my leg is broken.

Shoot a flare if you can. I'm not sure exactly where you are, but I think I'm close.

Okay. Watch. And Adam, please hurry. I'm not sure Brett can hang on much longer.

Is he conscious? Cover him with snow if you can.

The flare shot up and Adam headed toward it. The climb was steep and he had to stop frequently to rest his swollen ankle, to catch his breath. The wind was determined to suck it out of him. He fired two shots in rapid succession into the bitterly cold night air, waited and listened. He heard a reply and then a second one. He was close.

Damn this weather. Can't see my own hands in front of me.

Twice Adam nearly fell as he swollen ankle continued to complicate his climbing. His backpack shifted. It didn't make any difference what he tried, he couldn't stand without the aid of his walking stick and that made it impossible for him to rebalance the backpack. Its weight had shifted to the same side as his badly sprained ankle. His left shoulder begged for relief. He dropped the backpack, removed the rope from his belt, tied it to the backpack, and fastened that around his waist. It was easier dragging it. A couple of times it got hung up on undergrowth and he had to cut it free. Panic knocked. I should have found them by now!

He began to shout only to have the wind suck his breath away and all sound with it. Blindly he stumbled along, trying to telecommunicate.

Nothing. The receiver was silent. Then he slipped and fell flat on his face.

"Damn it, Adam. You nearly took my head off!" Running-water said.

"Where's the chopper? I kept looking for it. No wonder I walked into you," Adam said, relieved.

"Up there," Running-water said, pointing up beyond his head. "In the tree."

It hung there, a large bird of prey, waiting for its victim, a deadly enemy should it decide to let go and swoop down out of the tree.

"Got to get you two out here and fast. I think that chopper just moved," Adam said, as he examined Brett.

He had a weak pulse. Using his flashlight, Adam noted that Brett's eyes were fixated. Death was there, clutching his victim, squeezing out the life force. Adam cut open Brett's jacket and shirt. Both were red with frozen blood.

Adam's hands flew over Brett's limp body. He concentrated trying to direct his own healing energy. It didn't work. Finally, he just let his hands go where they would. They began to glow a pale blue and then as the floated over the internal injuries they turned bright red. The heat continued to build and Adam cried out in pain.

"What's wrong?" Adam, answer me!" Running-water said, trying to lift himself up.

"Quiet. Be very quiet. Mind talk with your sons. They will give you strength," Adam said.

The skin on the back of Adam's hands cracked and blood oozed from the lesions only to be quickly frozen. Despite the pain, Adam pressed them down hard against Brett's wounds, forcing them to stay still. A glowing blue light emanated from Adam's whole body, filling the whole area in a soft fluorescent glow. Then it went out. Darkness again engulfed them. Those who searched the darkness from the train suddenly saw a sharp bolt of light flash down from the darkened sky. It struck Running-water. He screamed in abject terror and then went quiet.

He saw them, the Ancient Ones, circle dancing, chanting. The drumbeat increased as did the cadence of the chanting. Its loudness penetrated his being, hurting his ears as it did so. He felt it massage his heart and he sat up. A small fire burned in front of him. Adam was nowhere to be seen.

"It can't be. I must be dreaming," Running-water thought as he looked out at a perfect circle that had been drawn around him—a circle created by many dancing feet. "No! It can't be. Maybe I am dead."

"I wouldn't count on that," Adam said, kneeling down beside his soul brother.

"What the hell happened? The last thing I remember is you telling me to be quiet. Brett! How's Brett?" Running-water said.

"He's still alive. The wind is picking up and we need to get out of here and fast. That chopper may shake loose from that tree. I've set your leg and put a brace on it. It's not much of a brace but it will have to do. Do you think you can stand?" Adam said.

Struggling to get up, Running-water said, "Man, I don't know. Give me a hand and we'll find out."

After some jostling for an awkward balance, they were both standing. Adam had made a crude crutch for his friend. The problem would be the depth of the snow as they returned to the waiting train. One misstep and both could go down, break another leg, or re-break the one that had just been set. Running-water stabilized himself. Adam removed the folded stretcher from his backpack, and then carefully rolled Brett on to it, strapped him in, covered him with his own coat, and then tied a rope to both ends of the stretcher, making it a sled. He would place the rope under his armpits and across his chest, making it a crude harness.

He remembered another time when he had put on a harness. It seemed a thousand years ago. He was plowing a field for Jedediah, Running-water's paternal grandfather. The plow got stuck and he gave it a yank and it came tumbling head over heels and slammed into his back.

I must remember not to yank on the stretcher-sled if it gets stuck. Go back and set it free.

CHAPTER THIRTY-TWO

It was too late! Like a giant prehistoric bird, it was upon them. Its impact knocked them to the ground. The helicopter-bird had swooped down out of its nest to claim its prey.

"Running-water are you okay?" Adam said, pulling himself up with the aid of his walking stick. His ankle was screaming with pain.

"Yeah. Just the wind knocked out of me. What about Brett? You see him anywhere?"

Both of them began yelling Brett's name. A very faint, 'here' came from beneath the chopper. It had tumbled head over heels and had landed on its rotor blades, pinning Brett beneath. Frantically, Adam began digging in an effort to free him before he suffocated.

"Better stop digging that way."

"You say something, Running-water?" Adam said.

"No. Why?" Running-water asked.

"Better stop digging that way. You'll cause the chopper to sink and crush him."

"Huh?" Adam said.

"You haven't learned much, have you? Don't dig around the blades. Dig around and beneath your friend."

"Running-water stop playing mind-games. Damn it! I haven't got time for this," Adam said.

"What the hell you talking about? If you're hearing voices, they aren't from me," Running-water said.

Adam slowly dug around Brett. His body gave way and he sunk. Adam grabbed the rope and inched his way back from beneath the chopper. A short tug set Brett completely free. Crawling on his hands and knees, Adam pulled Brett clear of the teetering chopper. Every muscle and sinew ached from the strain.

The wind had picked up again and its fierceness nearly knocked Adam down as he attempted to stand and pull the harnessed stretcher-sled and still hang on to Running-water. They had to keep moving or freeze to death.

"You know where you're going?" Running-water said.

"Look for marks on the trees. Check every few yards with the flashlight. If you're not sure we'll stop and double check. No use looking for my footprints. There won't be any," Adam said.

Adam stopped several times to check Brett, who floated in and out of consciousness. Concerned about Brett's body temperature Adam realized he had to do something and do it quick. Taking Brett's head between his hands, Adam allowed their heat to build. They reddened and grew hot. Brett moaned in protest. His eyes fluttered open.

"Listen to me very carefully," Adam said. "You must concentrate. You're badly injured. I'm trying to keep you alive and I want to put you into a very deep trance. I want you to think of a time when you were a small child, of something that pleased you very much. Do you understand?" Adam said.

Brett opened his mouth but was unable to speak. Adam accepted that as meaning he had understood. Adam began to hum, still holding Brett's head between his hands. A blue glow surrounded Adam as the humming increased in pitch. Brett's eyes opened wide and then closed. Again Adam moved his hands over Brett's abdomen; growing red hot they cracked and bled and Adam struggled to stifle his own pain. Even though his cry was lost in the howling wind, Running-water felt his friend's pain and shuddered.

Unable to stand up by himself, Running-water managed to crawl to Adam and reaching up he placed his hand on his soul mate's shoulder. Instantly Adam was surrounded by blue light; its intensity seemed to light up the whole mountain. Vital energy flowed down Adam's arms, through his bleeding hands into the injured Brett. Where Adam had been kneeling, the snow was red.

Those who kept their vigil at the train had seen the blue light and had wondered what it was. One among them knew and was grateful. It meant her husband was alive and he had found his two friends. Daphne went to the other women who had arrived at her private car.

Isha had been the first to arrive. She was distraught, frightened, and worried. Her husband was missing. Her children, in New Mexico, compounded her distress. She missed them. Julie was next to arrive and acknowledged Samuel, her husband, as she sat down. He remained the ever watchful guard; he remained at his station by the door, gun visible and ready. Patricia Livingston was the last to arrive.

Daphne offered the three women hot tea and sweet bread. She brought pillows and blankets for all of them. They would remain together. Sometime after midnight, Daphne roused herself, sensing a great urgency, she checked the others. She gently shook each into wakefulness.

"Adam needs us. Come! Join me and form a circle. Quickly. There's not much time," Daphne said.

Unsure of what had happened, Julie and Patricia did as they were told. Isha knew her sister-in-law was going to set up a Medicine Wheel. As soon as they formed a circle, Samuel also realized what was going on and joined the women. He had seen Adam create such a circle at Esaugetuh's ranch in Quebec. Unfortunately, the car was not wide enough for them to dance a song of life; therefore, they sat, joined hands, and began to hum.

Ah! Um! Ah Ummmm! Filled the car, growing louder with each round.

The Brothers felt the humming vibrations and went to Adam's private car. One opened the windows and the outer door and then sat down, forming a circle with the remaining Brothers. Soon the two groups were in sync and the vibrating sound floated out into the night sky, competing with the howling wind, and finally, defeating it with a thunderous roar.

Dutch, in the engineer's cabin, heard the sound. Taking an engineer with him, he got Will and the Royal Canadian Mounted Police Officer and headed for Adam's car. Michael Lane was nowhere to be found. Once they were seated, they began to hum and melded into the harmonics already in motion.

The vibrations bathed the mountain. The train's glow floated out through the darkened night, giving light to the refugees. As the vibrations hit the mountain they created a ripple effect and that was a mistake. The 'woompf' under Adam's feet told him. Quickly he covered Brett's face with the Buffalo skin coat; yelled at Running-water to keep his mouth closed. "Swim with it. Try to get to an outer edge."

He didn't have a chance to say more. It hit them fast, roaring down upon them, scooping them up, throwing them down the hill, crashing through scrub pine. Even though he knew he should let go of the stretcher, Adam desperately clung to it. He'd come too far to give up now. Flying over the tops of brush and through tree limbs, they fought for their lives. The stretcher had become a sled and became airborne. It raced along the very edge of the roaring avalanche. Adam wasn't sure at what point he lost contact with Running-water. He hoped the leg in its make-shift splint didn't get caught. If it did Running-water could be buried and would suffocate. He tried sending a thought message. There was no response.

At a hundred miles an hour, it was soon over! He and Brett had landed with a thud at the base of the railroad trestle. A few feet more and the avalanche would have hit the train. Adam struggled to right himself; sat up, shook off the snow, rolled off of the stretcher, and checked Brett. He found the sought after pulse and heaved a sigh of relief.

A sputtering, coughing, and cussing Running-water shook himself loose from the impacted snow. Placing his hands behind him, he pushed down as he heaved himself forward. "What the hell?" Running-water said, realizing he was sitting on top of someone. He rolled over on to his good side and frantically began pushing the snow away from the body. He knew if it was Adam or Brett he'd have very little time to get the snow from his face and get the air passages open.

He was so occupied with flinging the snow off the body beside him he didn't hear Adam calling him.

"What are you doing? You gone loco?" Adam said as he crawled over to Running-water.

"God! I thought you were buried in the snow. Where's Brett? He okay?"

"He's still alive. Who's that?" Adam said.

"Well, I'll be damned. There's no head. It must be Charles," Running-water said.

"You think you are up to some telecommunicating?" Adam said.

"What do you want me to do?"

"I've lost the radio so we'll have to try and contact Daphne to let her know where we are. Give me your hand; clear your mind of all thought, except one. Simply think 'beneath the trestle.'"

Placing a finger on the bridge of Running-water's nose, he slowly drew it downward as he hummed. Adam placed his other hand on top of Running-water's. A faint blue glow showed itself. It didn't strengthen. Adam had used so much of his energy in trying to save Brett's life he was not getting through. Running-water's injuries were sapping his energy. Nothing. Once more he cleared his mind, directing the energy to Running-water. Still nothing.

Adam rolled over on all fours, and then stood up, trying not to put any pressure on his swollen ankle. From a distance, he created a grotesque figure trying to do a pirouette. Finally, balanced, he lifted his arms upward, pointing his hands toward the train. Concentrating, he tried to send a message to Daphne. Something was blocking his attempt at making a telepathic connection. His hands began tingling, vibrating like a tuning fork. The vibrations traveled his body, filing it with renewed energy. Adam realized the people on the train were in a medicine wheel sending out their combined energy to him. That was why he and Running-water couldn't connect. Relaxing, he allowed their energy to bathe him, to engulf him, and to warm him. Again he attempted to send his wife a message. This time she heard.

"They're below the trestle. We need to get to them quickly. Find rope," Daphne said scrambling to her feet.

"We got a small crane and winch on board. We can use that to lower someone down," the now sober engineer said. "I'll back the train on to the trestle."

The engineer returned to the train's engine and eased the train onto the trestle until the flatbed holding the small crane and winch were just off center. Uncertain as to the exact spot where Adam was located, Dutch decided to go down. Slowly he creaked his way to the bottom of the ravine. Straining to see through the swirling snow, he called out Adam's name. The howling wind was so loud he couldn't hear. Barely able to see, Dutch inched his way along the treacherous river bank. One slip and he could end up in the icy waters.

A floodlight aimed from the train was of little use. It created a crystalline shimmer through which no one could see. Dutch felt something give way as he inched his way along. He had hit Brett and his groan brought Dutch to a standstill. Easing himself down on his knees, Dutch began to pat the ground around him. He felt the stretcher and then realized he had found one of the three.

"Adam!" Dutch yelled.

"I'm right here. You stumbled into Brett."

Dutch double checked the stretcher to make sure it was suitable to be hoisted up to the train. It was. The end of the cable was fastened to it and using a Cobra two-way, Dutch radioed the engineer to begin to pull them up. He decided he would ride the cable up by standing on its hook If the stretcher began to slip he'd be there to tighten it. The cable began to move and the stretcher was eased off the snow. They had risen a few feet; the wind angry at their audacity, lashed at them, causing them to swing back and forth. On a backswing, the wind caught Dutch; almost knocking him from his perilous perch. A steel wire thread broke piercing his left hand, embedding itself deep into the flesh. The pain was unmerciful in its assault. Dutch yanked his hand away. The sudden movement again nearly toppled him. Blood spurted in his face. Wrapping his arm around the cable, he pulled out his shirt, ripped a piece off, and tied it around the hemorrhaging wound. By the time they reached the top, Dutch was a bloody mess.

Fighting excruciating pain, Dutch managed to ease himself over the trestle's railing. Samuel helped him lower Brett down onto the flatcar. Once they had the cable disconnected, they carried him to Adam's private car where Dr. Bach was waiting for them.

Patricia Livingston rushed to her husband. Delirium had set in and he didn't recognize her. For the first time in her life, she felt a sickening panic, terrorizing her in fear not known to her before now. Dr. Bach gently removed her from Brett's stretcher, cut the straps holding him, removed the buffalo-skin coat and made a quick examination. Without an MRI he couldn't be sure of the extent of the internal injuries. That left him with exploratory surgery as his only option. Next, he examined Dutch's bloody hand, folding back the layers of torn flesh, he could see the bone. With a quick jerk, he yanked out the remaining piece of steel cable. Dutch gritted his teeth.

"Have to clean this out before I can stitch you up," Dr. Bach said.

"Leave it alone, Doc. Got get Running-water and Adam. Both are injured," Dutch said.

"No way. You've not just ripped flesh, but the muscles and tendons. There's a good possibility you'll not have use of that thumb. Sit still; shut up, this is going to hurt. I don't have any Novocain."

"I'll get Adam and Running-water," Samuel said.

"Once you are down there, go east about twenty feet. Take a light with you and wear heavy gloves or you'll rip your hands on that damn cable. One of the wires is broken. Try to keep it steady. The whole thing could snap. And watch out for the river. One misstep and you're a goner," Dutch said.

"Didn't I tell you to keep your mouth shut?" Dr. Bach said, pouring alcohol over the gaping wound.

"Holy shit! You trying to kill me? Jesus Doc, you could have given me warning."

As Samuel climbed up onto one of the girders of the trestle, sweat poured down his round face. He felt wet beneath his clothes. His breath came in short almost hurtful bursts. Finally, with both arms wrapped around the girder, he forced himself to look down into the dark abyss below. Fear had him. Heights frightened him; looking out from four hundred feet above the ground down into total blackness absolutely terrorized him He was sucking air. In desperation, he reached out, grabbed the cable, and pushed himself out from the girders. He knew he was never going to get to the bottom of the ravine. He hit the snow-covered ground with such force he was sure he had broken something. His tightly clinched jaws ached. He struggled to steady himself but fell flat on his face anyway. Cussing, he got up, and began yelling, "Adam, I am here!"

"Easy. We're right here. Get Running-water. He's got a broken leg."

Unsure if Running-water had enough strength to hold on to the cable, Samuel strapped the two of them together once he had Running-water's feet firmly planted on top of his own. Aiming his flashlight up toward the train, Samuel turned it on and off three times. The engineer, who had been watching, caught the faint glow and began to pull them up. Agonizingly slow, the crane labored to bring up its two charges. The wind enjoyed its chance to slap around two more victims. The swirling snow bit into their faces, forcing them to keep their eyes closed. Something Samuel had already done. At the top, Samuel was slammed into the top girder of the trestle. It was then that he opened his eyes; seeing eager hands waiting to help them.

Samuel untied Running-water, climbed up over the railing, turned, reached down to get Running-water but missed. The splint on Running-water's leg caught and he cried out in pain as the broken leg was twisted. With Herculean strength, Samuel grabbed Running-water, heaved him up and over the railing, and in a seamless motion slung him over his back. The splint-bound leg stuck out giving him further problems. After some jostling, Samuel had everything under control and headed back along the tracks. He stopped. He thought he had heard a sharp crack—a rifle shot. He didn't move, listening. Nothing but the howling wind. He moved on. With his charge across his broad shoulders, Samuel lumbered down the tracks like an ancient buffalo.

When Isha saw her husband she gasped. Bringing her delicate hands to her face she tried to muffle the sobs that chocked her. She folded herself around him, kissing him over and over. Dr. Bach gently pulled her away. He took a quick look at Running-water, checked his vitals, and quickly returned to Brett, the more severely injured. They had forgotten about Adam.

CHAPTER THIRTY-THREE

Screaming, earsplitting screaming filled the car. Everyone froze. The quadruplets. Daphne rushed to them. Blue radiated around them, flashing not so much in anger but more in panic. Daphne realized that they had forgotten Adam who was still at the bottom of the ravine.

Dashing back into the main room Daphne yelled, "Oh my god! Adam! He's still down there. Quick! The screaming stopped.

Running to the end of their private car Daphne flung open the door, not waiting for the steps to be lowered, she jumped from the car. She tried to run, but the snow was too deep. She was reduced to a trudge. Trying to see what was left of Samuel's tracks wasn't much help. The wind and snow had covered most of them. Even though the crane was only a few cars ahead, it seemed miles away to her. Still not over the birthing process she was weak. Several times she stumbled, barely catching her balance. She caught her foot on one of the ties and fell. The rail spike cut deep into her knee. The pain was so severe she couldn't move. Fighting to remain conscious Daphne thought "I *can* do this! I must! Get up! Get going!" Instead of stifling her scream, she let it come as she struggled to get to her feet. It gave her relief. Not bothering to shake the snow from her clothes she trudged on, keeping her head down as she tried to avoid the lashing wind and biting snow.

Reaching the middle of the trestle where the crane was parked, Daphne climbed up to the cab, hit the starter button. Nothing. She hit it again. With protest, it kicked in. Using a flashlight she searched for the lever to lower the cable. Finding it, she quickly engaged the lever and then climbed down. The pain in her knee was excruciating. She felt sick to her stomach. As she climbed up to the edge of the trestle railing every nerve in her body was consumed by pain. Twice she slipped on the wet railing, grabbing hold of one of the girders to steady herself and twice the wind beat her back. Continually she repeated 'I can do this' as she clung to one of the beams. She wrapped an arm around the beam and with her free hand aimed her flashlight out into the dark, searching for the elusive cable, hoping to see its shinny wires. Once she thought she saw it swing by but wasn't sure. She waited; she saw it and jumped.

Panic seized her. Nearly paralyzed with fear she clung to the cable as the wind pushed her around and around, a puppet on a frayed string. She remembered Samuel saying the cable could snap. Further terrorized, her heart raced. She gulped air; it's cold penetrating her lungs. An involuntary shudder nearly toppled her. And just as quickly it passed and she was no longer afraid. She no longer felt the cold wind lashing at her nor did the snow blind her any longer. Her body warmed and the pain in her knee subsided. She marveled at how good she felt. Weightless, she floated in the darkness. She was sure if she could see herself she would be glowing. It was then that she realized her sons were sending her massive energy.

Oh my god! It's true. I feel them. I must remember to ask Adam about this. She vaguely remembered him saying something about an informed universe; she couldn't quite remember. With a thump, she hit the ground. The pain again stabbed at her.

Isha went to be with the quads. The blue light surrounding them startled her. It was the same kind of light she had seen surrounding her own twins, but more intense. She looked down at them, checking each one. Their eyes were wide open and intensely fixed. They did not blink when she moved her hand in front of them. Frightened by this, she touched the first born on his neck to get a pulse. A flash of blue light arced from him to her and she felt intense vibration. Instantly she saw her own babies and both were radiating an intense blue light. She realized they were talking, more a whispering than normal speech. Not only could she see and hear them, she understood what they were saying. They were sending energy, vibrant life-saving energy, to Adam and they were healing Daphne.

"Oh no! Now Daphne," Isha thought, rushing from the bedroom.

"Samuel! Hurry. Daphne needs help with Adam!" Isha said.

"Not without me," Dutch said. "Anybody seen Michael Lane? We sure could use his help. Where's Will? Damn!"

Pulling on a fur-lined parka, Isha rushed to the end of the car and like Daphne before her, she didn't wait for the steps to be lowered. She jumped. Samuel and Dutch were right behind her. When they reached the crane they found that its motor had stalled out and that it had unloaded all of its cable. The wind screamed at them and for a brief moment, they were sure they heard it snarl, *who do you puny humans think you are? You dare to challenge me?* It received an answer as a bright blue light flashed across the sky.

A lifetime passed before them as Samuel struggled to get the crane started. The motor groaned as it kicked into reverse gear and began the rewind of its long life line. Dutch climbed up to the cab of the crane and shouting at Samuel asked, "You remember if Brett and Running-water were located north of south of the train?"

"What do you mean?" Samuel said.

"Were they still located toward the rear of the train when you found them?" Dutch said.

"Toward the rear. Why?" Samuel said.

"Want to make sure Adam hasn't moved. Shoot flares just to the left of that area. They'll help light up the area and maybe we can see down there. Don't want to hit them," Dutch said.

Four flares were sent up, one after the other. Using night vision binoculars, Dutch saw two people waiving. He also saw something else coming up fast. The cable had clumped and a huge knot of it was about to hit the railing of the trestle.

"Kill the motor," Dutch yelled at Samuel.

But Samuel didn't hear. The knotted cable struck with a loud thud and the trestle shook. The force was so strong that the crane came loose from its moorings. Samuel jumped, landing on the flat car. The crane toppled forward, smashed through the trestle railing, and fell into the ravine below, hit the snow-covered earth, and bounced once into the river.

"Samuel, you okay?"

"Okay."

"We can't leave them down there much longer. They'll freeze to death. Get to Running-water and ask him if he knows the whereabouts of rope, lots of rope," Dutch said to Samuel, as he helped him down from the flat car. "Glad you're okay."

Dutch watched Samuel lope out of sight. Then he continued his vigil looking down through the swirling snow, straining to see. Once the flares had burned themselves out, black forbidding darkness was his reward for his watchfulness.

Samuel and Will came trudging back; each carrying large coils of rope. Michael Lane followed, carrying a chair and blankets.

Damn! What the hell am I doing? I'm supposed to whack this guy. Missed him once. I don't dare try another shot. He set the chair down. Of course, I can't leave him down there to die. I won't get paid. The key to his payment was an announcement in the Canadian papers that Adam had been killed.

After tying a Prusik Knot [1] to one of the girders, Samuel tied the other end to the chair, looping it under and around the seat and then up the back for added security. Dutch lowered it to the ground. Next, using a fisherman's knot, Dutch tied two more ropes together. About four feet from the end of one, he tied another double knot. If he began to slide it would act as a stop. Then following Samuel's example, he tied one end to one of the girders. He pulled the rope, testing it, making sure it was secure. Even though time was running out for those below, he knew that a hasty rappel was dangerous with the high winds. He decided to do a body rappel. He passed the rope between his legs, then around one hip, and diagonally across his chest. Then he ran the rope over his shoulder back along his arm to his hand. It created a brake. He double checked himself by putting his weight into the rope and pulling. He felt it tighten around his chest. He was ready. He climbed back up on the girder, looked at the knot there, and then lowered himself over the edge. He planted his feet firmly on one of the wide beams. He was grateful for the hardhat with its built-in light he had found inside the cab of the crane. He began his descent.

Fighting to maintain his balance as he was body-slammed into the girders by the virulent wind, Dutch thought of past rappelling experiences. Rappelling in the dark was not new. Most of his experience with the Navy Seals was carried out in the dark. The winds gusting at a good fifty to seventy miles per hour was a different story. Not even rappelling out of a Black Hawk in Afghanistan compared to this. At times the wind was so strong it sucked his breath out. He hit the ground hard, nearly being knocked over by a ravenous gust of wind.

Once he had his balance he disengaged himself from the rope, fastened it to the bridge and then searched for the chair. He spotted its small strobe light blinking. He reminded himself to thank whoever thought of that detail. Calling out to Adam several times he became concerned about the lack of a response. He had just one flare with him and that was to be used as a signal to the people above to begin pulling up the rope. He couldn't risk using it and having them pull up the rope and still not finding Daphne and Adam. Shielding his eyes from the stinging snow, he strained to see.

There!

He thought he saw something, a darker object just above ground level. He headed for it. It was an old tree stump. Again he called out for Adam. Again no response. The howling wind made it impossible to hear. He squatted down, squinted, trying to find a sign. Then he saw it; a faint blue glow, close to the ground. He headed for it.

Adam was using his energy to keep Daphne warm. The blanket Dutch had strapped to his back was most welcome. Adam quickly wrapped his wife in the blanket. With Dutch's help, they headed back to the chairlift. Again the small strobe directed them. Daphne was strapped into the chair. Dutch took care to protect her injured knee; then he shot off the flare. Slowly the chair began to ascend. Its movements were jerky as those above put their backs into the effort of pulling. Hand over hand, Samuel, Will, and Michael pulled the rope taking care not to let it slip. Once she was at the top, Samuel lifted her and the chair over the railing and gently sat both down. He could see the toll all of this had on her: the delivery of four babies, the helicopter crash with her brother on board, her husband's injury as well as her own injury. She gave him a new respect for women.

"Don't you worry," Samuel paused. He didn't know what to call her. "Don't you worry, Mrs. Adam." He gently untied her from the chair, picked her up and carried her back to her private car. Dr. Bach was waiting.

He slugged his way back to the trestle. Had anyone been watching they would have seen a great buffalo moving across a snowy plain; head down, he trudged along the tracks. He would save Adam even if it cost him his own life. Wasn't Adam the only person in the world who had shown him respect, that is, until he met Julie? Even back at Karuna House, Adam had not mocked his size or his need for food. He remembered one night in particular. Joseph who thought he ran the place had berated him, insulted him, and belittled him in front of everyone. It had been after their ten o-clock meditation hour. His stomach had growled. As they marched out of the meditation room, Adam had called him aside. Said he was going down to the kitchen to have a snack and had asked him to go along. Joseph was furious. And there was the time he was trying to find Adam in the woods in Quebec. He'd made a fool of himself bellowing. And then when he proposed marriage to a prostitute Adam never said a word of criticism. Instead, he had congratulated him. Yes, he'd gladly die for this man.

For the two men waiting below the trestle, time had slowed—like waiting for your turn in a doctor's office. Your turn never seemed to be next. There was always someone ahead of you. When the chair was returned to the ground, Dutch quickly strapped Adam into the chair. Removing the laser from the chair, he signaled those above. Its beam reflected off the falling snow, giving a faint red glow in the air. Those who were watching from above saw it and began to pull. Dutch gave Adam a salute as the chair began its long slow trip to the top.

Dutch untied the other rope and wrapped part of it up under and around the shoulder of the injured hand. It was a safety thing. If his good arm and hand got tired he could lean back to rest and still be held.

Satisfied, he began the four hundred foot climb back up the trestle. The iron girders were slippery making the climb even more difficult.

He had experienced cold before but not like this. His face was numb. He had to breathe through his mouth because his nostrils were frozen shut. Instead of abating, the storm bent on revenge for whatever wrong it had perceived, blasted him unmercifully. Battering him from side to side, the storm drove him into the metal girders. Dutch cried out as he felt the bone snap in his arm. Desperately he hung onto the rope with his good hand and leaned back to recoup. He fought to stay conscious as the searing pain shot through him. He saw blood oozing through the sleeve of his coat. He watched the patch grow larger as it froze to the sleeve. He had always envisioned he would die in some clandestine operation. It had never occurred to him that a storm would kill him. Consciousness floated out into the darkness, returning when the storm again smashed him into the girders. The trestle seemed to sway, grumbling at the load it had to bear as the heavy snow from the avalanche continued to push against its pinions. At times Dutch thought he was twisting in the wind and at other times he was sure he was falling into the icy waters below. Movement was an uncertainty. He tried to think of something. Anything that would take his mind off the pain. It didn't work. The pain was all-consuming, eating deep into past memories of other painful injuries.

He was back in Columbia, flying low over the jungle, searching for drug runners. He was part of a Columbian-US team. They had taken flak from ground fire and he had been hit in the leg. He'd used his knife to dig out the bullet. He'd puked his guts out as he poked around in the split flesh of his leg with his knife. Bullets he understood. Shattered bones he did not.

Dutch was barely aware of being hauled over the railing, of helping hands grabbing him, holding him. The trestle began to sway. They felt the vibration as it moved. Samuel and Will Rexford lifted Dutch into the cab of the engine. Samuel notified Adam that everyone was back on board. The engineer slowly moved the train off the trestle and headed back toward Vancouver.

The avalanche and the falling crane had weakened the trestle. The high winds and the continued pressure from the still moving snow of the avalanche began to rock the trestle. Those on the train felt the movement and just as the last car was off the bridge, the engineer increased the speed and breathed a sigh of relief when he knew he was on solid ground. A huge roar from buckling steel told them the trestle had collapsed into the river four hundred feet below. The vibration sped along the train. The engineer leveled his speed and the injured matched their own rhythms with the muffled clickity-clack of the cars. Samuel put his shoulder under Dutch as Will Rexford lifted him up. They carried him back through the train, through the bloody mess in the passenger car. The copper smell of spilled blood and urine assaulted them. Dutch moaned as they sat him down to open the door to the next car. Dutch wasn't a lightweight. His 190 pounds seemed to increase with each car they went through until they reached Adam's private car.

Floating in and out of Dreamtime, Dutch was bombarded with little remembrances, flashing bits of jerky movie film from an old sixteen millimeter. Glimpses of his ex-wife, of Will Rexford, and of an unknown daughter slithered along the memory paths of his brain. There was no recognition that someone had ripped his clothes off. He was unaware of Dr. Bach desperately trying to stop the hemorrhaging that had begun again in the warmth of the train. Several times Dr. Bach had tried to clamp off a shattered vein without success.

"He's losing too much blood," Dr. Bach muttered.

There was no nurse to pat his sweating forehead. He wiped away his perspiration on the sleeve of his white jacket. Just when he thought he had a good clamp, the vein slipped away. Exasperated, Dr. Bach pulled off a glove and went at it with bare fingers.

"Gotcha, you little bastard," Dr. Bach said, finally completing a successful clamp. Still irritated he turned to those who waited, he said, "I need a type O. Anybody a type O? He needs a transfusion and damn soon!"

"How do you know Dutch's blood type?" Samuel said.

"Oh shit! Do I have to give a first-aid lesson? He's wearing a medic alert. Find somebody. Come on, damn it! Hurry up."

"I'm type O," Will Rexford said

"This isn't going to be easy. I have to do a make-shift peripheral line. Don't have the necessary equipment to do a standard blood transfusion. This will be painful and dangerous," Dr. Bach said. "I have no way of checking for the RH factor or for antibodies."

He pulled out a long section of medical plastic tubing from a box he had ripped open. From another box, he grabbed two hypodermic needles, removed their plungers, and added one to each end of the tubing. He made sure the tubing and needles were well married. Modifying an old technique used in World War II, Dr. Bach next inserted a syringe to act as a pump. Carefully he pulled back the plunger and then pushed it back in. He felt the small air flow at the end of the needled tubing. He was ready for the intravenous insertion.

"Okay. It'll take a couple of hours to get three-quarters of a pint of blood if we are lucky. It will be slow. Once I insert this needle into your arm, you must not move. You understand?" Dr. Bach said.

"Get it going, Doc," Will Rexford said. "I've been here before."

"Not like this. So don't get heroic! Samuel, when I tell you I want you to pull the handle to the syringe, very slowly. You think you can do that?" Dr. Back said.

"Sure."

"I mean very slowly."

"I got it! Jesus! I'm not totally stupid." Samuel said.

"I've numbed Dutch's arm as much as I can."

"Is he conscious? If he is I can put him in a deep trance. That'll make your job easier," Adam said as he hobbled over to the makeshift operating table. It was all he could do. His healing energy had not returned

"Do your thing, Adam," Dutch said.

Adam bent down, whispered something in Dutch's ear, and gently blew into his eyes. Once he had tuned into Dutch's body rhythms, Adam increased the pitch of his humming. Dutch's eyes remained open; he could hear, but he felt nothing.

Dr. Bach knew he had very little time to make the repairs to Dutch's arm. The light was not good and that bothered him. The movement of the train posed still another issue. And that bothered him. The fact he didn't have the necessary equipment bothered him. His insertion of the needle into Will's arm was harsh.

"Jesus, Doc. You trying to push that damn needle right through my arm?" Will Rexford said.

"Sorry."

The other end was inserted into Dutch's arm with less force. Dr. Bach told Samuel to pull back the handle of the syringe. Each held his breath, waiting for the blood to flow. Dr. Bach gently tapped the tubing near the needle. The blood began to flow. Both of them exhaled in near unison. Anxiously they waited to see if Dutch was receiving the necessary blood. It seemed it would never get there.

"Come on, damn it! Take!" Dr. Bach said. "Finally! Okay. I'm ready. One of you hold his arm. I don't want to take a chance of it jerking.

With a swift yank, Dr. Bach had set the broken bone. Then he began the repair. After an hour, he was still cleaning away the mashed flesh, pulling back the layers as he sopped up blood so he could see if the two pieces of bone had gone together. They had. Next, he cut away tissue that could not be saved. It was cut and stitch. Cut and stitch. He double checked his stitching; added a couple more as a precaution. He gave Dutch a shot of antibiotic. Because he didn't have plaster with which to make a cast, he used two rolls of gauze and Duct Tape. With methodical precision, he taped the arm to Dutch's chest. And when it came time to remove it, it would hurt like hell. Dutch was very hirsute.

As he pulled off his surgical gloves Dr. Bach said, "I've enough morphine to get him through the night. Tomorrow will be hell for him."

"What's your prognosis?" Adam said.

"If he heals without complications, in a week I'll put a different cast on his arm. I don't dare do anything close to permanent until I see how he's healing. He lost a lot of blood, but his greatest danger is infection. The bottom line is I'm not sure how much use he will have with that hand and arm. Just can't say. How long before he comes around?"

"I can release him now. You want to give him a shot of morphine? If you want to hold off on that I'll stay with him and hypnotize him again. Not sure how long I can keep him under. He's highly trained and he may reject it. In the meantime, you better get some rest yourself. Is Will Rexford going to be okay?"

"Will's fine. He's strong. We'll watch Dutch to see if he develops an abnormal temperature or breaks out in a rash. If he does, let me know right away. Samuel, get the inspector or that Michael Lane to help you take Dutch back to his compartment? And be careful. Don't jar him," Dr. Bach said. Turning to Daphne he said, "Let's take a look at that knee."

He cleaned the cut, carefully examined the knee cap. Without x-rays, he couldn't be sure if it was cracked. It wasn't dislocated. He made a gauze bandage for the wound, taped it on, and then gave Daphne a shot of antibiotic. Dr. Bach took another look at the splint Adam had put on Running-water's leg. He saw no reason to change it. He added some duct tape to further secure it. With Isha's help, Running-water returned to their private car.

Daphne and Adam hobbled to their bedroom. Adam sat on their bed, close to Daphne. Gently he put his arm around her, and with his free hand stroked her cheek. She was so absolutely beautiful he had difficulty in concentrating. His azure blue eyes reflected his appreciation. "Thank you," he whispered. "I would not have made it without you. You are the bravest, and the most beautiful woman I've ever known. The miracle is that you chose me."

She looked up, kissed him. "I know. But there's a real miracle you should know about. Your sons, our sons, screamed when we had forgotten you. They sent me energy to climb that awful bridge. Adam, I was so afraid and I hurt. Suddenly I felt warm, actually wonderful."

The quads glowed at the recognition given to them, but their parents didn't see this. Adam was busy hypnotizing her so she could rest. Once he was sure she was in deep sleep, Adam slipped out the door and went to Dutch' compartment. Inside, Adam removed Howahkan's obsidian amulet from around his neck and laid it in the center of Dutch's forehead. He opened the medicine pouch of his father, Esaugetuh, took some of the fine powder, and sprinkled it on Dutch's hairy chest. He lit a bundle of sweet grass and slowly smudged Dutch's six foot two frame. Had there been others present, they would have seen a faintly glowing blue orb surround Adam and would have heard a low pitched humming. The guardian at the door heard and knew Adam was working to help Dutch heal.

A commotion outside the compartment door ended the humming.

Michael Lane was insisting that he was going to enter the compartment. He was steaming. "I'm in charge of the investigation and I'll go where I damn well please. Now move aside."

Samuel insisted he was not going to enter Dutch's compartment. To emphasize his point, Samuel removed the Uzi from his shoulder.

"Look, little man, when it comes to Adam, I'm boss. Wherever he is, I am. I don't need you here. Dutch is not your concern. As far as I'm concerned you have no authority on this train. It's private! You understand? So shove off!"

Lane heard the release of the safety on the Uzi as Samuel stepped directly in front of the door of Dutch's compartment.

"Have it your way."

He turned and walked away. Stubborn bastard. I ought to pop you. On the other hand, it might be more fun to watch you bleed out.

Adam opened the door.

"Mind telling me what that was all about?"

"I don't like that man. There's something about him. He's not going to tell me what he is or is not going to do. Was I wrong?" Samuel said, concerned that maybe he had overstepped his authority.

"No, Samuel. You did just fine. And thank you. I'm going to go back and check on Daphne again. You mind coming along?" Adam said.

He was as delighted as a child who had been given an extra scoop of ice cream. That Adam had thanked him was enough for a whole day's high, but having been asked to join Adam put him in orbit. Samuel lumbered behind Adam as they headed into the next Pullman, on through the car which housed Running-water's extra-large compartment and then to Adam's. He kept his Uzi at the ready. Julie would have to learn that he was always on call when it came to Adam's safety.

After all, Adam had done so much for him. For starters, he gave him a renewed sense of self-respect, of self-value as Adam called it. The rest of The Brothers may not appreciate the gift given to them—the chance for a new life— but Samuel did. It was because of Adam that he had lost a hundred pounds of fat, got into shape, and for once in his life, held his head high. He had given him a sense of hope! He might be a slow processor, but he was not stupid by a long shot.

Once he had checked Daphne and finding that the large bump on her knee cap had begun to go down, Adam decided it would be safe for him to go back and stay the night watching over Dutch. Before leaving, he checked on his sons. With Brett and Running-water out of commission, and Dutch down Adam's personal defenses were nearly eliminated. Daphne and the quads were vulnerable. Adam asked Samuel to guard his private car. Samuel grabbed Adam, hugged him, and swung him around.

"Yes! Yes! Don't you worry. Nobody will get by me."

As Adam left, Samuel took up his position in front of the door. He sat down, propped himself up against the door, Uzi on his lap. Just let someone try to get by me. Around two in the morning he thought he saw a figure scurrying along the corridor coming toward him. It was Julie. She had hot coffee and donuts.

She watched her husband stuff the donuts into his mouth and wash them down with large gulps of coffee. Snuggling closer to him she whispered, "Samuel, you're all I got now. I want you to know I'm the luckiest woman in the world. No matter what happens or wherever you go, I'll always be there for you. You are my world."

Samuel thought his heart would burst because it was beating so fast. Yes, there is hope!

Several times during the night, Dutch moaned, and each time Adam laid his hand upon the Wisdom Keeper's amulet that remained on Dutch's forehead. When its vibrations steadied Adam withdrew his hand and Dutch quieted. Its power fascinated Adam. Hard as he tried he could not comprehend its seemingly magical powers. He knew it came from the other side, a gift from the spiritual world. He accepted that and quietly gave thanks for this blessing.

Mid-morning found Dutch awake but unfocused. Sweating profusely he still felt cold. His arm had no feeling. The rhythmic movement of the train no longer soothed him. He hurt. He didn't like the smell of the room. He felt the urge to relieve himself. He tried to sit up, to get up but couldn't. He forced himself to focus. Adam was holding him down.

"Damn it, Adam, let me up. I gotta piss."

"Guess you're going to live, after all," Adam said, helping Dutch to stand.

---

[1] Named after Dr. Karl Prusik, An Austrian music professor during World War I. This particular knot is used to safeguard a loaded rope in a rescue.

CHAPTER THIRTY-FOUR

Morning was late in opening her eyes. A glimmer of blue sky appeared when the train pulled back into the station at Vancouver. The grays of the ugly storm gradually moved out the morning held the promise of a day of new beginnings. They had been ordered to stop at Vancouver. Adam had anticipated a negative reaction from the law enforcement and the railroad officials but the harshness and rage stunned him. Even Runningwater could not muster an argument against the tirade that was let loose upon them. And again, Michael Lane was nowhere around.

"Where's Lane. He should be talking to these people. That's his job. Get the Monty in here to see what he can do," Adam said into his two-way as a husky man moved closer to the train. Adam stepped into the vestibule. The man had a wispy red mustache and a bilious disposition. He yelled over a bullhorn.

"I'm sick and tired of you weirdoes and your special treatment. Get off that god damned train or I'll have your asses taken off."

"Knock it off, dirtbag, and be damn quick about it. Who do you think you are?" Patricia Livingston said, stepping down one step in front of Adam. She felt his holstered gun as she brushed past him.

"I don't care who the hell you are, bitch. You're not in charge here. Open your mouth once more and I'll drag your sorry ass off those steps and have you locked up."

"Try it!" Patricia Livingston said.

He moved toward Patricia and reached out to grab her arm. He felt burning pain. A swift kick to his throat silenced him.

"I'm sure your superiors will have plenty to say to you, especially after they see my report on television. Every word you uttered has been recorded," Patricia Livingston said.

"This one has something to say," Michael Lane said, appearing from around the corner of the car. "You're done here," he said to the injured man.

The agent wobbled off, still clutching his throat. It would be several hours before he would be able to speak. He was sure his larynx was ruptured. Even though Michael Lane had been paid to take Adam out, he didn't abide by the mistreatment of women and that included foul language.

"Excuse me, Ms. Livingston. I want to speak to that agent,"

He followed the injured man; when they were out of sight, he stopped him. The inspector never saw it coming. He gurgled just once and fell to the ground. Michael Lane pulled the blade of his knife from the base of the man's brain With a quick twist, he had severed the brain stem. He wiped the knife on the dying man's coat. He didn't search the man, didn't look for a billfold, or gun, or badge.

Keep it clean. No prints. Killing that shit head, felt damn good. I don't need a screw up like him. Had enough of those lately. My *man* is going to be pissed because I've not whacked Adam yet. Better make a call.

He didn't realize he was actually breathing hard. The excitement of the kill gave him a rush. He felt so alive. But first things first. Don't blow your cool. Casually he ambled back to the train, whistling *The Best Things in Life Are Free.* In this case, it was a free kill.

The Royal Canadian Mounted Police Officer had appeared; nodded to Michael Lane who then spoke with the officials there. Both men boarded the train as it slowly moved on toward Blaine. In a matter of minutes, the train arrived at Blaine where it was immediately parked on a side track.

As coordinating investigator, Michael Lane met with the task force. In quiet, authoritative tones he told them of Adam's heroic rescue of Brett Montana and Paul Dakota, leaving the details of the location of Charles' remains until last. He was careful not to take credit for any of the heroic actions or the discovery. As he began to tell those gathered about the collapse of the trestle he was interrupted by a Royal Canadian Mounted Police officer.

"Sir. There has been a message from the Minister of Public Safety and Emergency Preparedness. A communiqué had been received from the American Secretary of Homeland Security."

"So. What's the issue?" Michael Lane said. Annoyed by the interruption.

"In a display of Inter-American cooperation, any further inspection is immediately terminated and the train and its passengers are to be allowed to cross the Border immediately. The RCMP will complete the investigation."

Michael paled. He didn't respond. He boarded the train. He would have to change plans. Struggling to control his anger and to regain his composure, he went to find Adam.

"Evidently you have very powerful friends in government. The Ministry has released you and your group. I've notified the train's engineer that he can move out. Better make sure everyone is on board."

"Please extend my thanks and appreciation to your government," Adam said.

"No problem," Michael said, opening the door to jump down from the train before it picked up speed.

"I've detected that you are not happy. Maybe you'd like to ride along for a time and talk about it," Adam said. "The choice is yours."

The train was picking up speed. Michael Lane couldn't believe his luck. He made a quick decision.

"Once Running-water is up and about I'll have him take care of your legal paperwork if there should be a challenge for your return to Canada," Adam said, grabbing Michael's hand and pulling him back onto the vestibule. The door clanged shut behind him.

"No need. I'll notify my superiors that I'm staying on board for a while longer. I'm not sure what I should say about myself right now beyond the fact that I'm still pissed about having my vacation slot changed. Friends had to change their plans. Caused quite a bit of a mess. Guess you can understand that. You were telling me about your powers and something of your origin. Mind continuing with that?"

CHAPTER THIRTY-FIVE

Adam and Michael Lane walked forward to the dining car. Adam towered over him yet Lane did not give the appearance of being a small man. His short cropped black hair added to his military demeanor. They sat down at a table. Coffee and donuts were brought by one of the waiters.

"It's difficult to define my powers, as you call them. I prefer to view whatever they are, as abilities. There's much I don't know. As to whom I am, I'm a bastard born to a white woman, fathered by an Indian and according to some that makes me a half-breed; sometimes rejected by both societies. Both my mother and father were rejected by their families. Evidently, there had been some kind of an arrangement made between Esaugetuh and the man who married my mother—the man who raised me as his son. A large sum of money was provided to him to ensure his business success. I had always sensed there was a distance between him and me. It wasn't that he was outright cold; it was just a lack of warmth—the kind of warmth I saw between other fathers and their sons," Adam said.

"That must have frosted your balls," Michael said. "Anyway, how did you meet up with this Esaugetuh, the man whom you now call your father?"

"When I was a child my parents and I spent every summer on an Indian reservation in Canada. The women were always whispering about a powerful shaman. I used to imagine what he looked like, even pretending I saw him standing on a hill not far from our log cabin. The man who raised me refused to talk about him or even acknowledge his existence. Wondering who he was stuck with me. After college, working as a freelance writer, I set out to find out about him," Adam said.

"And when you found him, he told you who he was?" Michael asked, making sure his questions were not too probing.

"No. It was only recently that I learned Esaugetuh was my real father," Adam said.

"I don't understand," Michael said.

"Esaugetuh allowed me to find him in Florida. Even then he didn't let on as to who he really was; nor did he let on that he was the mysterious shaman for whom I had been searching. I eventually suspected he was the shaman so I stayed with him, learning from him, lapping up every word like a cat licking up spilled milk. I argued, cussed, fumed. I had never been so challenged. One day when I awoke he was gone. I tracked him down at a conference at Mesa Verde, Colorado. I really don't know why but it was there that he publicly decided to adopt me. That didn't set too well with some of the older generation. After making a public show of me, he took off again, leaving me there, wondering why he made a public spectacle of adoption. I thought it was cool, being adopted by an Indian."

"Then what happened?" Michael said. He was finding Adam's story interesting, actually fascinating and that was not good. One of his key principles was not to get emotionally involved with a client or with a target. He found it was too easy to like this man.

"I tracked him to a casino in northwest Washington. It was then that he really took me under his wing and began the task of teaching me the ways of the shaman. I guess he needed to know that I had the will to stick with something. We spent weeks in the deep woods of the Pacific Northwest. Months flew by and I had all but forgotten the people I knew as my parents and the woman I was supposed to marry. He led me on a spiritual journey down the northwest coast of Washington and Oregon and from there into the mountains of Nevada where on a sacred mountain I began my vision quest."

"I've heard of such a thing but haven't the foggiest idea as to what it actually is. What is it, anyway?" Michael said.

"It's a time of denial, a time of spiritual evolution, a transformation. In my case, it was also the arrival of my spirit guide, the conferring of spiritual wisdom," Adam said.

"The two of you didn't remain together?" Michael said.

"When I came down from the mountain he was gone. And that began my search all over again. I wish I could have been smarter, stronger. Something. Maybe he'd still be alive," Adam said, his voice trailing off as he remembered the ugly scene of the decaying body of his father at Karuna House.

"I'm sorry. I didn't mean to bring up bad memories for you. It must have been hell finding your father like that. Man, I'm sure I would have puked my guts out."

"Then," Adam continued, "from a letter he left I learned he was my real father, that he had been the one who had provided the monies for my pleasures—the very money I used to search for him. My white father told me the money came from my grandfather's estate."

"So, when did you discover you had these magical powers, I mean, abilities?" Michael said.

"Not magical. There's no hocus-pocus involved. I'm a healer. I've been told that such abilities come from the amygdala in the brain," Adam said.

"The amy—what?"

"Amygdale. It's the primitive part of our brains, and some of those abilities I possess are part of a broad category of paranormal effects called anomalous perturbation." [1]

"Explain."

"It means that I can create an effect on a person that I intend to influence," Adam said.

"It's rumored you can do some really heavy duty stuff like throwing lightning around, reading peoples' thoughts, and making people fear for their lives. It's said you can throw a grown man across a room by just raising your hand," Michael said. He had to know the strength of Adam's powers. What he should expect if there was a confrontation. While his mind wandered he sensed Adam's focus on him. He looked at Adam and was caught up in the intense presence of Adam's azure blue eyes.

They were wondrous eyes, all-knowing, penetrating. Too late he realized he should have avoided their gaze and he tried to look out a window, but he could not resist the total serenity he was feeling when he looked at them. Michael Lane knew his soul had been scanned, searched to its depths. His sense of serenity quickly moved to a different level, one of discomfort; an ill-ease formulated itself into a terrible sense of having been found out.

His breathing labored as his heart thumped against his ribs. He was sure he was suffocating. Desperately he tried to suck in air. Perspiration formed and matted his black hair. He face paled against its blackness. His lips quivered. Anxiety had him.

"Easy! Just relax. Take deep breaths," he heard Adam say. The voice coming from far away.

Adam placed a hand on Michael's shoulder and passed his hand in front of his eyes. "Breathe in on one; out on two. You'll be fine."

There was an instant change. Michael felt warm, comfortable as his breathing steadied, he said, "Man! Sure don't know what started all that."

"Perhaps you have personal issues that you have not resolved and something I said triggered the hyperventilation."

"Don't think it was anything you said. Sometimes I hyperventilate especially when I've been under a lot of pressure. Never this bad, though. What does the shaman recommend?" Michael said as he attempted a smile, feigned as it was.

"Begin by accepting who you are," Adam said. He raised his right eyebrow to indicate that Michael should know what he meant.

"Sorry to interrupt, Adam, but we're not far out from Seattle. What do you want to do? Continue on or stop," Running-water said, as he hobbled up to their table and slid into a seat next to Adam.

"Hmm. For how far do we have clearance?" Adam said.

"I can answer that," Michael Lane said, glad for a change of subject. "You have clear track as far as Seattle. If you wish to continue on after that you'll have to run with a regular schedule or make some other arrangements with AMTRAK. When you disembark, you'll have to return the train to the CNR."

"Why? Adam owns it!" Running-water said, his lawyer instincts kicking in. Lane made him uncomfortable. He couldn't quite put his finger on it, but there was something about him—maybe it was—,"

"Hmm. Have we passed Mount Vernon?" Adam said; his question brought Running-water back to the issue at hand.

"No! No, we haven't. You want to stop there?" Running-water said. It wasn't so much a question as it was a challenge.

Ignoring Running-water's change in tone, Adam said, "Yes. See if there are enough eighteen wheelers to accommodate us. We'll need a side track. If there's not one available, then we'll have to go to Seattle."

"Okay. I'll see to it," Running-water said, getting up to leave.

To ease his friend's disposition, Adam said, "You can do that from here, can't you?"

"Sure. No problem."

A side track to accommodate an extended stay was not available, but there was ample tracking at a little town just south of Mount Vernon; a processing plant had available track that could accommodate the train. Running-water made the necessary arrangements. Once the train reached the area, and after some necessary switching, backing up, and switching again, the twenty car train was sided along the northwest side of the town. Railroad officials were notified that they were off the main line.

Because of the notoriety of the "Death Train," local and county law enforcement agencies were notified. Samuel, under the supervision of Runningwater, set up safe parameters for the train and its occupants. A 24/7 security detail was quickly put into place with the remaining Brothers and Samuel sharing responsibility. Since three of The Brothers had betrayed Adam, those who remained were not issued weapons; they were equipped with walkie-talkies. Michael Lane, excluded from the security detail, did not protest; rather he busied himself filling out reams of reports. Even though these occupied him, he couldn't help dwelling upon Adam's comment, 'Accept who you are.'

Wonder if he would accept me if he knew? That was just too damn close when he scanned me. Got to be more careful. Can't let him get to me.

---

[1] A term coined by the Science Applications International Corporation (SAIC) and originally referred to psychokinesis.

CHAPTER THIRTY-SIX

Running-water eased himself from his sleeping wife's arms and slipped out of their compartment. Being careful not to make noise with his crutch, he hobbled along the sleeping car until he came to an exit. Carefully opening the door, and easing the steps down, he stepped into a chilly pre-dawn. He walked along the south side of the train, checking to see who was on guard duty. He counted three of The Brothers. And that was as it should be. When he walked around the backside of the train he found no one there.

Damn! I assigned three of The Brothers to be out here. They're gonna get their butts kicked. We don't ask much of them. You'd think they'd want to be involved.

The hair on the nape of his neck and arms crawled. He pulled one of his twin Glock 31's from its holster. Took it off safety. He waited. Nothing moved. Cat-like, he backed up against a wheel of the train. Quieting his heart, Running-water listened to the early morning sounds searching for something out of place. Then he heard. His muscles tightened and his finger stroked the trigger of the Glock. He thought he saw a shadowy figure, sensing its presence. He squeezed the trigger. Nothing. "Jesus!" He thought, "now what?"

Machine like, he quickly checked his gun. It wasn't jammed. He pulled the trigger again. Nothing.

"What are you doing out here?" Isha said.

"My God! I just tried to kill you," Running-water said, grabbing his wife, and holding her so tightly she cried out.

"What are you saying?" Isha said, struggling to free herself from her husband's grasp.

"Twice I tried to fire my pistol and twice it didn't fire," Running-water said.

Next time, my brother, make sure of your target before you fire.

Running-water knew who it was, and replied, "I don't understand. Why didn't the gunfire?"

Just be grateful it didn't.

Running-water stared into the mist, straining to see. He knew there wouldn't be anyone there who had spoken to him, at least not anyone he could touch and feel. Yet, he couldn't help but look and listen. It had been that way between them from the very beginning. Sometimes he still reacted with surprise. It had taken them both some time before they realized that their souls were inextricably connected, that they were in every sense of the word, 'soul brothers.' That fact was really driven home for Running-water during Adam's battle with Moon-Woman—which was really a battle for his soul—a battle she lost. He didn't know why she popped into his mind. He shuddered.

My god I owe him so much; not only did he save my life, my very soul, he has now saved the life of the one to whom I have given myself, my Isha."

Isha followed her husband's gaze and she too knew she would see no one. But for a very brief moment, she did see a blue aura glowing ever so slightly in the fresh morning mist. And she knew there wouldn't be anything physical there. She had learned much from this man that served another—this man whom she called her husband. She understood that there are powers beyond what most people consider normal. And she was just as sure that she had just experienced that power. She embraced her husband, seeking his strength.

Gently he pulled her closer to him and he felt her wrap her legs around him as she sought him. Words were not necessary between them. The morning came alive with bird song and gentle sea scented breezes. And for a moment they forgot where they were as they became one.

CHAPTER THIRTY-SEVEN

Running-water again wondered where the three Brothers were. He had assigned them to guard the back side of the train. Checking the Glock, he slowly walked along the cars, searching for clues, any clues as to their whereabouts. Isha walked with him, her arm entwined in his. She dismissed a shudder as being caused by the chill in the morning air. Spring couldn't come soon enough for her.

"There—! What's that?" Isha said, pointing to a heap lying along a ditch that ran parallel with the railroad tracks.

Running-water signed for her to squat and then lay down. He handed her one of his guns. Carefully he unsnapped the holster of his second Glock, trying not to make any noise. He hobbled his way over to the heap. An instinct he knew all too well told him death had found its prey. Using his good leg, he pushed one of the bodies over, turned on his flashlight, and carefully looked at the face. It was one of the Brothers. His throat had been slit. The same for the other two. The cuts were smooth, and continuous, suggesting they had been made from behind. Checking the ground surrounding the three bodies, Running-water was puzzled. The ground should have been darkened with their blood. It wasn't.

"My god, what happened?" Michael Lane said, stepping out from between two of the cars. "Thought I heard a noise."

Stepping back from the bodies so he could look directly at Michael Lane Running-water said, "Maybe you got some idea about that yourself?"

"How's that?" Michael Lane said.

"How long have you been out here?" Running-water said.

"Just came out. As I said, I thought I heard a noise. They helped load the train back in Toronto didn't they?" Michael said, trying to be casual.

"Can't say for sure. Only Adam knows that," Running-water lied, "Why? Would that be important?" He wondered how Lane knew about the loading procedures back in Toronto.

"Oh, ah--- no particular reason. Just searching for a motive," Michael said.

The questions made him feel uncomfortable. Whew! Got to watch it. That was too close. Don't get too eager.

"You say you thought you heard a noise?" Running-water said.

"Yeah. Thought it was the wind at first. Sounded like a groan. Guess I was right, huh?"

"How strange. My husband and I were making rounds and we heard nothing from either side of the train," Isha said.

She didn't like this man. Hadn't liked him since he gave her that silly smile when they first met. It sure cooled him down when she told him her husband was standing right behind him. It didn't bother her if someone called it 'woman's intuition. Odd that he could hear a noise inside the train with its engine running and heat flowing through the vents.

Running-water was engrossed in studying the three dead men, looking for any detail that might be helpful. He didn't realize that Michael Lane had stepped directly behind him. The light from the cook's window shone on something metallic in Michael's hand. Like the sharp-eyed eagle, Isha caught it. "My god, he's got a knife and is going to kill Running-water," Isha thought.

There was a flash and a pop, nearly simultaneous. Michael Lane spun around, a look of total disbelief on his stricken face, and then fell forward. A bullet pierced the base of his brain, traveled upward, and exited through the front lobe.

"Isha?" Running-water said.

"He was going to slit your throat. Just as he did those poor souls," Isha replied, nodding toward the dead Brothers.

"But—but how did you know?" Running-water said.

"I saw the knife in his hand."

"Give me the gun," Running-water demanded.

The cold tone in his voice startled Isha and warned her not to disagree with his demands. Yet, she felt he could have at least expressed some gratitude for just saving his life She would not be intimidated.

"Why?"

"Because the gun is registered in my name. I am Adam's official bodyguard. I have a permit to carry a concealed weapon. The local authorities will have to be notified. They'll be an inquest. Days, even weeks could be involved. There could be a trial and that could drag on forever. You have our sons to tend. They have been without their mother long enough. It's time you went to them. I want you to leave immediately. Gone before I call the police. I'll have Samuel drive you to the airport."

"Just like that. Dismiss me and I just saved your life."

"This is just the beginning. Things are going to get worse. I've felt it for some time. I've got to know you are safe. Can't have you taken as a hostage."

Disgusted, Isha stomped off. She would do as he said.

The fact that there was no visible blood and the fact that the bodies were stacked on top of one another made a strong case that they had been killed elsewhere. That bothered Running-water. If they had been killed at some point on our way from the Border, why had Lane waited until now to dump them? There was any number of places he could have thrown their bodies overboard between Blaine and here. None of this makes any sense.

Having called Samuel to unload the stretch limo, Running-water watched it being backed down from a flatbed. Samuel, now dressed in his chauffeur's uniform, patted his side, indicating to Running-water that he was armed. He waited, at attention, by the car. Two women dressed in hooded garments and veiled stepped off the train. Immediately, Samuel opened the door to the limo. Each carried a small bag and neither spoke to Samuel as they got in. As soon as they were secure, Samuel turned the limo around and headed it away from the train. He flicked its lights at Running-water who gave him a thumb's up.

Running-water watched until the limo was out of sight. He punched in 911 on his cell phone. No service. Disgusted, he climbed into the SUV that had been unloaded so the limo could be used. He turned on its Global System. Nothing. Deciding that the train was blocking his attempts at transmission, Running-water drove to the main street. He found the local police station, parked the SUV, and walked up to its entrance. A sign taped to the door read: In case of an emergency call 911. "What a joke," Running-water thought as he looked up the street.

No patrol cars in sight. He noticed a little restaurant and headed for that. Inside, he was told there wasn't a public telephone. Should have known better. Any place that has a sign on its restrooms that says for 'customers only' wouldn't have a public phone.

"Don't suppose you have a phone in the office I could use?" Running-water said, laying a twenty on the counter.

That brought results. He was handed a phone from beneath the counter. The cook stayed within hearing. He had recognized Running-water as one of the 'crazies' from the train. Running-water dialed 911 and told the operator the situation. He emphasized that he would wait at the restaurant for the police and go back to the train with them.

"Thanks for the phone," Running-water said to the cook. "I'll have a coffee, black."

As he sipped his coffee he noticed the cook had moved to the other end of the counter and was using the phone. Running-water figured he was calling someone to come into work. Fifteen minutes turned into a half hour. Since no one had showed up he decided to return to the train, thinking that perhaps the dispatch had misunderstood and had sent the police directly to the train. As he slowly pulled in alongside the train, he wondered why there were no police cars around.

Damn! Now what?

CHAPTER THIRTY-EIGHT

Adam met Running-water as he boarded the train. Quickly he told Adam about the discovery of the three dead Brothers and about Daphne shooting Michael Lane. He didn't reveal quite everything that had happened. Some things are personal. Immediately he cleared his mind of those thoughts, remembering that Adam could tune in. Much to his dismay there had been no police at the train.

"Why didn't you tell me you were sending Isha and Julie away? I would have sent Daphne and our sons with them," Adam said. The tone was not one of rebuke but a subtle sadness that his friend had not thought of others.

"Oh shit! It never occurred to me. I just knew I needed Isha out of here. I didn't take time to think about anything else. I just knew if she remained she would have to go through an intensive investigation. And since she saved my neck, I just wanted to—,"

"You're right, of course," Adam said. "I would have done the same thing." His thumbs-up reassured Running-water.

"Samuel took Julie with him. It was Isha's idea. Because Julie is married to one of The Brothers it might be safer if she were not around. I sent them to New Mexico to my mother's. My uncle Gordon Rapport will protect them."

"There I things I want to discuss with you. Have Will Rexford meet the police if they ever arrive. Have him delay them for a while. Dutch's is still healing doesn't need any hassle." Adam said, indicating that Running-water should follow him.

Once they were back at Adam's private car, Adam offered coffee.

"I want to put you through a healing session before I discuss with you my plans. Put your leg up on that stool," Adam said.

Lighting a smudge bundle, Adam wafted it around Running-water. Then he placed both of his hands on Running-water's broken leg. His hands warmed quickly as they hovered over the broken bone. They didn't grow as hot or as red as they had when Adam did his first healing back on the mountain. That was a good sign.

"Good. You are nearly healed. Won't be long before Dr. Bach will be able to remove the cast."

Running-water sipped his coffee in silence as Adam paced up and down the floor. Suddenly he stopped, looked directly at Running-water, looking deep into his friend's soul, lingering there, judging. Running-water shifted his torso, somewhat uncomfortable by the intensity of Adam's scan. He wondered what he was searching for.

"It is time for you to leave me. Everyone must go immediately. Dismiss the staff. I cannot allow any further threats to you, your wife, to my family, or to anyone associated with me. I had hoped that once we were back in the United States we could find a home and the killing would stop. I was—I am so terribly wrong. No, don't even bother to put up an argument. Take Dutch, Will Rexford, and Dr. Bach with you. Now it's my turn to ask the favor," Adam said.

"Of course I will take care of them. Do not worry about that. Have you told Daphne?" Running-water said.

"Told me what?" Daphne said, walking in from their bedroom carrying two of the quads. Handing them to Adam she continued, "I'll be right back and then you can tell me."

"Maybe I better leave and come back later," Running-water said.

"No. Stay. You are part of this family."

"Okay. I'm back. Now, what is it Adam is supposed to tell me?" Daphne said as she cuddled the two boys she held in her arms.

"Running-water has sent Isha back to New Mexico. Take our sons and go there. Your mother will be expecting you. Pack what you need for the flight. Nothing more. Running-water is going with you and will look after you," Adam said.

"And just what are you going to be doing?" Daphne said.

Running-water recognized the signs and tone in his twin's voice. She was not going to buy into any of Adam's orders. And knowing his sister, he knew that she was about to let it fly. Desperately he wanted to leave.

"Family arguments should be private," he thought.

You are part of this family. You are my wife's brother, Adam said, answering telepathically.

Turning to his wife, "Daphne," he said raising a finger, " you will do exactly as I say. The SUV will be ready shortly. The jet at Bellingham is being fueled as I speak. You are not to use public transportation. Brett will be your pilot. Patricia Livingston, Dutch, Will Rexford, and Dr. Bach are to go with you. Do not attempt to contact me by cell phone, land phone, or computer."

"Give me a few minutes to throw a few things in a bag for the boys."

Running-water was stunned by his sister's total compliance. She didn't even raise an eyebrow. She didn't ask why she was being sent away. Within minutes she returned with a flight bag, one baby strapped to her back, another fastened to her midriff, and carrying the other two on her hips. These she handed to Running-water.

"I'm ready. Let's go."

She exited their private car, down the three steps, and into the waiting SUV. Not once did she look back at Adam nor did she say anything. Patricia Livingston was the only one who looked back. There was no one there. She was sure that there was a faint blue aura where he had been standing. Running-water was perplexed by his sister. She was not the Daphne that he knew. He tried to telecommunicate with her. No response. Not even a sense of her being. Then he heard Adam's voice.

It's better this way, my brother. She'll be fine once she lands at Albuquerque. Keep her safe. Your mother and uncle will be waiting for you. Speak to no one. Go now. Leave me to my business.

Bellingham's airport was a short drive north. So preoccupied with what had happened, Running-water didn't notice the beautiful scenery or the sparkling lake as they whizzed along Interstate 5. Will Rexford was driving. Everyone was into his own personal thoughts. Only the quads seemed to be alive. They offered a distraction for Running-water. The blue aura surrounding them brightened and faded in and out.

Wonder if they are talking to one another.

Of course, we are. We have a question for you. Will you disobey our father?

Running-water thought his imagination was playing games with him.

Will you? They spoke with one voice.

A man must do what he has to do.

That does not answer our question. Will you disobey our father?

He sat there. As he shook his head in disbelief, his long blue-black hair came unbraided and fell over his broad shoulders.

We're waiting!

You know I have sons of my own and that I long for them and yet I am compelled by your father's wishes to protect you and your mother. How can I break a vow? It is a great worry.

Did you not make an earlier one? Certainly, that comes first.

Yes! Damn it! We are soul mates. I cannot leave him unprotected.

Running-water had his answer. As soon as he had the others on the plane he would return to the train. So preoccupied with planning, he was unaware that he had walked out to the runway without his crutches. He helped Daphne on board with her sons. Like a drill sergeant, he checked to make sure everyone was secured. Returning to the cockpit, Running-water gave some last minute instructions to Dutch and Brett and then left the plane.

He hurried back to the SUV and watched the plane until it was out of sight. Reaching into a side pocket of the SUV, he pulled out a knife and cut the brace away from his leg. It was more difficult than he thought. Finally, he had chipped away a crack and was able to use the knife to cut a slit the full length. Then he pulled it apart, tossed into the back seat. He got out, and gingerly put weight on his leg. No pain, it felt wonderful. No more cast.

No communication. Leave him alone. Well, we'll see which one of us is the better Indian. Entering the Interstate he headed south. The car phone buzzed. Someone else had decided to be disobedient. It was Samuel and he was on his way back from SeaTac Airport. They agreed to rendezvous at the same small restaurant from which he had made his 911 call. As he entered the town, he swung by the train. The lack of a police presence surprised him. He was sure they would be there. Strange that they've wrapped up their investigation so soon.

As he drove on into town he was amazed at how such a small town could support so many eateries and banks. The street paved now probably was once brick. The buildings were all connected. Something right out of the old west. The storefronts were nondescript leftovers from the 1800s. In one of them was Olsen's Café. Pulling the SUV into a space on the main street, Running-water waited for Samuel to arrive.

Once Samuel had the limo parked, he joined Running-water and went into Olsen's Café. A few people were seated at old wooden tables covered with green and white oilcloth. Two men were seated on backless stools at the small counter. Running-water and Samuel sat down at one of the two booths toward the back of the restaurant. Like the tables, their tops were covered with the green and white oilcloth. They gave their order to the same man that had been behind the counter earlier. Again Running-water noticed he stopped and used the phone.

I just don't understand Adam. Sometimes I wish he'd explain things.

He's a complicated man. Even I do not always understand him.

"Well, I'll be damned. How long have you been able to telecommunicate?" Running-water said.

"Is that what just happened? Or is Adam playing games with us because we didn't do what he said?" Samuel said.

"Let's find out. I'll send you a thought message. Try not to concentrate. Just keep your mind relaxed," Running-water said.

They sat there and waited. There was no response from Samuel. Running-water was about to say something.

You're right. Adam is concerned about our safety.

"What took you so long? Hot damn! That's it!" Running-water said.

"What?" Samuel said.

"That's why Adam's father selected each of you," Running-water said.

"I don't understand," Samuel said.

"Simple. Each of The Brothers can telecommunicate. Wonder how many of the others realize that?"

Before Samuel could reply, they were interrupted by two police officers.

"You from that spook train?" Officer Neigh said.

CHAPTER THIRTY-NINE

"How come you two are out by yourselves? We thought none of you weirdoes ever left that *death train*," Officer Neigh continued. His hand caressed his gun on his right hip.

"Easy, Charlie," Officer Wayland said, "They have a right—,"

"Don't easy Charlie me. Christ sakes. We don't need their kind here. It's nearly spring and these weirdoes have overstayed their welcome," Neigh said. "Time they moved on." His nostrils actually flared.

People in the café got quiet. Knowing Neigh had a bad temper, some scooted out a side door to avoid him. They knew all too well if you got into it with him you ended up with your head split open. Why the town tolerated him was anyone's guess. A child, in a highchair, whimpered.

"Actually you are right. However, I think it would be a very good idea if you spoke quietly. You're scaring that child," Running-water said.

"Tough. Let it cry. Who gives a rap shit?" Neigh said.

"I do. Sit down!" Running-water said, tapping the underside of the table with his Glock.

"Damn! Charlie, you gone and done it now," Wayland said, sliding into the seat next to Samuel. Instantly he felt the barrel of Samuel's automatic pushed against his side.

Wayland began to perspire and his breathing labored. "Damn it, Charlie, sit your fat ass down. And do it now." Both were surprised at the force of his voice.

"That's good advice, Charlie," Running-water said, tapping the underside of the table again.

Charlie sat down. His pock-marked face showed through his scrubby beard. No one would ever say he had a handsome face. Resentment showed in every line around his deep-set dark eyes.

"I called 911. Waited over thirty minutes and then I had to leave. You ever go over to the train?"

"Why'd you call 911?" Wayland asked.

"To report four dead bodies over there—behind the train. They were piled on top of one another in the ditch."

"You putting us on?" Charlie said.

"No. I told the dispatch I'd wait and I did. No one showed up. I thought maybe the police would still be there but when I just drove by they weren't anywhere around."

"We're not on duty yet so we ain't heard nothing about it. You say four bodies? Probably some of them immigrants that work the fields. They get into it once in a while, especially if some of the illegals try to take the jobs from the legals," Wayland said.

"You two stay put while I step out to make a call," Charlie said.

When he returned he was even more aggressive. His demeanor reminded Running-water of a pit bull, ready for the kill. His nostrils actually quivered.

"Talk. And you better tell it straight. I've called for back-up. Even if you shoot Wayland and get a shot off at me, you'll never get out of here alive," Charlie said.

"Sit down, and shut up! There's no one left in here to impress," Running-water said.

"Do as he says, Charlie. Jesus, maybe you don't give a damn if you get your head blown off, I do," Wayland said, feeling another jab in his side from Samuels's gun.

"First of all, I haven't any reason not to provide you necessary information. Remember, I'm the one who called 911. I thought you had come here to meet with me since you had not shown up when I turned in the call. Besides calling for back-up did you ask about my 911 call?" Running-water said.

"No such call was turned in. You better be through playing games. What the hell's your problem? You on something? Shit, you people are all alike. A bunch of damn whackos," Charlie Neigh said.

Another policeman walked in. Running-water noted a different air about him and didn't see any other 'back-up'.

"I'm Captain Macerate. You wanna tell me what's going on?"

"I'm Paul Dakota, an attorney. I called 911 to report three dead men in a ditch along the north side of our train. Actually, there are four. I shot the fourth man as he turned to face me. He had a knife. Probably the same knife used to slit the three men's throats. The cell phone service was not available so I came here to use the phone. I also said I'd wait here for the authorities. That was several hours ago. Charlie here tells me that no 911 call was turned in. I don't understand. You can check it out with the cook. I gave him a twenty just to use his phone."

"Now look here Mister, I don't know what your game is, but before coming here I personally went over to your train, walked all around it. I found no bodies, no sign of any struggle," Captain Macerate said.

"Did you talk to anyone on the train?" Samuel asked. He was surprised by his assertiveness.

"Yeah, some tall guy who said he was the chef. Said he heard nothing and saw nothing."

"Did you ask to talk to Adam?" Running-water said.

"Who's he? The cook said everyone had left the train except for some monks and they were in the dining car eating. I looked in and sure enough. There were four monks in there, heads bowed in prayer," Captain Macerate said.

"What did this chef look like?" Samuel asked.

"Tall guy, shaved head. Maybe thirty. Had real blue eyes. Seemed normal enough," Macerate said.

"I'll be damned!" Running-water said.

"What?" Samuel said.

"Adam's playing games with us, Sam. Sure sorry about all of this, captain. Our boss has been testing us. In addition to being his attorney I head up his personal security team," Running-water said.

Samuel was taken aback by that. No one had ever called him Sam. He was about to comment when he thought he heard something. He shook his head, and then he understood. The word 'quiet' came through.

"Hot damn! I am special. His eyes lit up with recognition and a smile spread itself across his broad face. Pleasure filled his inner being.

"Well, no harm done, I guess. I wouldn't stay out on the streets too late if I were you. Some of the locals are a little jittery because of all the rumors going around about that damn train. Sure wish you'd move on," Captain Macerate said.

"I appreciate your patience and understanding. Thank you. And we won't be here long, Captain," Running-water said.

Captain Macerate, Charlie and Wayland left the café. Samuel was so excited he could barely contain himself. He sucked his food down in massive bites, swishing hot coffee around in his mouth to cool it before swallowing.

"Easy Samuel. We're not out of the woods yet. There's a gas station out by the Interstate. Meet me there in about twenty minutes. Stay alert!" Running-water said. "I want to have a little chat with that cook."

Running-water waited until Samuel slid behind the wheel of the stretch limo. Its logo on its dark metallic blue sparkled under the street lights. As Samuel eased the oversized Lincoln out into the main street, Running-water paid their tab.

"Who'd you call after I used the phone?" Running-water said as he laid one of his twin Glocks on the counter.

"My wife," the cook stammered.

"Uh huh. Why?" Running-water's dark eyes glared at the cook. "Don't suppose she works the local 911 line, now does she?"

"Ah. Yeah."

"Next time you might just find your butt in jail. That includes your wife."

Stepping out into the street; he looked around, and then got into his vehicle and headed back to the train. Instead of parking at the train, Running-water left his SUV a block away and walked to the train. Immediately he went to the ditch and it was as the Chief had said. No bodies. His eyes caught a small area of recently scuffed up dirt. He squatted to get a closer look. Two sets of footprints. One set left a heavy indentation in the dirt. Adam's. He moved the bodies. I'd guess the other set belonged to Captain Macerate.

CHAPTER FORTY

Samuel had gotten as far as the main road out of town when he realized he was being followed. As he stopped at a red light a truck pulled up behind him. It was a large truck, sitting high up off its oversized wheels. And that placed its headlights level with the rear window of the limousine. With its tires peeling, the truck came up alongside the limo. The driver raced the truck's motor causing it to rock back and forth. Samuel ignored the challenge. Continuing his role as chauffeur, Samuel slowly moved the limo through the light when it turned green. A passenger in the truck, as it stayed alongside, rolled down the window and began shouting obscenities as he shot Samuel the bird. The truck sped ahead as the young man, still leaning out the window, continued to shout and shake his fist.

When Samuel pulled into the gas station where he was to meet up with Running-water, he saw another oversized truck pull up to the next set of pumps. He waited. No one got out. Samuel got out of the limo, put plastic into the eager mouth of the pump, and as he turned to unlock the gas cap, he casually pulled back his jacket to reveal an automatic. The truck sped away.

"Hot damn!" Samuel said as he topped off the gas tank and then returned the hose to its proper slot. Before getting back into the limo he took time to look around. His gaze, slow and deliberate, checked the numerous vehicles in the Park 'n' Ride and for an instant, he thought he saw a taillight flicker. Getting back into the vehicle, Samuel drove it away from the pumps, backed into a slot next to a

Tourist Information Stand. He killed the motor and doused the lights. Leaning his seat back, readjusting his gun, and losing his belt a notch, Samuel waited for Running-water. As he waited, his thoughts turned to Julie. He closed his eyes trying to imagine her face. He blinked away his tears of loneliness, a feeling he had not felt since their marriage. That was just enough of a distraction. Two figures dressed in black, crawling on their stomachs, inched their way toward the limo.

Running-water turned into the side road to the gas station; his headlights flashed across the two crawling figures. They froze until they were sure he had driven on by. A ways down the road, he turned off his lights, stopped, got out, and circled back toward the gas station. The limo burst into flames. The first figure had used a paintball gun and fired a ball filled with gasoline: the second figure tossed a lit match.

Panic seized Samuel as he desperately tried to get out of his seat belt, something he forgot to do when he eased his seat back. He heard it, a voice.

Don't get out of the car, don't open the windows, and don't open the door. Stay put. The car will not burn up or explode.

The familiar voice calmed him. He waited. Within seconds the flames burned themselves out. For a moment he wondered if life wasn't like that. It just burned itself out. He shook his head to get rid of that thought.

Running-water came up behind the tormentors' car. He was so quiet not even insects crawling on the ground felt any vibration from his movement. Their car was parked beneath a lamp post with a burned out bulb. Sliding under the rear of the car, Running-water attached a rope around the axel. Inside the car, the bass thumped so its occupants didn't hear him. He looped the other end around the lamp post and tied it off. And as he had arrived, he quietly slipped back into the shadows and waited.

Because Samuel had remained in the limo, the driver of the car got nervous. He shoved his car into gear and hit the accelerator. When the light pole came crashing down on top of them they thought they had been bombed. Jumping out of the car, two of them huddled together as they looked at the lamp post on top of their car.

"Jesus! Just look at this friggin' mess. My old man is gonna kill me," the driver said.

The other didn't have time to reply. A rope from out of the shadows pulled them together, holding them so tight they couldn't move. Running-water tied them to the window frame of their wrecked car. Slowly he walked in front of each one, pulled down their pants and with a swift flick of his knife cut away their shorts.

"Oh shit!" one of them said, "He's going to cut off our balls."

Running-water, using a can of spray paint, sprayed their private parts a bright yellow. According to Esaugetuh, 'specific humiliation is fit punishment for those who would humiliate others.' Yellow was appropriate for their cowardliness.

Going over to the limo, Running-water spoke to Samuel.

"Make sure the clerk in the store has called the Highway Patrol. Have her call the power company. The downed line could cause some serious trouble.

Meet me back at the train. Go to the engineer's cab."

Samuel waved him off and went into the store. He found the clerk cowering behind the counter. After some quiet persuasion, she called the Patrol. He drove back into town and met Running-water as directed.

"Why did Adam send everyone away? We're supposed to protect him," Samuel said.

"He wants us out of danger. Evidently, he knows something we don't. But believe me; we are going to find out!" Running-water said. "Tomorrow, Samuel."

CHAPTER FORTY-ONE

Little prickly sensations raced through Adam's body. As the night dragged on, they grew in intensity, becoming sharp and painful. Whatever limb was being affected would jerk violently. He felt he was being bombarded. Vague images from his Vision Quest raised themselves up in memory—images of being plunged into the bowels of the earth, spit out and shot into the non-ending heavens. The old weakness engulfed him. Adam fought to stay conscious as he got out of bed. He managed to stagger to his chair, sat down, and waited.

The morning was slow coming. Patiently he waited for a change in the continued drop in his physical energy. It always had. This morning it was taking longer. Much too long! He had to relax, to calm his being so it could regenerate itself. He pushed a button and the music of R. Carlos Nakai, one of his favorite Native musicians, filled the air. "The Great Mystery Hears Me" bathed his soul. Adam cranked up the volume. He felt the vibrations massage him. Slowly he turned in his chair so he could look out the window at the early morning sky. Before him lay vast open acreage, no furrows there. "No amber waves of grain" fluttering in the morning breeze. Nothing to capture and hold his interest. Nothing except the nothingness itself.

A small speck appeared at the far end of the field. At first, Adam thought it was an insect on the train's window. Its motion told him it was not. As it came closer it picked up speed. Spiraling upward from the ground, growing in size until it dominated the landscape.

It seemed to be propelled by rearing its head back and forth in the air. Early morning sunlight slithered between its vast circles. Suddenly the thing's head stopped, bent down and looked directly at him. It was an old face, wrinkled and leathery.

And the Nakai song played on.

It was Nakai's song that gradually drifted into the sleeping Running-water's subconscious. Slowly he moved his long legs upward, pushed against the air in isometric exercise. Clinching his hands together, he pulled until the muscles in his arms felt the tension. He laid back, his naked body enjoying its freedom from the night's blanket. Lazed by the quiet humming of the train's heart, he was in no hurry to rouse himself from the pleasure he was feeling in his groin. His thoughts turned to the last time he and Isha had sex. She made it so good for him. No woman had been able to satisfy him until now. The music became a pleasant intrusion as he tuned into it. He realized it was coming from Adam's private car.

Dressing quickly, strapping his guns on, and not bothering to wake the snoring Samuel, Running-water ran toward Adam's private car. He saw the monster weaving back and forth along the side of the car. Quickly he flung open the door

My god! Adam's transformed himself into a dirt devil. He immediately squatted. It wasn't Adam's head. It was Esaugetuh!

CHAPTER FORTY-TWO

Running-water listened as the gravelly voiced dirt devil hissed at Adam.

"You are in great danger, but you already know that, don't you? And there you sit. Is that all you are going to do?"

"If you refer to the recent deaths, that situation has been ameliorated," Adam said.

"You still haven't learned much, have you? If the danger has been ameliorated, as you claim, then why would I have just told you that you are in grave danger?" Esaugetuh said.

"I don't understand. Explain.

"You are experiencing energy drains, are you not?"

"Yes."

"And they have worsened?"

"Yes."

"Well, why don't you recognize that as a grave danger? Why aren't you concerned? Why are you trying to find its cause?"

"It's just a part of my continued transformation," Adam said, "But why are you here, now, as a dirt devil?"

"Pampsychism [1] and don't change the subject. I am old, have traveled far, and time is at a premium. Seek the cause of your weakness and you will find your enemy," Esaugetuh said.

"Doesn't it come from within? I mean my weakness."

"Always the questions. When are you ever going to learn to take some things at face value? I just told you, you are in great danger and you make assumptions. Have I not taught you to change your perspective?" Esaugetuh said, stirring up a great cloud of dust.

Okay, so I have to change my perspective, but I still have to ask my questions," Adam said.

Just like the old days. Only now he blows dust rather than smoke from his pipe. He always did that when he was pissed at me. But now even his words are sepia.

"Yes, but ask the right questions. Why does someone want you dead?" Esaugetuh said.

He spoke with such force that the wind shook Adam's private car. Dust was everywhere. Adam could not see out of the window. Running-water was rocked on his heels.

"Hey! Don't get yourself in such a huff. I remind you that I am—,"

"Listen to what I'm telling you or I'm out of here," Esaugetuh said.

"Okay. Okay. For crying out loud. So, who wants me dead?"

"They do!" Esaugetuh said. "Find out why and who's behind them."

The dust devil rose up above the train, swirled for a moment, and then was gone. Town's people, who had come out to watch, were fascinated by the display. The old timers said it had been years since a dust devil of that magnitude had been seen. It caused almost as much excitement as when they saw steam coming up out of Mount Baker. And those who were of such a mind said it was an omen and it wasn't good.

"Man, that was something else," Running-water said, making his presence known.

"You been there long?" Adam said.

"Long enough, my brother. So who is the 'they' that want you dead? And why?"

[1] Pampsychism is the idea that some sort of world soul is present in everything.

CHAPTER FORTY-THREE

"I hear Samuel bellowing. So the two of you are in cahoots. Okay, since you are both here, I want to take a drive. We'll be gone for a couple of days. Pack some supplies. How soon can you be ready?" Adam said, ignoring Running-water's question.

"How about in twenty minutes?" Samuel said, entering Adam's private car. "Man, that sure was some dust storm. Nearly knocked me over. Didn't realize the wind was up that strong."

"Should I pack some extra hardware?" Running-water asked.

"Isn't the limo still well supplied?" Adam said.

"Yes. Yes, it is," Samuel said.

"Bring it around in a few minutes. Say nothing to The Brothers. Don't even acknowledge you notice them," Adam said. "I need to speak to the staff. I want them away from the train for a couple of days. Give the chef the keys to the SUV. He can drive the rest of them into Seattle."

Samuel left, leaving Running-water to pursue his question. "Adam—,"

Adam signed for Running-water not to speak. Silence was to be maintained until they had left the area. Setting the CD player to play continuously, Adam inserted another CD, changed the volume, and then signed for Running-water to seal the car and to follow him to the waiting limo.

As Running-water opened the passenger side at the front of the limo, Adam signed for him to sit in the back with him. It concerned Running-water that his friend was so pale and wane—looking almost old. Whatever plagued him, its toll was beginning to show. He said nothing. Adam had directed Samuel not to drive through the town but to take the back road to the Interstate and then head north. In spite of its weight, the limo hit seventy miles per hour within seconds of it entering the Interstate. A few miles out, Adam told Samuel to take the next exit and to continue until told otherwise. And during this time he did not speak to Running-water. And Running-water did not reveal anything about the recent episode in town or at the one at the gas station.

CHAPTER FORTY-FOUR

After leaving a small village a few miles east of the Interstate, Samuel was directed to turn on to a side road that eventually wound them up a mountain, switch-back style, and dumped them into a hundred-acre private estate. The grounds, despite some obvious neglect, were awash with flowering vegetation. Tulips and daffodils provided a plethora of color among leafy ferns quietly reflected in several small ponds. A meandering brook, whose waters sparkled diamond-like, gingerly splashed over aged smooth rocks. Some of the giant trees were almost certain to be old growth judging by their girth and height. Spring was most welcome. Winter, having extracted its toll, was finally coming to an end.

At the highest point of the mountain property stood a large three-storied rectangular structure of mauve marble and gray quarry slate. It's front was laced with giant windows on each of the three floors. The top floor windows each had a small balcony. A set of massive white oak doors with a thin portico claimed the front entrance. The mansard roof, now overrun by moss, was once white Mediterranean tiles.

The main building, according to the real estate listing, contained fifteen thousand square feet of living space divided into meeting rooms, private sleeping quarters, offices, kitchen, large dining room, a large laundry, and a private chapel off the larger entrance foyer. Two separate waiting rooms and a larger room the listing called a ballroom.

The building reminded Adam of his old academy. Times were good then and maybe that's what attracted him to this monastery. Upperclassmen even referred to the academy as The Monastery. Halcyon days. How innocent they were, how so very naïve and yet not one of them thought of themselves in any way other than being totally sophisticated.

After all, were we not all wonderful? A bemused smile crept along his lips. Most of the boys at the academy went off to Europe or to The Cape for their summer break. Not Adam. His parents always took him into Canada to summer with the Indians at the Baskatong.

Originally built for a sequestered monastic group in the mid-1800s, The Monastery had been used as a preparatory school for young ladies, a mental hospital, and finally as an exclusive hotel for the very wealthy. The absence of human occupation had wreaked havoc with the grounds as well as some of the outbuildings. Of these, the smokehouse seemed to be in the worst shape. There was a stable big enough for a dozen horses, a five-car garage, and a powerhouse. The main building, from the outside, didn't seem to be in bad shape. A good pressure cleaning would get rid of the dirt and grime. Hopefully, the tiled roof contained no cracks and that no sustained water damage had been done to the inside.

Adam and Running-water got out of the limo and indicated that Samuel was to join them. He took his time getting out of the car. When he emerged, he had an Uzi in his hand.

"The realtor hasn't arrived yet. We can walk around the immediate grounds," Adam said.

As they poked around in some of the outbuildings, Adam turned to Samuel and said, "Samuel, I have a favor to ask of you."

"Name it."

"I'd appreciate it if you did not mention our trip or this place to The Brothers. For now, I'd like to keep it our little secret," Adam said.

"No problem. My mouth is shut," Samuel said.

It always pleased him whenever Adam spoke directly to him. He liked it even better when Adam asked him to do something. The uniform from the days at the Esaugetuh Institute at Toronto furthered his self-esteem. He looked good in the light blue uniform and its snappy cap. He knew he looked good—not as good as Adam or Running-water—but good. Julie liked him in the uniform. She said it accentuated his tight ass. Then she'd giggle as she pinched him.

Man, I miss her; miss her smell, her touch. And with that thought he was running the very mouth he said was shut. Had he been in the South he would have been told he had a 'gate mouth.'

"Adam, what's going to happen to Julie and me? If you are buying this place, where are we going? What will we live on? The money you gave me when I was one of The Brothers won't last a year. Is there room for us with you? My god, Adam, I just don't know what would happen to us. There aren't that many jobs for chauffeurs."

"Don't worry, Samuel. And by the way, we miss our wives, too. It's better that they're away from us for now. There is still much danger," Adam said.

Samuel blushed because he forgot that Adam could read his thoughts. He was about to say something when he received a mind-thought from Running-water telling him to be quiet.

"It's alright, my brother. We each have our questions, and they should be expressed. How long have you and Samuel been able to telecommunicate?" Adam said.

"Since yesterday. At the café," Samuel blurted. "You're right I do have another question, but you said we each had questions. What's yours?"

Samuel was taken aback by his sudden boldness. He had no idea what had come over him. Never in a million years would he have asked such a question of this man whom he totally adored, idolized,—no worshiped.

"Don't worship me, Samuel. I'm just a man, like you. True, I do have certain abilities that others do not seem to have, but like you, I too can bleed, cry out in pain, long for my woman, and can die," Adam said, ignoring Samuel's question.

"And since questions are in order, I have one," Running-water said.

"And it is?" Adam said.

"Samuel, do you communicate with the other Brothers telepathically?" Running-water said.

Running-water's lawyer voice surprised Samuel. He stood between them, dumbfounded.

"Well!" Running-water said, looking directly at Samuel.

"You think I'd try to harm Adam?" Samuel said.

His feelings were hurt and his whole mouth turned downward suggestive that he was about to cry. My God! Doesn't he know that I'd die for Adam?

"I know you would, Samuel," Adam said. "What are you getting at Running-water?"

"Well, I know you think The Brothers are behind the attempts on your life and someone is directing them. I agree with that. Even though Joseph and Thomas are in prison I feel that someone is feeding them information about our activities. Remember when the chopper came down out of the trees and pinned Brett under it. Didn't you think it odd that it didn't burst into flames? That you didn't smell gas? The storm didn't put us down, Adam. Someone had punched a hole in the gas line. Fortunately, Brett realized that and had begun to set us down. Otherwise, you would have found our remains," Running-water said.

"Michael Lane could have been responsible for that and he could have been the source. Too bad Isha was such a good shot. We'll never know," Adam said.

Turning to Samuel, Adam said, "So you have just realized you are a telepath? How do you feel about that?"

"It's strange. Scary and exciting at the same time. Will I get better at it and be able to read people's thoughts like you?" Samuel said.

"Maybe. My father was always telling me to change my perspective. He told me that so many times I thought he had burned into my soul, but I did forget. We can look at Samuel's new revelation a bit differently. Suppose Samuel is a conduit?" Adam said.

"A conduit?" Running-water said.

"It's possible for Samuel to be transmitting information without being aware of it. What kind of dreams have you been having, Samuel?" Adam said.

"Do I have to say?" Samuel said, red-faced, and feeling mortified that someone should know his private dream world.

"Not those dreams. Others you have not understood or seemed strange to you?"

"Well--- yeah. I wake up with a headache."

"I would like to do a mind scan if you have no objections. That will tell me what I need to know."

Surprised by Adam's asking Samuel permission to do a mind scan, Running-water wondered what he was up to. Generally, Adam just did the scan and no one was the wiser.

You'll soon know, my brother. Be patient.

And like Samuel, Running-water's face reddened.

"Caught me," Running-water said.

"Yeah, just like the old days, don't you think?" Adam said, giving Running-water a friendly cuff aside of the head.

Samuel agreed to the scan. While Adam was doing the scan, he planted a new command at the subliminal level. Later he would reinforce that while Samuel was in a deep hypnotic state.

"Our friend, here, is an open vessel. Whatever he sees or hears is transmitted to someone else. He's been programmed. I've planted a little surprise for whomever it is. We'll know who when we return to the train," Adam said.

"So you finally believe The Brothers are involved in the attempts on your life?" Running-water said.

"You got a better idea?" Adam said.

"You think it's one or more than one, or all of them?" Running-water said.

"Not sure. Time will tell."

A woman on a Harley drove up. She slid off the bike with practiced ease. She called out. "Hello. I'm Liz from Specialty Realty. Sorry, I'm late. An accident had traffic tied up."

"No problem. I'm Adam. This is Paul Dakota, my attorney, and this is Samuel, my chauffeur, and personal bodyguard. We've been looking around and I'm anxious to see the inside. Shall we?"

Liz removed her helmet and shook her long silver-gray hair loose. She was a petite woman maybe in her fifties. As she removed her black chaps that matched the rest of her leather, Adam noticed she had a 357 strapped to her side. Catching his look, Liz said, "I never go anywhere in the wilds without it. A gal never knows what kind of beast she might meet. Know what I mean?"

"Yes. Don't blame you."

"By the way, this place has quite a history," Liz said.

"So I've read. How long has it been vacant?"

"At least four years. For a while, there was a caretaker here. My agency just got the listing last week and I've not had time to get a crew in here to clean it up. I did a quick tour yesterday. The place is dusty. I didn't notice any structural damage, but I'd still have a full inspection if you're really interested in buying it," Liz said.

"We'd not be here if our intent was not serious," Running-water said. "What's the asking price?"

"Twenty million."

"Is that firm or is there room for negotiation?" Running-water said.

"The price is firm. But you never know. It's your call to make a lower offer," Liz said, pushing open the heavy oak doors.

Immediately Liz went to the windows, pulled back the dusty maroon velvet drapes, and opened the blinds. Sunlight poured in producing an excellent Doppler effect. She was right about the dust. Furniture, covered with large white sheets, was stacked in one corner of the stairway. The stairway had beautifully hand carved newel posts and turned balusters. The steps were carpeted in a complimentary burgundy carpet that had seen better days. She waited while her clients took in the interior landscape. One thing in this business she had learned: don't talk your client to death. Besides being quiet gave her a chance to check them out. He was even more handsome than he looked on television. When she'd gotten the call from Adam, she checked out his credit. She wondered why his name had never appeared in Forbes' Wealthiest.

As the four of them climbed the stairs to each of the two upper floors, it became apparent that there should be an elevator somewhere. Samuel opened a door and was about to step in. Fortunately, he didn't. It was the elevator shaft. The elevator was at the basement level. They went through every room in the building, checked every closet, and bathroom. Adam even poked his head into each of the five fireplaces, stopped to admire the ornamental columns and colonnades in the third-floor sitting rooms. He imagined the decorative caps with carved eagles. Running-water was busy taking notes, jotting down things Adam mentioned or wondered about as well as some points of his own. He was not surprised when Adam signaled him to buy the place. As a precaution, Samuel was not privy to that decision. Adam wanted to make sure the block he had subliminally planted worked before revealing what he was actually doing—buying a home—a place where he'd make his final stand. Adam had Samuel join him back at the limo, leaving Running-water to close the deal.

Liz nearly fainted when Running-water handed her a check for twenty million dollars. Her commission would allow her an early retirement. She grabbed Running-water around the neck, and kissed him.

"Thank you! My God! Yes! Thank you, thank you," Liz said as they walked back to her Harley. "I need to phone in. Do you mind?"

"No problem. I'll be with Adam in the car.

Adam was waiting for him. Samuel was in the back seat, asleep.

"I've put him in a deep sleep. He'll wake up in about an hour. In the meantime, he'll not hear what we say. Do we have this place?"

"It's yours. Now what?" Running-water said.

"I'll explain later. Here's Liz. "Liz, do you think it's possible for us to spend the day and night here?"

"Don't know why not. The owner has accepted the offer. Here are the keys. Don't know if you can get that generator cranked up or not. I'll let you know the closing date, okay?"

"No problem. You think you could speed up that closing? I'm sure you have verified the validity of that check I just gave you," Running-water said.

"I'll do my best. Is there a number at which you can be reached?" Liz said.

"Running-water will give you a number. I want to get a large crew in here to get this place back in shape and to make some major renovations. When we get together for the closing could you have a list of contractors, carpenters, electricians, and plumbers available for me? I'd like to use local people as much as possible," Adam said.

"You going to re-open it as a hotel?" Liz said.

"No. Get back to me on that closing," Adam said.

After Liz sped away on her Harley, Adam said, "I don't want to go back to the train until after dark tomorrow. It will be then that we find out if the remaining members of The Brothers are involved."

CHAPTER FORTY-FIVE

Running-water went to the outbuilding that held the large generator. Fortunately, instructions for starting it were taped to the side of the generator. It took him a little time to find the valve to turn on the propane, pump it, and hit the start button. The battery was good; the generator fired up. Inside, Adam had uncovered some of the furniture and dust covers from lamps. They were beautiful Tiffanies. He guessed they were originals. He pulled the chains on two. The lamps came to life, a welcome sign, casting rainbows along the walls, and ceiling. Adam made a return trip to the kitchen. The large gas stoves and ovens worked once he got the pilot lights lit. That's where Running-water found him.

"You check the water?" Running-water said. "Might need to run it a bit."

"What the—,"

Samuel was bellowing. He had awakened, had looked around, and didn't see anyone. Nothing seemed familiar to him. It didn't occur to him to use his cell phone.

"Here! Up here," Adam shouted, "Bring up the gear, will you?"

"We're spending the night? Where are we? I don't seem to remember," Samuel said, dropping a couple of large bags on the steps.

"Yes, we spend the night. Were you able to get everything from the car? Adam said.

"One more trip should do it. Sorry about falling asleep. You didn't answer my questions. And how did we get here?" Samuel said.

"We're at an old monastery. It's been closed for quite some time. You drove us here. Adam put you into a deep sleep after hypnotizing you and that's why you don't remember. You'll be fine," Runningwater said. "I'll give you a hand with the rest of our gear."

"No problem. I can get it," Samuel replied. "Thanks for the offer."

He trudged back down the steep slope to the limo. Man, that's a first. Guess I'm not just a mule anymore. Oh man, I'm sure dumb. Drive the damn car up to the house or whatever it was that Runningwater called it

Because the sun had begun its descent, the moon felt safe in showing herself. Her companion, Earthshine, [1] stuck around for only a short time— a nervous suitor. A heavy evening mist quietly blanketed the landscape giving privacy to the mythic couple. The twinkling night lamps lighting the valley below were extinguished by the mist.

Spring at this altitude was still not warm. Feeling the dampness penetrating the old monastery, Adam lit a fire in the fireplace of the great room. He watched its flames create dancing shapes on the opposite wall and across the vaulted ceiling. Not grotesque shapes—oh no— but a parade of past visitors— elegantly dressed ladies whose long silk gowns gracefully scraped the marble floor as they entered or left a room. Potbellied, mustachioed men with long cigars sat around in fine leather chairs sipping aged brandy. And what a wonderful world it was. But then that was when it had been a grand hotel. Had Adam tarried a bit and had he listened he could have heard those who had first lived here; he would have heard prayer chants of the monks beseeching their Maker to help them stay the course in their quest for spiritual understanding. But then again, he had not tuned into the informed universe to accept what knowledge it was willing to share. Much had been missed. And yet, he knew it was the very reason why he was where he was— to finally come to grips with his own spirituality. Had he but tarried a while longer, some understanding of one of his myriad harassing questions may have been possible. The fire required his attention.

Once he was certain the fire had taken, Adam went from room to room throughout the mansion turning on all the lights, pulling back the heavy velvet draperies, and opening the Venetian blinds at every window. Instantly the monastery became a beacon, lighting the underbelly of the low cloud-mist. The people in the valley below looked up at the mountain and wondered about the halo glowing in the night.

Adam returned to the main floor and the great room where his two companions were seated. He surprised them by bringing out a bottle of aged brandy from his backpack. And as was his custom he offered each a glass. The warmth of the fire, the warmth of the brandy, and the warmth of friendship lessened the burden of the task before them. It wasn't what was said or unsaid, but the mutuality of their trust that bound them to one another. Here Adam would make his stand. Like Running-water he began considering the possibility of someone controlling The Brothers.

"Samuel," Adam said, breaking the silence, "Look into the fire? Take your time, look closely, pay attention to each of the flames as it laps its way into the air. Breathe in deeply and exhale slowly. Keep watching the flames as you breathe in and out. Imagine the flames growing larger and larger until that is all you can see. When they are as large as the wall in front of you, close your eyes."

Samuel's eyes closed as deep sleep once more blanketed him. Adam watched his breathing and waited until it slowed to a normal rhythm. Then he signed for Running-water to follow him outside.

"I want to try distance visualization. Our senses are transducers. Every thought we have is a unit of energy. Everyone actually experiences that same energy. We experience this energy not just with our minds but with our whole bodies. Our skin is a wonderful antenna picking up all kinds of information and reporting it to our brain. Conversations that never stop go on all the time inside each of us. It's because of this that someone has been able to tap into the energy of Samuel. To be really effective, I want us to join our energies. By doing so we can connect in such a way that will allow us to see who it is that is using Samuel as a conduit. You game?" Adam said.

"Absolutely. What you're suggesting is an energy meld. We did that in your fight with Moon-Woman. Let's get at it."

"Once you're under, look up at the low clouds. I think we have enough luminosity so they can act as a screen. Project what you see there. It'll be like watching a movie on one of those old drive-in theaters," Adam said.

Running-water was a good subject and went under immediately. He felt the warmth of the fire bathing Samuel face. A light flashed and it startled him. He was moving at a tremendous speed. Everything was a blur. He heard Adam's voice reaching out to him.

"Slow down. Easy. Look around you. Note where you are, look at buildings, streets."

"How the hell do I slow down? Man, this is so unreal. I'd forgotten what it was like," Running-water said.

"Focus on a single object. Once you have it in focus, move to something else. Pretend you're a video camera."

A tall, free-standing smokestack caught Running-water's attention. Focusing, he saw an outline of a lighted tulip. The image was reflected on the bottom of the low clouds just as Adam had said. The whole concept fascinated Running-water. He wondered if he could see Isha and his sons.

Maybe I can go home if I see who's behind this mess. The image flickered. Desperately Running-water tried to recover the image of the smokestack. It was no use. Anger rushed over him; then embarrassment and shame took their turn.

"Damn! I'm so sorry, Adam. What now?" Running-water said.

"All may not be lost. The smokestack is a good indicator that our target or targets are where the train is. I may be able to tap into Samuel's energy pattern and see who's using it. It's a long shot."

"Isn't there a danger in doing that? Whoever is behind the attempts on your life will know you have found out."

"That's a possibility. It's a chance we have to take."

"Didn't you say you had planted a surprise for who's using Samuel as a conduit?" Running-water said.

"Yes. I suspect it may be one of the remaining Brothers. Of course, it could be more than one. But I still sense they may be being used. That's why I wanted to do the visualization. It may have provided a clue," Adam said.

Back inside, Adam bent over Samuel, whispered something in his ear. Samuel yawned, stood up, stretched, and looked around.

"Must have been that brandy. Sorry about dozing off again. Everything okay?" Samuel said.

"Everything's fine Samuel. We're getting ready to bed down for the night," Running-water said.

Their sleeping bags were rolled out. Running-water closed the blinds, pulled the drapes shut, and locked the sliding doors to the room. There simply was no way he could make the whole building secure so he had decided to make the great room as secure as he could. He began to shove a large over-sized couch against the door.

"What are you doing?" Adam said.

"Securing the room. I also need to make sure we have an escape route in case we need it. Have you forgotten the mess we had in Arizona? Man, I can still smell the gasoline pouring into our motel room."

"I'll help you."

"And I'll help," Samuel said, shaking the sleep from his large frame.

A good full hour later, Running-water was finally satisfied that the living room was secure as it could be without electronics. He had set some booby traps around the windows and had selected one as their escape. Finally, he was ready to call it a night. He would, as he always did, take the first watch. Samuel would take the second, and Adam the last. He sat down on the floor, against the wall facing the windows, and just out of the glow created by the burning embers.

Four hours later, Samuel took over the watch. The night ended without incident. Adam had opened the curtain and blinds to one of the windows and was watching the morning sunrise when his cell phone buzzed. That brought Running-water and Samuel to their feet, guns ready. Liz, the realtor was on the phone. The owners of the estate had kept all the deeds, surveys, well logs, the as-builts, and the history of ownership making it easier for the land-title search. The title was clear of any encumbrances. In accordance with state law, Liz had turned the check over to an Escrow company. Everything fell into place so it was possible for them to close that afternoon. Adam agreed to meet at a bank in the village at the base of the mountain.

The stretch limo with its eagle monograms caused quite a stir as Samuel maneuvered it down the main street of the village. Some people came out of the local coffee shop to watch it as he turned into the parking lot of the bank. One remarked that they didn't get many of them in town Someone had called the bank and told Ruby, the manager about the limo. She and her two tellers looked out the window to see what all the fuss was about. Liz on her Harley roared in, dismounted, went over to the limo, and knocked on the window.

"Must be the people who are buying the old monastery up on the hill. You see that glow up there last night? Sure was strange. When Liz called she was so excited I could hardly understand what she was saying. Amy, you better call the town clerk and have her come over," Ruby said. She was a large woman, tall, full-figured. She wore her auburn hair cut short.

"So Adam, what are you going to do with that old wreck? Make it a hotel again. Can't say the town ever benefited much from that," Ruby said extending her hand as she greeted Adam. "Goodness we haven't had this much excitement since they made a movie here years ago."

"I'm going to make it my home, a home for my wife and four sons."

The meeting was affable. Within minutes, Adam had become the new owner of a hundred-acre estate. At Adam's request, Liz had a list of local carpenters, plumbers, and electricians ready for him. Running-water's legal talents were an asset to the interviewing process. By late afternoon they had hired a large crew and had established a work schedule. Much remained to be done but Adam's desire to be back to the train shortly after dark precluded any further activity at the Monastery.

---

[1] Earthshine occurs whenever a crescent moon is on the horizon at sunset. Look between the two horns of the crescent moon for a ghostly image of the full moon as an ashen glow. This natural phenomenon is caused by clouds.

CHAPTER FORTY-SIX

The remaining six Brothers panicked when they realized they were alone on the train. Like mice, they scurried from one part of the train to another. They scrambled to locate the service staff. None could be found. Even the cook's quarters were empty. The engineers were missing. Thinking that there was a meeting going on in the dining room, they rushed there. The smell of decomposing bodies repelled them. They fled back to their compartments. Some locked their doors. They wondered who was keeping the train's system running. In desperation, Christian, the most aggressive of the remaining six, demanded that everyone meet with him. They had to dispose of the bodies in the dining car. If the police came it would be awkward for them. After much argumentation, they dragged the four bodies from the train, dumped them back into the ditch from which Adam had removed them. It didn't occur to them who they were burying until they shoved the last one into the ditch.

Seeing Michael Lane's body sent three of them into total panic. What happened? Wasn't he the one who was supposed to have killed Adam? Who killed him? Hadn't The Master told them everything would be all right? Allen, Anthony, and Christian returned to the dining car, leaving the other three to complete the job of covering up the bodies. In the dining car, Anthony opened all the windows while Allen went back to his compartment for a room deodorant. Christian had retrieved an aromatic incense from his compartment and had lit that. The door to the dining car was flung open. It didn't matter that flying insects could get in. Getting rid of the terrible smell was all that mattered to them. They scrubbed down the tables and chairs.

"Do you ever wonder about Samuel?" Allen said.

"What do you mean?" Anthony said.

"Well, he used to be one of us. Ever since he became part of Adam's inner circle he's been different," Allen said.

"You know The Master said for us not to worry about Samuel. In fact, didn't he say Samuel was helping more than he knew," Christian said?

The three of them waited, not knowing what else to do. The three who had completed the burial returned. Paul, the oldest of The Brothers, went to the cook's car to prepare something for them to eat. At sixty, he had learned not to push the envelope. Quite some time ago he had decided it was easier to stay with this collection of misfits than to go back to the real world.

Strange that Christian, Anthony, and Allen were so shaken up when they saw Michael Lane's body. Death isn't all that big a deal. It's just something you have to go through.

Collectively The Brothers decided that they would go to Adam's private car. They couldn't get in. They exited the train, stacked up some boxes and tried to peer into one of the windows.

"How stupid can we be? The windows are all blackened," Christian said, stepping down from the boxes. "No use trying to break the windows. They're bulletproof and shatterproof."

"What now?" Anthony said.

"Let's go to Samuel's compartment," Christian said.

They found no one there and the same held true for Running-water's compartment. The whore along with Isha and Daphne was gone. The nosy newswoman was nowhere around either. Glad that she wasn't, they returned to Christian's compartment. Allen and Anthony sulked.

"It's not supposed to be this way," Anthony said, "None of this was supposed to be this way. None of it!"

"Why was it necessary to kill our three comrades? Tell me that," Allen said, "I don't like it."

"Who gives a rat's ass," Christian said.

They didn't understand. Understanding was not one of their strengths. They were so dumbed by the events of the day that they didn't notice it. The sea fog had slipped in, making everything around them surreal. The street lights played a game of hide-and-seek with the wisps of fog as they floated in off the water. The blue lights along the underbelly of the train created a Van Gogh painting from his Blue Period. And if they had taken the time to look, to peer up through the wisps of fog they would have seen a living *Starry Night*. Preoccupation destroys opportunities to experience the world. And it was that preoccupation that Adam counted on.

The Brothers didn't see or hear the limo as Running-water drove it to the back side of the train. Once he had it parked, he cut the motor and waited for Adam to exit or say something. They sat there for thirty minutes and then an hour saw its time go by. Nothing was said. The deafening silence weighed in on him and Running-water decided to break the silence and turned to Adam but was quickly signed to remain still and to be quiet.

Adam opened the window separating the driver from the passengers. The sleeping Samuel lay on the seat with a blanket pulled up under his chin. Adam, reaching in front of Running-water, titled the rearview mirror so it reflected the sleeping Samuel. Satisfied that the mirror was at the best angle, Adam, looking directly at Running-water, sent a telepathic message.

Soon, my brother, there will be plenty of action. Watch the far end door of the second sleeper car.

Nodding his head, Running-water quickly checked his guns. He shifted his position so he had a better view of the sleeper car. He felt vibrations and realized that Adam had lowered all the windows in the limo. As the vibrations increased, Samuel began to move. Adam, watching intently through the rearview mirror, saw Samuel sit up. As he did he groaned as the vibrations took hold of him. Hearing the groan, Running-water turned to look back at Samuel. His concern brought him a sharp knuckle aside the head. Adam pointed to the door, signing that he was not to take his eyes off the door.

The humming now a high pitch, vibrated through Samuel's body. His head began to sway back and forth, slowly at first, and then rapidly. His head stopped moving. His body jerked epileptic-like. It stopped. For a few minutes, he sat perfectly still. His eyes were open, glazed over, and unseeing. He slid across the seat, looked out the open window, and then opened the car door. He waited a moment, then got out of the car, quietly closed the door, and leaned back against it. The vibrations began again and this time they were faster. Samuel put his hands over his ears as he cried out in pain.

Hearing Samuels cry, Running-water opened the car door to go to his aid, but Adam yanked him back into the car.

I said not to take your eyes off that damn door. And I meant it. Damn it, Running-water, do as I tell you or you may end up getting us both killed. I've got to concentrate on Samuel to make sure he's not hurt.

Allen, Christian, and Anthony jumped out the far end door of the sleeper car. They were screaming, jumping up and down, tearing at their clothes. Naked they rolled around on the ground, desperate to extinguish the flames they thought were consuming their bodies. In their desperation, they rolled into the same ditch in which they had reburied the four bodies.

"Throw dirt on me. Don't just stand there like dumb-ass idiots. Can't you see I'm on fire?" Christian screamed.

Obediently they began throwing dirt on Christian and then on one another and in doing so, completely unearthed the dead bodies in the ditch. At that point, Adam stopped the vibrations and made a call on his cell phone.

Samuel, released from his hypnotic state, got back into the car and curled up on the seat and went back to sleep. Adam had Running-water drive the limo up closer, and turn on the headlights. They watched the three naked, terrified, and screaming men throwing dirt on one another. As police sirens pierced the night air Adam had Running-water douse the car lights. Flashing lights glowed eerily in the sea mist as two police cars pulled up to the back of the train. Running-water turned the headlights back on; eased the limo toward them, flooding them with the high beam halogens, stopped, and waited. Adam rolled down a window and waited. Captain Macerate sauntered over to the limo.

"What's the problem here?" Captain Macerate said.

Stepping out of the limo, Adam said, "We're just returning from a camping trip in the mountains and found those three screaming and yelling. The way they are carrying on you'd think they were on fire."

"Hey Captain, you better come and take a look at this. There's a mess of dead people here," Officer Charlie Neigh shouted.

"Get those loonies into a car. And for Christ's sake, get something to cover them up, Captain Macerate barked.

Seeing Running-water and Adam huddled in quiet conversation, Macerate immediately interrupted them. "I have some questions for you. It's Dakota, right?"

"Yes, Paul Dakota."

"A couple of days ago you claimed you saw dead bodies in a ditch. Is this the location?"

"Yes. I can't understand why you didn't see them when you came over here to investigate. Unless, of course, you didn't come here thinking I was just a nut cake, one of the weirdoes," Running-water said.

Macerate couldn't let the implications go. It infuriated him.

"Look, smart ass, one more crack like that and I'll throw your sweet ass in jail. I was here. It was dark and that's why I didn't see the bodies. Looks to me like they've been covered up and just maybe one of you covered them up so I wouldn't see them. Do either of you know who they are?"

"At least I would have had a flashlight to look around. Guess you didn't," Running-water said, ignoring Macerate's threat.

"Yes. They are part of a group called The Brothers that has been traveling with me," Adam interrupted.

"And just who are you?" Macerate said.

"I'm Adam. I own this train. Perhaps it would be a good idea if you questioned those men you have in custody as well as the rest of the people on my train," Adam said.

"Your train? You own this thing?" Macerate said.

"Adam owns the train," Running-water said.

"I didn't ask you," Macerate said.

"If you want to talk to my client you'll do so through me or you won't talk to him period."

"Your client?"

"That's what I said. If you can't handle this investigation perhaps I should call the State Attorney General and have him send in a team of investigators," Running-water said.

"Is that a threat?" Macerate said

"Anyway, you want it. You want cooperation you begin by being respectful."

"If those bodies have been there for at least two days, aren't you losing valuable time in gathering evidence?" Adam said, "If you wish to talk to me further, you'll find us inside. I'll arrange with my security team to let you on board."

CHAPTER FORTY-SEVEN

Captain Macerate was pissed. No one threatened him and no one dismissed him. Tell me how to do my job, will they? Just wait and see. Son-of-a-bitch! How in the hell is it that I always get saddled with weirdies? And now Doc Baker is probably pissed because he has had to miss his TV program. Tough shit.

Maybe it was his name that made him basically disagreeable. All his life he had to put up with name-calling and with people poking fun at him. He'd often thought of changing his name to Machete. At least that didn't mean *soft* because of excessive soaking. His days in high school were pure hell. He dreaded PE. He begged the coach not to make him shower with the other guys. It was always the same humiliating comments about his personal body parts.

An old Ford pick-up pulled in behind the train. A man, shoulders bent with age, coat collar turned up and a slouched hat plopped on his head slowly emerged from the truck. Unlike the coroners shown on television, he didn't carry a shiny mental case. He had an old black satchel. It reflected his attitude: what was good enough forty years ago is good enough now.

"Well! Where in hell have you been? Took you long enough to get over here. You think I want to be out here all night?" Macerate said. "Jesus, you only live three blocks from here.

"Don't get your pants in a sweat. Where're all these bodies you were blabbing about?" Doc Baker said.

Even though he had been coroner for forty years, he had only dealt with a couple of murders and two suicides. That didn't mean he didn't know what he was doing and he was not about to be rushed. While he looked over the site, Macerate paced up and down. Impatient by nature, he felt the coroner was deliberately being slow.

"Well!" Macerate said.

"Well, what?" Doc Baker said. His speech still had a bit of a Southern drawl even though he'd lived here years.

"You know damn well what!" Macerate said.

"Three of the men had their throats slit. From the looks of the cuts, and I can't be too sure at this point because of the shape they're in, I'd say they were clean, continuous slits from ear to ear. No jagged edges. Because of the apparent depth of the wounds, I'd guess they were caught from behind, had their heads pulled back and swoosh," Doc Baker said.

"Swoosh?"

"Slit. Most likely a professional. Possibly someone with military training," Doc Baker said. "The other one has a hole in his head. Guess you could say he'd been shot."

"Shit! I can see all that. Tell me something I don't know," Macerate said, "for instance how long have they been dead?"

"Well, it's hard to say for sure but I'd say at least two days, maybe three. The puzzle is why is the one who was shot still clutching a knife," Doc Baker said.

"So?"

"Well, it suggests that maybe he's the one who knifed those other poor souls and someone shot him. And that's even more interesting," Doc Baker said.

"More interesting?"

"Uh huh. Why did he have the knife in his hand when he was shot from behind? It doesn't appear he was defending himself. Maybe he was getting ready to kill someone else? If so, who? And, who shot him? And if he killed the other three here, where's all the blood? They must have bled out somewhere else. Better have a forensic team called in."

"Don't you think I know that? The sheriff has already been called."

"You know the guy that standing on the platform? He's been watching every move we make?" Doc Baker said.

"How in hell should I know? Probably another one of the weirdies.

"No, I don't think so. I saw him get on the train just as I pulled up. I suggest you—,"

"Don't even go there. If one more person tells me how to do my job he's going to find his sorry ass in jail. And that includes you," Macerate said, stomping off toward Adam's private car. He knew he wouldn't arrest the coroner. It just burned him up when people started telling him what he should or should not do. Jesus. The way people carry on you'd think I just started this frigging job.

Doc Baker shook his head. Someday that disposition of his is going to get him killed.

As he stepped onto the platform to Adam's private car, Macerate was confronted by the man

251

standing on the steps. He was a tall thin angular man. Even his face was angular.

"You got business on this train?" E.I. Hyoid said.

"Who the hell are you?" Macerate said, "I know you've been watching."

"E.I. Hyoid, Chief of Detectives, Northern Railroad. And if you expect to board this train, you'll check your weapons."

"Guess you can't tell I'm a police officer. Now out of my way, I'm here to see Adam," Macerate said, feeling the veins in his neck bulge.

"So you are. However, that fact gives you no authority on this train or on this railroad. You and your men have made a mess of the crime scene. I will not tolerate any further contamination. Is that understood?" Hyoid said.

"Now look here. My men and me responded to a 911 call and as such it's our—,"

"Your first response, once you had those obviously deranged men in custody, should have been to secure the crime scene. That was your second mistake," E. I. Hyoid said.

"Second mistake? How the hell you figure that?"

"You should have contacted the Railroad immediately since the bodies were on railroad property it becomes railroad jurisdiction. Now then, do you or do you not want to speak with Adam? If you do, hand over your weapons."

"Okay, get on with it. Here are my gun and mace," Macerate said.

Samuel opened the door and pointed his Uzi to where they should sit down. Macerate took his time in checking out his surroundings, made note of the high tech surveillance equipment. He zeroed in on the shuttered and curtained windows. His old fear reared its ugly head.

He got up to open a window, but a jab from Samuel's Uzi ended that. Reluctantly he sat back down, trying not to think about the closed windows and the closed door. He always drove his patrol car with a window slightly open, even in the dead of winter. The blinds in his office were never drawn. The window in his one bedroom apartment was left open at night. True, he had it rigged with an alarm, but it was still left open. He slept with a light on.

He looked around trying not to think of the closed windows and door. He spotted two men sitting at a small table. Wonder who those guys are? More weirdoes. Sure wish someone would open a window. It's hard to breathe in here. No air. Damn! Can't stand it.

"How about opening a window or two in here. The air is stifling," Macerate said, loosening his tie and unbuttoning his collar.

Adam and Running-water walked in from another car.

"Sorry about your discomfort. Of course, you may have a window open. I wouldn't have liked being locked up in a dark closet for hours on end either," Adam said, opening a window and indicating that another window should be opened.

Macerate's mouth dropped. How'd he know I was locked up in a dark closet when I was a kid? Jesus, this guy creeping me out.

A commotion at the door brought everyone to attention. Three dirty, naked men filed in, their heads bowed, and in handcuffs. Their nakedness and muddiness didn't seem to have an effect on them. When Samuel pointed his Uzi toward the floor, they sat down immediately.

The two Brothers seated at a side table, got up, went to their comrades with water. Once they had given them a drink they asked to cover their nakedness. Adam immediately provided blankets.

"I'm sure you have many questions, Captain. Perhaps I can help clear up some of them for you," Running-water said.

Before Captain Macerate could reply, the door opened. Samuel jumped in front of Adam, and Running-water pulled his guns.

"Mind if I join the party?" Will Rexford said.

"Wondered where you had gotten off to. Where have you been?" Running-water said.

"I left the train at Bellingham. Had some things I had to do. I see you have taken care of some of the issues," Will Rexford said, flashing his boyish grin.

"Suppose you begin by telling me who you are and then explain what you just meant by 'taken care of some of the issues,'" Macerate said.

Ignoring Macerate, Will said, "Adam, the Secretary sends his regards."

"You'd better answer my questions mister, or your ass will be sitting in my jail," Macerate said.

"The Secretary?" Adam said.

"The Secretary of Homeland Security," Will Rexford said.

"What's your connection?" Running-water said.

"I'm a special agent. Dutch had asked me to come on board. By the way, where is he?" Will said.

"He's away on business," Running-water said. He wasn't sure why he just didn't tell him Dutch was in New Mexico.

Macerate was beside himself. He would not be ignored! He stood up, shaking his clenched fist at them, he opened his mouth to speak but was unable to do so. Terror filled his eyes. Hyperventilating, he fell forward. Adam caught him and eased him down to the floor.

"Damn! What's got his shorts all twisted?" Will Rexford said, leaning down, and looking at the sprawled figure on the floor.

"Breathe in and out, slowly as I count." Adam slowly began to count backward. " You'll be fine."

The spasm subsided and Adam did a quick body scan. Finding nothing that indicated a physical issue, Adam helped Macerate to his feet.

"You better get your anger under control. If you don't one of these days it will be the cause of your death. We are not your adversaries. Please try to understand that my friends are very protective of me especially since there have been so many attempts upon my life. Your accusatory tone has set them on edge," Adam said.

"I—I just need some air. Open another window. Please," Macerate said.

Adam opened another window as well as the door to his private car. Turning back to Will Rexford he said, "Suppose you tell me what's going on. Why were you assigned to my train and without my knowledge, and by whose authorization?"

Ignoring the sharpness in Adam's tone, Will Rexford walked over to a sofa, sat down, stretched out his long legs, rubbed his crotch and then leaned back. Slowly he looked at all those present. As he looked at the men, he paused on each one, analyzed each before moving on to the next.

"Adam, a glass of your aged brandy would be nice about now. Take the chill off, don't you think?" Will Rexford said.

Adam retrieved a bottle of brandy, a tray filled with small snifters. Running-water couldn't believe his eyes. Adam letting someone boss him around. Samuel and Hyoid refused. Adam provided glasses to the two seated Brothers.

"Would you release Allen, Anthony, and Christian from their handcuffs so I may give them a glass of brandy?" Adam said.

Macerate unlocked each and returned to his chair under the open window.

Then Adam bent down to the three on the floor to offer them a glass. As he handed each a glass, Adam looked at each man, each had betrayed him. And he wondered for what reason.

Stealing quick glances at each other as they sipped their brandy, they too wondered. They wondered about this man called Adam. Why hadn't he just killed them instead of having them beaten? Surely he could have killed them himself. What really puzzled them was that they detected no malice coming from him. Adam's hands began to tremble. Because his back was turned toward the others, they didn't see that.

"Macerate!" Adam's voice boomed, vibrating from all sides of the car at once.

Stunned by the command, Macerate spilled his drink down the front of his uniform. Will Rexford came to rapt attention. "Why were these men beaten?" Adam said.

"What?" Macerate said. Gaining his composure, he continued, "I didn't know they were. Give me a few minutes. I'll be right back."

"How'd you know they were beaten?" Will Rexford said, sipping his brandy. "I don't see any marks on them."

Running-water thought Rexford's comment was strange. He made a mental note to be more alert.

"Not now, Will. Not now," Adam said.

The thought of anyone being beaten tore at Adam's conscience. He remembered a beaten Running-water and the struggle to save him. An image of Running-water's smashed face, swollen eyes, and broken ribs came crashing down upon him. Tears welled up. He could still see Running-water's soul leaving his body. He shook his head to clear the ugly picture. He actions were noticed.

I'm fine, my brother, don't fret, Running-water said telepathically. *"By the way, what's with Will Rexford?"*

Memories are hard to erase, Adam replied ignoring the question.

"While Captain Macerate is out, suppose you explain where you have been and this business of the Secretary of Homeland Security. On whose authorization were you assigned to my train and without my approval?" Adam said.

"And be specific," Running-water said, still wondering why Rexford exhibited surprise that Adam knew the three Brothers had been beaten.

"I've been cleared to answer your questions. Dutch Masters is a former operative. When he realized your ranch in Canada was being used as a terrorist training camp, he gave me a call. Once that operation was shut down, it soon became apparent that you were still in considerable danger. My superiors thought it might be connected to a terrorist cell in Toronto that was seeking revenge. Once I joined you at Blaine, I recognized the man you know as Michael Lane. Needless to say, he wasn't. The real Michael Lane was found with his throat slit."

"So who was it that Isha took down?" Running-water said.

"Apparently some guy off the streets that had been hired as a hit man. Isha didn't kill him, I did," Will said.

"You did?" Running-water said, wondering if Will had also watched him having sex with Isha. The thought reddened his face. A slow burn began to build.

"I was under the car. Once the trajectory of the bullet is determined, you'll realize that Isha didn't hit him. I know he killed those three men," Will said.

"And do you know where they were killed?" Adam said.

"They were killed in one of the lavatories on the train. Have the police check under the train; they'll find lots of blood there," Will said.

"But why were they killed?" Adam said.

"Thought maybe you could answer that one," Will said.

The door to Adam's private care flew open as Macerate shoved two of his officers inside; both landed on the floor. Macerate, livid, screamed at them, "You stupid bastards! This will cost you your jobs. Just you wait!"

"Easy Captain," Adam said.

"These two idiots used their nightsticks on their backs while they were still handcuffed. Now there'll be all kinds of investigations, reams of reports, and lawsuits. Jesus, what a mess! By the way, how did you know they had been beaten?"

"Yeah, how'd you know?" Will said.

That set off an alarm in Running-water once again. Surely he knows Adam is a healer, especially after the helicopter accident, Daphne, and Dutch's injuries. Something's wrong!

Adam, concerned about the injured men didn't respond. He was busy letting hands float over their backs. Sensing internal bleeding as well as broken bones he opted to try to stop the hemorrhaging. His last seizure left his energy nearly depleted. He had to struggle to heal himself and he wasn't sure of much impact he had on their injuries.

"There's a good chance that an artery or kidney has been pierced by a broken rib. I believe there's a clinic here. Take them there and have them checked. Surgery may be required," Adam said, remembering the internal injuries Running-water had suffered.

"That's one of those managed health care places. Doubt if they'd take these guys. I'll call for an ambulance and have them taken north to a hospital," Macerate said.

Macerate made the call and shortly two medical teams arrived at the train. A preliminary check by the medics confirmed Adam's suspicions that they were seriously injured. They were transported to a hospital. Captain Macerate accompanied the two emergency vehicles. He thought he could talk to the injured men and maybe convince them not to bring a lawsuit. He didn't get that chance. The men were whisked away into surgery after their examination.

Once they were released from the hospital he'd have them transferred to the county jail. He was really torked-off because he didn't get a chance to 'interrogate' them. His anger did not abate on his way back from the hospital. All he could think about was the investigation that most certainly would be held. It might even ruin his career. His car swerved. Desperately he tried to regain control. The steering wheel locked and he couldn't turn the wheels. The car accelerated. He was doing eighty. He stomped on the brakes. Nothing. He reached to turn off the ignition. It was too late.

The truck driver saw a man's face contorted with absolute rage. His eyebrows met in the middle of his forehead creating deep ruts. His mouth torn open and stretched to its maximum extension. As Macerate's car slammed into the semi, the driver saw his stomach and intestines regurgitated out of his gaping mouth.

Vomiting as he slid across the passenger side of his truck, the driver pushed on the door and jumped, rolling into a water-filled ditch. His truck shoved the car across the road, into a field, where both exploded. A huge plume of smoke filled the air, followed by a massive fireball. The truck driver tried to stand up but was forced back into the water because the heat was so intense. He didn't know what his cargo was and he didn't care to find out. Remaining in the water-filled ditch, he ran from the scorching flames. Gasping, he stopped, looked back, and vomited again.

"Holly Mother of Jesus," he said, crossing himself.

Cars slowed as their passengers gawked at the burning carnage. No one saw the driver, now huddled in the ditch. No one stopped to help. Someone had called 911. A deputy sheriff on his way home from his day's tour of duty stopped. He found the truck driver, bruised and shaken.

CHAPTER FORTY-EIGHT

The county sheriff, who arrived with the HAZMAT team, found the license plate of the burned-out car. A quick check on his computer identified the vehicle as one assigned to Captain Macerate. It would take time before they knew if it was the Captain's remains in the car. Those there assumed they were. A radio dispatch to the Chief of Police verified that Macerate had been on his way back from the county's only hospital. Both the Chief and the Sheriff agreed to meet back in town at Adam's train. When Adam and his entourage first arrived in town, he had made a point of calling on Chief William Warren. The Chief, a firm believer in proper protocol, waited for County Sheriff Laurence Vegan to arrive. He didn't have long to wait.

Both men were told to deposit their weapons. Samuel was most persuasive and with a bit of a flourish, he personally escorted the sheriff and police chief into Adam's private car.

"Death sure seems to be a part of your life," Chief William Warren said, shaking hands with Adam.

"It weighs heavy. I have specific information about the four dead men found in the ditch along the side of this train," Adam said.

"Good. But unfortunately, we have news of yet another death. Captain Macerate was killed in a head-on collision with an eighteen-wheeler," Sheriff Vegan said.

"The truck driver fell asleep at the wheel?" Running-water said.

"No. The truck driver said that Macerate's vehicle suddenly swerved, hitting him head-on," Sheriff Vegan said.

"Odd, don't you think?" Will Rexford said.

"I'm sorry, we haven't been introduced," Chief Warren said.

"Will Rexford, Homeland Security."

Both the sheriff and the chief's eyes widened in surprise. Both wondered what Homeland Security was doing here. Neither spoke. Wonder why Rexford didn't at least pay a courtesy call at my office. Just because he's out of DC don't make him better than other folks.

"I killed one of the four men found in the ditch. He is a known assassin. He killed the real Michael Lane in Vancouver as well as the three Brothers. He was about to kill Paul Dakota and that's when I shot him. The three Brothers were killed in one of their compartment's lavatory. If you check under the train you'll find their blood. That's why there's not a large quantity of blood at the scene."

"You got proper identification, I suppose," Chief Warren said.

"Yes," Will Rexford said, handing over his identification.

"What is Homeland Security doing on a private train and involved in a murder investigation?" Sheriff Vegan said.

"National security. Can't tell you more than that," Will said.

"National security be hanged. It's downright impertinent not to make a courtesy call at the local level. Seems to me that even Homeland Security would follow proper protocol," Chief Warren said.

He didn't like this man and he didn't care if he knew it.

"If I had one of my highest ranking officers in a questionable accident, I'd be there trying to find out what happened. A little less protocol and more investigation would be appropriate," Will Rexford said.

"Why do you say it's a questionable accident?" Sheriff Vegan said.

"First, I didn't hear you say that there were other vehicles involved. Nor have you said that the truck driver reported noticing a blowout of a front tire," Will said.

"Why a front tire?" Running-water said.

"A rear tire would not have caused the car to swerve." Turning to the Sheriff, Will said, "Have you had the areas searched for a spent cartridge?"

"Don't see any reason to," Sheriff Vegan said.

"Did your man have a drinking problem or suffer from some illness?" Will said.

"No, not that I know of," Chief Warren said.

"And you don't think it odd that the Captain's vehicle should suddenly veer and smash into a truck?" Will said.

"Hmm. Guess I better take another look. Just thought it was an unfortunate and tragic accident," Sheriff Vegan said, getting up to leave.

His radio was squawking when he opened the door to his cruiser. Dispatch had information. Immediately, the sheriff returned to the train, where he was again met by Samuel.

"Tell Adam that the three men in the hospital are dead. I'm on my way there now. As soon as I know something I'll be back in touch."

Adam grimaced at the news. It would be nearly impossible to find out why the three Brothers were using Samuel as a conduit, and for whom. He had Samuel bring the limo around. He then called Sheriff Vegan and asked him to wait for him. Running-water and Will Rexford piled into the limo. They caught up with the sheriff just as he was turning to head north. He pulled over, secured his vehicle, and climbed into the front seat with Samuel.

"Push it!" Adam said, using the car's intercom. "I need to get there and fast."

"Ask him if he thinks there's a crime there," Sheriff Vegan said.

"I think there's cause for concern," Adam said.

"Okay, I'll notify my man there to secure the bodies," Vegan said.

The stretch limo eased into a smooth hundred miles per hour. Samuel loved the feel of its powerful engine. He had turned on the emergency lights. The sheriff placed a portable red flashing light on the roof of the limo. Other vehicles moved over as the speeding car approached. At the hospital, Samuel slowed the Lincoln to an easy stop.

They were taken to the area where the bodies of Allen, Anthony, and Christian were. Adam pulled back the sheet on each body, identified it and then slowly passed his hand over each man's head. A minuscule thread of electromagnetic energy from each was brought together by Adam in an effort to form a mirrored projection. Unfortunately, it was not strong enough to give him a clear image of who was using them as channels to Samuel. The figure, shadowy and dark, remained distant. Too much time had passed for there to be a strong electromagnetic energy field left in their brains.

"Now what?" Running-water said.

"Since they were under my care, authorize the autopsies, and once you get the report, have their bodies cremated," Adam replied.

"Would you like the hospital chaplain to come in?" Sheriff Vegan said, "I'll have their next of kin notified if you like."

"There are no relatives. Each was a street person, homeless, and a discarded soul. For a time, they found a degree of creature comfort and companionship in my home in Toronto. Two of the twelve Brothers—both societal derelicts, murdered my father. And some, despite my kindness, chose to betray me. It makes me ask, where does charity end?" Adam said.

"Well, I don't know where charity ends, but around these parts, we have a saying: 'If a dog bites you; you don't let him bite you twice,'" Sheriff Vegan said.

Adam opened a leather pouch he had slung over his shoulder. Carefully he took out some sage and sweet grass. He sprinkled the sweet grass over each body and then lit the small sage bundle, smudging its smoke over each body. The sheriff was about to say something but was silenced by a look from Running-water.

"I don't know the strength of the spirit of these men; however, to be used by another demonstrates a weakness. And perhaps that's why they were homeless and lived on the streets. Yet, I cannot believe that they did not have value, that they did not have individual worth, and that in some way they shared that with me. My father, Esaugetuh, must have seen something, must have sensed something as good in each man. Otherwise, for what purpose did they live? Maybe C.S. Lewis is right. There are 'bent' ones," Adam said.

"Amen to that, my brother," Running-water said.

He had brought his flute and he began to play. And for its duration, it worked its magic. For a fleeting moment, Will Rexford thought he saw an eagle fly into the room and land on Adam's outstretched arm. The hair on the nap of the Sheriff's neck moved because he thought he heard the low growl of a cougar and Samuel would argue that he saw its shadow cross the wall of the room. The three of them had felt the spirits. those shadowy guides of those who believe. The two who were soul brothers accepted that which was. But the others? They didn't understand.

"Sheriff," Adam said after a pause, "would you mind if I took a look at the spot where Captain Macerate was killed?"

"No problem. You thought of something I should know about?"

"It just doesn't add up. I'd like to talk to the truck driver. You know where he lives?"

"Yes. We can stop at his place on our way back. He lives in town."

It was a short drive to where Macerate hit the truck. Adam took his time looking around. The burned out police cruiser had not as yet been removed. He looked inside; Macerate's remains had been removed. He walked around the truck still trying to get a sense of what had happened.

"Sheriff, did you say the driver was found in a ditch? You know where?" Adam said.

The sheriff pointed out the general area. Adam waded into the water-filled ditch. He sat down on the edge of the bank, looked back at the spot where the vehicles had burned. He pictured the moment of explosion in his mind, picking up a sense of the driver's reactions. Satisfied, Adam signaled he was ready to return to town and to talk with the truck driver. Samuel brought the limo up.

Sam Curler was hesitant to talk without his attorney present. He was a small man and the size of Adam and Running-water intimidated him. Sheriff Vegan assured him that he was not a subject of investigation and would wait for him to call his attorney. Adam explained the nature of his visit and asked permission to place him under hypnosis.

"Why do you want to do that?" Sam Curler said, his voice quivering.

"Often when one is involved in trauma as you have been, details are sometimes blocked out. Those details may be important in helping us determine what caused Captain Macerate to swerve his vehicle into your on-coming truck," Adam said.

"Well, I guess it would be okay. I probably don't need to call my lawyer. What do I have to do?" Sam said.

"Think of something that you really enjoy, a place. Visualize it. Zero in on its location. Once you have done that, I want you to count backward with me, beginning with ten. Good. Now pretend you are at your favorite place watching a movie. Describe each scene as it appears on the screen. Be as detailed as possible."

Sam began to describe the fearful contortions that Macerate experienced just before the moment of impact, that he was desperately trying to turn the steering wheel, that he was stomping hard on the brakes. That blowing his truck's horn and flashing the headlights had no effect on the Captain.

"When I count to ten, you will wake up, feeling very relaxed," Adam said, beginning to count.

Sheriff Vegan and Adam thanked Sam Curler for his help and returned to the limo. Adam asked him to sit with him in the back of the limo. Will Rexford moved to the front with Samuel.

"Sheriff, I think Captain Macerate was murdered. It might be a good idea to have what's left of his vehicle checked for tampering. I strongly suggest you check your own vehicle each time before you drive it. And keep in constant radio contact with your dispatcher," Adam said.

"Explain," Sheriff Vegan said.

"Because of your involvement with me, you may be in danger. The three men at the hospital had been used telepathically to garner information about my doings from my chauffeur. I had subliminally planted a counter trigger in Samuel's subconscious. The reason the three men were dancing around, pulling off their clothes was because they thought they were on fire."

"What's that got to do with Captain Macerate or me?" Sheriff Vegan said.

"Whoever is behind all of this may have thought the Captain was too close to realizing there was a hired assassin on board my train and that he may have passed that information on to you."

"Thanks for the concern. I'll be in touch," Sheriff Vegan said as Samuel pulled the limo away from the sheriff's car.

"You're being unusually quiet, Paul. What's going on?" Adam said.

Being called by his Christian name snapped Running-water back to attention. Looking at his friend, Running-water sent him a telepathic message.

Will Rexford. What if he's the real assassin? What if Michael Lane was who he said he was? I can't believe Isha missed Lane. She's just too damn good a shot. What do we know about Rexford? Nothing, other than he arrived with Dutch. And then there the business of his not knowing you are a healer? My god, Adam, he was on the train when you did several healings. It doesn't make sense."

Certainly Dutch would know his man, wouldn't he? Adam said.

People live double lives and some more than that. Have we had identification on Michael Lane? No! All we have is Will Rexford's word. Adam, I think I should break your imposed silence and get in touch with Dutch.

Maybe you are right, my brother. Do what you will.

Adam? What's with this Paul business?

Just practicing. It might be time we called you that. It may suit our business purposes better. What do you think?

"And does that mean that you are going to finally reveal your last name and use that from now on?

Maybe.

Samuel stopped the limo by Adam's private car, got out, and opened the door for his passengers to get out. Will Rexford had to be prodded awake.

CHAPTER FORTY-NINE

Running-water placed a call to Dutch who immediately became enraged at the suggestion that Will Rexford was anything other than what he said he was.

"Look, Dutch, with all this shit that's gone on, I have to be careful. Just too much has happened since you've been out of commission. Tell me about Will and be very specific," Running-water said.

The description Dutch gave of a blond long-legged hayseed was in keeping with the man on the train, but that didn't satisfy Running-water.

"Tell me something that only he would know, preferably something the two of you did that no one else knows about. If this guy knows the answer then I apologize in advance for being suspicious. I'm sure you'd do the same thing," Running-water said.

"Yeah, you're right, of course. He was the cause of my divorce. Only the real Will Rexford would know that," Dutch said.

"And that was?"

"Oh man, I hate this. Promise you won't spread this around. Keep Adam out of it even though I owe him a lot, it's embarrassing."

"Only two of The Brothers are still alive. I'll do my best not to give away your secret to Adam. So, what you do, catch Will with your wife?" Running-water said.

"Hell no. She caught us in bed together."

"What? Oh, shit! I didn't know you were—,"

"We were drunk. Hell, I didn't know who I was with. We're just back from a mission, went out on the town, and really tied one on. I had forgotten Elli was supposed to meet me. Anyway, to make a long story short, I was humping Will and singing my head off," Dutch said.

"What were you singing?"

"Of, for Christ's sake. You need to know the asshole of everything? It was an old Gene Autry song called "Back in the Saddle Again." Dutch said.

Running-water began to laugh. He laughed so hard he had to sit down. "Man I needed a good laugh. It's been really tight around here lately. Thanks, my friend."

"Oh, shut the hell up. Anyway, now you know. Elli never forgave me," Dutch said.

Running-water returned to Adam's private car where he found Adam amicably chatting with the two handcuffed police officers left behind by Macerate. Samuel was at his usual position as a security guard. Will Rexford was noticeably absent.

"What are you going to do with those two?" Running-water said, indicating the two policemen.

"They've told me quite a story. They were only following the late Captain's orders. In fact, they told me it was he who had them hassle you and Samuel while you were in town. Seems they even hired a couple of high school kids to push your buttons. Something neither of you told me. Anyway, I've contacted Chief Warren and he's on his way here to pick them up." Adam said.

"And what about Phillip and Faul?" Running-water said.

"It appears that the three murdered Brothers were not in cahoots with Joseph and Thomas and were about to spill the beans. That's why they were eliminated. The three at the hospital were killed to ensure their silence. Paul and Phillip have refused to be part of their inner circle and are now in danger. They were the last two recruited by Esaugetuh and were always viewed as outsiders. That's why they are still here. They will remain here with me until all of this is resolved," Adam said.

"So you are saying Joseph and Thomas are still trying to kill you, even from their Canadian prison?"

"Looks that way. I've asked Will to see if they have escaped or if they haven't, to find out what access they have to telephones, computers," Adam said.

Will Rexford sauntered in, plopped down in a chair, stretched out his long legs, and then pulled out a cigar and lit it. Neither Adam nor Runningwater had seen Will with a cigar. The fact was they didn't know he smoked. Both kept it to themselves.

"Both men are still in prison and have access to a telephone but not to computers or cell phones. Anything else you want me to do?" Will said.

"Not right now. It's time for lunch. I'll notify the chef we'll have some extra lunch guests. Will you gentlemen join me in the dining car?" Adam said.

Chief Warren met them as they left Adam's car. "I had a call from the coroner and his preliminary exam indicates that they didn't die because of the beating these two assholes gave them. Still not sure about the cause of death. You want to press charges against these two jerks?" Chief Warren said.

"They've told me they were following Captain Macerate's orders. I think they should face the consequences of their actions. They have to accept responsibility for their behavior," Adam said.

"I agree. I'll order an internal investigation and go from there. In the meantime, they are suspended without pay. And I can tell you right now, I will recommend that they be fired," Chief Warren said.

"Fine. In the meantime, perhaps you would unlock their handcuffs so they can eat and perhaps you will join us for lunch?" Adam said.

They were ushered into the dining car by Samuel. Chief Warren and the two policemen sat with Adam; the two remaining Brothers sat with the engineers and Running-water, Samuel, and Will Rexford sat at another table.

"Tell us, Will, how'd you and Dutch meet? Was it in the Seals?" Running-water said.

"We trained together," Will said.

"You go on missions together? I guess the two of you were always ready to get back in the saddle again back then," Running-water said.

"What's that supposed to mean?"

"Well, from the little Dutch has said, despite it being a rough and tumble business, you were always ready," Running-water said, smiling.

"It was that alright. Never knew where we were going to end up," Will said.

"Elli didn't like that, I'm sure," Running-water said.

"Elli? Who's that?" Will said.

A shot rang out and Will Rexford fell backward writhing in pain. Before he could pull his gun a second shot tore into his shoulder. Samuel was on top of him, gun shoved into his face.

"You bastard. What'd you do with the real Will Rexford?" Running-water said.

"I've nothing to say to you. No, tell this ape to get off of me."

"Okay. Have it your way. Take his gun and then let him up," Running-water said.

"You always shoot people?" Chief Warren said.

"Arrest this jackass. He's the murderer, imposter, and the real assassin," Running-water said.

"How do you know that? What evidence do you have?" Chief Warren said.

"I'm not at liberty to say, but believe me, I am absolutely certain," Running-water said.

"If Running-water says he's certain, then he is. Perhaps I can help?" Adam said, bending over the wounded man.

Adam ran his finger down the bridge of the wounded man's nose, whispered something in his ear. A glazed look came over the man's eyes.

"What is your real name?" Adam said.

"Scott Cooper."

"Who hired you?"

"A guy named Joseph."

"Describe him," Adam said.

"Never actually saw him."

"And where is the *real* Will Rexford?" Adam said.

"In the baggage car."

"Samuel go and see," Adam said.

"Ask him about Michael Lane," Running-water said.

"Why did you kill Michael Lane?" Adam said.

"He botched the job," Cooper said.

"And that was?" Adam said.

"To kill you."

"What happened to the real Michael Lane?" Adam said.

"He was Michael Lane," Cooper said.

"Who killed the three Brothers?" Adam said.

"Lane killed them."

"Why?"

"Joseph wanted them dead. That's all I know."

"And Captain Macerate. Did you tamper with his car?" Adam said.

"No. Joseph said he'd take care of him," Cooper said.

"How do you communicate with Joseph?" Adam said.

For the first time in a long time, Adam felt he was finally getting to the bottom of all the attempts on his life. There had been so many he had lost count. Maybe now he would be able to settle down, feel safe, and pursue his healing. Further questioning revealed that all communications between Joseph and Cooper had been through a PMB Suite in a storefront. That was verified when Chief Warren while searching Cooper, found a short letter with specific instructions. Cooper had his rights read to him, handcuffed, and taken away by two policemen who had been called to the train.

Adam was the first to hear the yelling. It was Samuel.

"He's alive! I've got him!"

Shortly, Samuel, with Will Rexford slung over his broad shoulders, boarded the steps to Adam's car. Will was cussing up a storm.

"God damn it! Samuel put me down. Jesus, I'm not an invalid."

Samuel dumped him on the floor. That brought another barrage of cuss words from Will.

"Since you are already on the floor, lay flat. I'll see if you have any injuries," Adam said.

"I didn't, but I might now after that big ape dropped me," Will Rexford said.

"Why did Elli leave Dutch?" Running-water asked.

"She found Dutch in a compromising situation. Why? Has she come back?" Will said.

"What song did Dutch sing to you?" Running- said.

Will's face turned bright red as he looked up at Running-water. *Back in the saddle again.* Say what the hell is this all about?"

"He's the real Will Rexford," Running-water said. Looking directly at Will and winking at him, he continued, "Don't worry I won't say any more about it. Okay, cowboy?"

With that issue settled, Chief Warren excused himself and returned to his office. In all of his twenty-five years in law enforcement, he had never seen such a mess. Seven murders, one shooting. He dreaded the paperwork. Hours would be required and he knew the county prosecutor's office would want pages and pages of detailed information. Forensic evidence would have to be systematically cataloged, interviews carefully recorded, background checks on each of the deceased completed, and a time frame for all of it would have to be developed. He hoped the sheriff's office would take over most of the work.

"Damn Macerate. He'd have to go and get himself killed. He was the one who was good with details. Now I have to do it. Damn!" Chief Warren muttered, as he shoved his car into gear and sped off.

"Any idea why Cooper didn't kill you?" Running-water said to Will Rexford.

"Man, I can tell you this. I'm glad he didn't. He was a strange one."

"Did he give any indication as to why he didn't kill you?" Running-water again asked.

"He said he had other uses for me and he'd be back."

"Hmm. *Back in the Saddle Again*?" Running-water said laughing.

"Now cut that shit out! Just wait till I get my hands on that big mouth. I'll fix his ass," Will Rexford said.

"Yeah, I bet you will!" Running-water said still roaring with laughter.

"Mind letting me in on what's so funny?" Adam said.

"It's a private thing, Adam," Will said.

And so it was. Adam turned his attention to Paul and Phillip, the last of the twelve Brothers. Paul, the older of the two, in his mid-fifties, was an enigma. During Adam's time at Karuna House, he was anything but visible. At Esaugetuh's ranch, he remained aloof, quiet, and pensive. Because he seldom spoke, Adam equated that with a desire to live a monastic life, spending his time in contemplation. Whatever it was that his father had seen in Paul, Adam was determined to find out. He would not be misled again.

Sensing Adam staring at him, Paul became uneasy. He shifted his six-foot frame, adjusted his gold-wire-rimmed glasses, found a spot on the opposite wall to fix his attention. As long as Paul could remember, he had never gotten used to people looking at him. He always wondered what they were thinking about him. Sometimes he even imagined what their snide remarks were. And there were snide remarks. On very rare occasions he would be told what the person was thinking. Obvious things as remarks about his green eyes or about losing his hair. Those comments were about as close as anyone ever got to being personal. No one bothered to ask him how he felt or what his thoughts were.

Ending the exaggerated long silence Adam said, "Paul why did my father ask you to join the group at Karuna House and how did the two of you meet?"

Paul's green eyes widened and his graying eyebrows arched as he realigned himself in the chair. It was hard for him to look directly at people, even when they spoke to him. But now he was determined to change all that. He looked directly at Adam, making eye contact. Adam's azure blue eyes offered no threat but seemed to offer an invitation to a quiet conversational response.

"I don't—,"

He was going to say he didn't remember but changed his mind. He remembered and all too well. Phillip who had been dozing came awake and got very attentive.

"It was on a very cold, bitter winter night. Maybe five years ago; might be less. I was lying in a gutter along the super highway leading out of the city. Car after car whizzed by. My body was numb and I was sure that I was slowly but surely freezing to death. All I wanted to do was to hurry up and get it over with," Paul said, surprising himself with his new found vocalization.

"It was that bad?" Adam said.

"Yes. I didn't have any reason to go on living. Yet—yet I didn't have the courage to take my own life. Everything I ever had, ever known was gone: career, family, and friends. Friends? Man, that's a laugh. They couldn't wait to see me go down. And down I went. A non-stop slide into total oblivion. Until—,"

"Until?" Adam prompted.

"Esaugetuh stopped. A hulk of a man got out of the car, picked me up, put me in the back seat of his stretch limo. An old man offered me a full glass of brandy. Then he did the damndest thing."

"What that was?" Adam said.

"He unwrapped the cloth from my feet and began to massage them. His hands were warm. Then he poured something over my feet pulled wool socks over them. The warmth of the brandy and my feet getting warm was a wonderful feeling. I took a good look at him and saw bright blue eyes looking at me, just as you are doing right now. And for some wonderful reason, I felt safe. I began to cry and I think I cried for days," Paul said.

"And do you know the cause of this crying?" Adam said.

"A broken man will have any number of causes," Paul said.

"And when you say, 'broken man' do you mean spiritually, physically, or psychologically broken?" Adam said.

"How about all three? Pick anyone you want," Paul said.

"I believe one's spirit or soul, when damaged, causes the other two. What broke your spirit? I'm talking about your inner spirit, your soul. The Self if you want to call it that. What caused you to lose your value of self?"

'I know that," Paul said.

"Then you must know if you don't have value for your Self then you wither and die. The Self is the essence of being. It is who you are," Adam said.

"It's so easy to say that, isn't it?"

"Okay, we'll leave that for now. Can you remember what my father said to you?" Adam said.

"Sure. I've tried to figure out what he meant when he said, 'You've got work to do.' Actually, it probably helped me survive by giving me something specific to think about."

"And?" Adam said.

"He never spoke to me again. And I never saw him again. Bradford was instructed to give me a place to sleep, clothes, and food. That was it, my plunge into oblivion. Karuna House offered me another form of oblivion."

"And before your plunge, what was your life like?" Adam said.

"I was a psychiatrist."

"Paul, what is your last name?" Adam said.

"It's Saenz. Dr. Paul Andrew Saenz. You going to look me up on that computer of yours?" Paul said nodding toward Running-water.

"Would that cause you concern?" Adam said.

"I can save you the time. I—I'm. Paul stopped, looked at Phillip, and then continued. "I'm responsible for the death of one of my former patients."

"Why do you believe you are responsible?" Adam said

"He went on a rampage, killed several people, and then blew his brains out. I should have known he was homicidal. I misread the signs They were all there for me to see," Paul said.

"Many times a doctor's patient dies, or does something foolish, but that does not necessarily mean the doctor did anything wrong. Why do you feel you did something wrong?" Adam said.

"The people he killed were my wife and daughter. I should have known that his interest in my family life was a ruse. He was young, seventeen, precious, charming, witty, and a master at deceiving people. The constant deception was the reason his mother brought him to me. I made the mistake of allowing him to know intimate things about myself and family. That's something a doctor should never do," Paul said.

"Intimate things?" Adam said.

"Yes. The things my family and I did together, what my wife did with her time, what my daughter liked to do. Where we went on vacations. Those kinds of intimate details."

"Your wife worked?" Running-water said.

"Yes, she worked at an elementary school. She and my daughter were killed at school. Of all the things we talked about, he never wanted to talk about his relationship with his father. It was a closed subject as far as he was concerned."

"Liar!" Phillip said, lunging for Paul. "You programmed my son to kill your wife. He changed after he started seeing you. You knew your wife was having an affair with the principal of the school. You bastard! I've waited to make sure it was really you. Now I'll finish the job you didn't have the guts to do."

Samuel brought the butt of his Uzi up, clipped Phillip under the chin. Phillip went down on his knees, his anger turning to sobs.

"Stay put," Samuel said.

Before Adam could intervene, Paul was on his knees beside the stricken Phillip.

"No Phillip. You are mistaken. My wife was the principal. Your son told me that you had molested him but I always was suspicious that it was just another of his stories. He sensed I didn't believe him. You've got to accept the fact that there is such a thing as a 'bad seed.' David was evil. He gloried in what he perceived as power over others."

"No! No! I'll never believe that. He was perfect," Phillip moaned.

"If he was so perfect, why did he kill and why did he kill himself?" Adam said.

The questions stunned Phillip. They were the questions he never wanted to face—had never faced. There it was in all its naked truth, screaming at him. He knew the real answer, but it was too late. His life was over. His wife had left him, remarried. And now The Brothers are decimated.

I wondered why the old man dragged me out of the slop house I was living in. Now I know..

Reading Phillip's thoughts, Adam said, "You're wrong, Phillip. My father would not have brought the two of you together so you could kill one another. Maybe he wanted the two of you to come together and realize you made the decision to throw your lives away. Maybe it was to have you understand that you can't be responsible for another's behavior," Adam said.

"And what did you do before this tragedy hit you?" Running-water said.

"I'm a physicist," Phillip said.

"Glad to see you said that in the present tense," Adam said.

CHAPTER FIFTY

Sheriff Vegan pulled up alongside the train. As he hurried along to Adam's private car he noticed the many dents made by the bullets from the train's ambush. He was still shaking his head when Samuel let him in. He handed over his gun without being asked for it.

"Wonder if you know what these tattoos mean? The coroner would like to know," Vegan said, handing Adam photos of the three dead Brothers at the hospital.

"Why would the coroner think I would know ---," Adam stopped, stared at the left arm of each of the three dead Brothers. His face paled --- "My god, it's true." His voice was barely above a whisper.

"What is it, my brother?" Running-water said, moving closer to examine the photos. "Looks like part of a flag. Wasn't there a 'Don't Tread on Me' American Flag?"

"Not like this. Notice that the straight line appears to have roots indicating that something is growing up out of the ground. The fact that there are only three branches or limbs on the right when viewed sideways become a three-pronged Devil's fork. The snake or serpent with its mouth open also is coming up from out of the earth. This is the symbol of chthonic powers [1]," Adam said.

"What does it mean?" Sheriff Vegan said.

"I believe it means a power from the other side has entered our world and has begun recruiting followers. I feel we are in for a very dangerous time. The three dead Brothers were executed because of some failing perceived by the evil one or they had served their purpose. Whichever, we need to be very cautious from now on."

"Let me see your arms," Running-water said to Paul and Phillip.

Neither had tattoos on their arms.

"Sheriff, can you find out about the three men who had their throats slit? If so, check to see if they have tattoos on their left arms and get photos if possible," Running-water said.

"No problem. I'll get to it right away."

"While we are at it, do you mind, Will?" Running-water said.

Will Rexford rolled up both sleeves and showed both arms. No marks. Not to be left out, Samuel followed suit. Again no marks.

"Might just as well check mine," Sheriff Vegan said, rolling up his sleeves.

And like the others, his arms were clean.

"I noticed you used the word 'executed' when you mentioned the three men who died at the hospital. You know something I don't, Adam?" Sheriff Vegan said.

"No. As I looked at the faces of the three I noticed how contorted they were and that reminded me of the description that Sam Curler gave of Captain Macerate's face as he hit his truck," Adam said.

Adam stepped out onto the platform as Sheriff Vegan left. Unease filled him as new concerns, deep-rooted, nagged at him.

Damn! How I wish Esaugetuh were here.

"Haven't you been told that he is always with you?" Running-water said, responding to Adam's unspoken thought. "What would you have him do?"

"I don't know but by God how I wish I did," Adam said.

"Why not call upon the spirits of our brothers, of our sisters, and of our grandfathers and grandmothers. Call upon your spirit guide and I will call upon mine. Surely you will find what you are seeking."

"Yes. But not here. The stench of death still lingers. The train is not clean. We'll return to the monastery. Have the boxcars emptied and have their contents delivered to the monastery. Send the train back to Vancouver; put it up for sale as soon as the authorities release it. Pay off the staff. Speaking of selling, have Karuna House, Syd's Bar, the sanitarium and the ranch been sold yet?"

"I've received a few offers on the mansion and the ranch. Nothing's been solidified yet. You getting antsy about cash flow?" Running-water said.

"No. I just want to get things consolidated. Unload the apartments and offices in Montreal. Also, get us out of the banking business. Less to worry about. We'll need all of our mental faculties to deal with the situation that's developing," Adam said.

"You really are concerned, aren't you?"

"This time, my brother, we are in for a hell of a battle. One of us or both of us may not survive. Have you filed those jointure papers I asked about?" Adam said.

"They have been filed. You think you are the one who will not survive, don't you? What makes you feel that way?" Running-water said.

"In case you haven't noticed, those around me are systematically being eliminated? And that, my brother, is why I sent you and the rest away. Whoever or whatever is behind these attacks has been deliberately weakening my immediate line of defense," Adam said.

"I take it, you didn't view The Brothers as a part of your defense? Samuel being the exception, of course," Running-water said.

"I didn't send them away so I could find out if they were involved. I figured if they realized I was alone, they might make a move," Adam said.

"As far as I'm concerned I think they are a part of the problem. It still mystifies me as to why your father brought them together. What are you going to do about Paul and Phillip?" Running-water said.

"Glad you didn't count me out even though I was used as a conduit by

whoever's behind this mess. As mean, sneaky and power hungry as Joseph is, I don't think he has the power to do all of this stuff. At least he didn't when we were at Karuna House. To get even with you, he could have hired someone," Samuel said as he joined Adam and Running-water on the platform.

"Where'd he get the extra money? I'm sure the money Adam gave him when he was booted out of Karuna House would have been used up in his legal fees," Running-water said.

"He had each of The Brothers sign over their money to him. I didn't do that and neither did the three found in the ditch," Samuel said.

"Do you have proof of that?" Running-water asked.

"Check their sleeping compartments. Somewhere there's got to be some papers. Whatever papers I had I kept under my mattress. A dumb thing to do, but in those days I was dumb. I can search if you want me to," Samuel said.

It was agreed that Samuel would search the deceased Brothers' compartments. Paul and Phillip, like Samuel, had not given their money to Joseph. Nor had they taken out any life insurance with him as their beneficiary. Running-water set about making preparations for moving the contents of the train to the monastery. Without the Brothers to help with the unloading, professional movers had to be hired.

Several phone calls later, Running-water, had a local company with enough available trucks to carry the contents from five boxcars. A security company was hired, Sheriff Vegan and Chief Warren were notified. Each had agreed to be part of the escort. Sheriff Vegan also assigned several of his deputies to escort duty. One boxcar would be unloaded at a time; trucks with its content would be identified by the number corresponding to the manifest. The license of each driver was photocopied. That was e-mailed to Sheriff Vegan so he could do a background check on each driver and their assigned helpers. Only one driver had to be changed. Each truck's tag number and registration, as well as a digital photo of the truck, were made part of Running-water's records. As each truck was loaded, Running-water personally sealed the trailer and assigned a member of the security team to guard it. The unloading went on through the night.

Running-water and Samuel were especially cautious with the unloading of boxcar seven. Each box, double checked against the manifest. The loaders didn't understand why there was so much fuss over boxes marked diapers, baby food, clothes, family photos, dishes, and foodstuffs. They were unaware they were uploading the much sought after treasure worth millions of dollars. Once all of its contents were loaded onto trucks, Running-water put Samuel in charge of their security. Satisfied with the night's work he returned to Adam's private car.

There he found Will Rexford busy writing a letter to Joseph at his prison in Canada. Adam had asked him to pretend he was Cooper who had revealed the language of any communication he had with Joseph.

He was to express his condolences over the loss of a Brother. Joseph would understand that the assassination had been successful. To hit him up for more money Rexford told him that the cost of the funeral was more than expected. That would incense him and eventually Joseph's anger would get the better of him and he would break silence and call. Adam would be ready for that call. The letter was sent via overnight delivery.

The chef's announcement that breakfast was ready brought a welcome relief. Three shifts of diners were set up. Truck drivers and their helpers were fed first, then the security people, and last Adam and his immediate group. Phillip was the first to speak.

"It is true, Adam, that I am a physicist, but what I didn't tell you was the areas in which I did my work. I worked in the area of the paranormal. I was specifically involved in distant viewing and teleportation. I have found watching you and your abilities fascinating and if there ever was living proof that such abilities exist, you are it. I would like to help you in any way I can to fight this force from the other side."

"Count me in, too. I dealt with phenomena related to psychokinesis. Wrote a book on it. My understanding is that you believe that there is a force contrary to your own and it wants to dominate. Is that correct?" Paul said.

"You could put it that way. It goes far beyond my domination. I believe it's much more serious than that," Adam said.

"I can't speak for Phillip, but I know that I have to demonstrate I can be trusted. I am sorry so many of The Brothers chose to betray you. You have wondered why your late father brought such a divergent bunch of derelicts together. Perhaps it was to separate the chaff from the wheat," Paul said.

"More likely to force the issue with this adversary. Your father probably thought he needed someone stronger, perhaps more powerful than he for this battle?" Phillip said. "Obviously he didn't realize they were a part of the enemy."

"You may be right about that. You realize that if you stay and get involved, it may cost you your lives. Are you prepared for that?" Adam said.

"Oh hell, Adam. I've been waiting years to die," Paul said.

"It's settled then," Phillip said, "We stay."

When they became aware of Samuel listening, they turned their heads away. He wondered why he made them nervous. Certainly, they knew he was Adam's personal bodyguard. He tried to remember any offense while they were at Karuna House. They sure act strange around me. I'll see about that later.

The noise of the eighteen-wheelers caught his attention and he stepped out onto the platform of the train. He watched as the curiosity seekers gathered. They found the presence of heavily armed guards unnerving. When their own Chief of Police, William Warren came into view they were sure that the people on the train had been arrested and everything they owned confiscated. With the arrival of Sheriff Vegan and several deputies, they were sure it had been a big drug bust. The hangers-on waited for the rumored arrival of the National Guard. The tall, long-haired Indian seemed to be calling all the shots. The morning sun bounced off his blue-black hair. His movements were closely watched by several of the female observers. They enjoyed the sensual movements that were so natural to him. A couple of the bolder women clucked at him in an effort to get him to turn around so they could get a better look, especially at his full crotch.

Running-water pretended not to notice even though he enjoyed open admiration of his physique. He was reminded of a past time when he played his flute and danced as the infamous Kokopelli. Then, the young women went wild, stuffing his loincloth with twenty dollar bills. He missed his Isha. Longed for her touch.

The long-haired blue-eyed one was not seen. Those who had heard he was some kind of a medicine man would like to have had him try and heal them. Others found the young man with straw-colored hair, the well-developed pectorals, and flashing smile of more interest. They had not seen him before. As he turned toward them, he humped the air, thinking it was what they wanted to see. And it was.

"Oh, honey, you are so hot," giggled one of the young women.

Another began to sing Rose Mary Clooney's 'Come ona my house, I give you everything'."

"This is sure better than the county fair," said an onlooker.

"You know," said another, "maybe that blue-eyed one was among those they found dead. That's why the Chief and the Sheriff are here. They've confiscated everything as part of their investigation. I heard that them poor fellas had their throats slit."

"Well, I think their terrorists. Man, can you believe that? Right here in our own town," a young man said. Remembering yellow paint and the embarrassment it had caused at school, he blushed, and quickly faded back into the gathering crowd.

With all the speculation going on, one, however, was content just to watch. He was an odd looking figure, clothed in a black suit and a long black cape that flapped open in the chilly spring breezes. His long white hair cascaded beneath a wide-brimmed black hat. He leaned slightly to his right, favoring his left leg. When he shifted his weight he used a black cane with a silver handle. His eyes were not visible because of very dark sunglasses that seemed to melt into his face and head. A little girl tugged at his cape, wanting to be picked up so she could see. He stepped back, and with a bony finger, indicated that the child and its mother could step in front of him. When the mother turned to thank him, he was gone. But then, she wasn't sure anyone had been there, to begin with.

The sound of large trucks shifting gears and reviving their motors announced the caravan was about to leave. That chorus was joined by the clang of train cars being bumped as the engine pushed them forward. Several maneuvers were required before it was turned around and headed northward.

A crowing rooster, who took his job very seriously, was joined by the whinny of horses from a nearby equestrian stable. Barking dogs chimed in as the escorted caravan eased its way out of town. Soon the only reminder of the death train and its group of weirdoes was the yellow crime ribbon that fluttered in the morning sunlight.

As the stretch limo snaked its way along the winding mountain road, Running-water watched the sparkling green river, full because of the early spring snowmelt in the high mountains. He marveled at its speed and wondered what secrets it carried along. How many of his ancestors had zipped along in their canoes? His mental reflections were broken by the ringing of Will Rexford's cell phone.

Will knew the call would be from Joseph. He pushed the speakerphone button so Adam and Running-water could hear. Then he answered.

"Not one dime more. I don't have any more money," Joseph said.

"Don't play me for a fool. I know you got plenty of money. You got those other poor assholes to give you all their money. And don't forget the life insurance policies. Now, pay up! Will said.

"Or what? You listen to me you greedy son-of-a-bitch. Not one damn dime more. You know what happened to Macerate can happen to you."

"You threatening me? Listen, you sick little prick, you can be had where you are," Will said.

The line went dead.

"Damn! A dropped call or else he hung up on me. Damn!" Will Rexford said.

"I don't think so. See if you can contact the prison and ask to speak to the Commandant," Adam said.

The prison Commandant was not available. Whoever answered the phone suggested calling back later. When Will asked if there was a problem at the prison the man on the other end tensed up. "Why do you ask that?" he said.

"I was just talking to one of the inmates and the line went dead."

"Which inmate?"

"Does it matter which one? Ah, there *is* a problem," Will said.

"Sir, if you could tell me the name it would be helpful. Sir! Just a moment. The Commandant will speak with you."

"This is Commandant Garrity. I understand—,"

"I'm Will Rexford, United States Homeland Security. What's happened?"

"An inmate was on a phone and suddenly caught on fire," Garrity said.

"This inmate have a name?" Will Rexford said.

"His name was Joseph Aeromonis. Is that the man to whom you were speaking? And why were you talking with one of our inmates?" Commandant Garrity said.

"Yes. That's the man to whom I was speaking. You used the past tense when you told me his name. Is he okay?"

"I'm afraid not. All that's left is a pile of ashes. My understanding is that he simply burst into flames. You didn't answer my question. Why were you talking with one of our inmates?" Garrity said.

"We believe he may have been involved with a terrorist group that tried to take over a ranch in Quebec Province. I was trying to get him to agree to a meeting," Will Rexford lied. "I'd appreciate a more detailed report concerning his death. I'll be back in touch. Thanks," Will Rexford said, ending the call.

"So it begins all over again. Too bad you didn't get to talk to him a bit longer. But I caught enough of his voice to know that was not Joseph Aeromonis, not the Joseph of The Brothers. Running-water, contact our sheriff friend in Pennsylvania. I'd like to talk to him." Adam said.

"So you do believe there is a connection to Moon-Woman?" Running-water said, opening his laptop.

"It could be just a coincidence. Just want to make sure," Adam said.

"Who's Moon-Woman?" Will Rexford asked.

"My aunt," Running-water replied as he turned his attention to his open laptop.

The sheriff's number was retrieved from the bowels of Running-water's computer. Sheriff Logan was delighted to hear from Adam. The cause of Moon-Woman's death had been listed as spontaneous human combustion. According to Sheriff Logan, there were only a few personal items left. A hairbrush, a pair of shoes, a dress, and what appears to be a journal of some kind. Adam arranged for those items to be sent to him by special courier.

The caravan—and that's what it was, consisting of the limo, an SUV, a couple of dozen trucks, two patrol cars, two deputies on motorcycles—snaked its way through the small village toward the mountain. The locals were used to log truck rumbling through town and didn't pay attention to the noise. Entering the compound, Adam noted, with satisfaction, the amount of work that had been accomplished in such a short time. Hiring enough workers to man 24/7 shifts had paid off. Hiring local people for much of the work cut down on wasted travel time. The long winding driveway had been paved; lights had been installed along its sides. Rock Cress, Primrose, Peonies, Lupine, and Marsh Marigolds mixed with a rainbow of tulips brought an elegant majesty to the grounds. Adam looked at each outcropping of plants out the open window of the limo. Once he spotted what he was looking for he had Samuel stop the car. He got out, went to the plants, bent down and sniffed at each one. Their fragrant blossoms pleased him. He got back into the limo and said, "They're called Daphne Odora and they are there for Daphne."

Once the caravan reached the upper level of the property they had to stop because of a massive iron gate. On each side of the gate were large clumps of Daphne Odora. The two deputies on their motorcycles pulled up alongside the limo and waited, unsure of what they should do. Runningwater exited the car, went to the control box and punched in a code. He waited until the gates, with their bald eagle crest, rolled back into a cement wall. This was something he had insisted upon. Gates that swung out allowed for vulnerability. He motioned for the limo to drive through; he climbed back into the car. The gates, their cameras, and intercom system had been installed at Runningwaters instructions. Now that they were moving in, he would have a control pad put in the limo. That way it wouldn't be necessary to get out. The less exposure for Adam the better he liked it. The road, besides a heliport that was under construction, was the only way to access the property. The back of the property was protected by a granite cliff that had a drop of several hundred feet.

"Did you secure the cliff?" Adam asked Running-water.

"No. It's a sheer drop. Just didn't think it was needed," Running-water said.

"There are people who can scale that," Adam said.

"I'll have sensors installed right away. Sorry about that slip-up."

"No problem. You up to doing some cooking?"

"Sure. What you got in mind?" Running-water said.

"We need to get food supplies. And while we are at it, let's have a feast for the work crews, the truckers, and the security detail. Something extra for a job well done. Agreed?" Adam said.

"Agreed."

"Good. Send Samuel back into the village to get supplies. No burgers or hot dogs. Get several roasts of beef, pork, chickens, several bags of potatoes, carrots, onions, garlic, green beans, eggs, milk, coffee, sugar, pastries, and whatever else you can think of. Send Will Rexford with him. Take cash out of the safe in the trunk of the limo. Give Samuel a couple thousand."

While the unloading progressed under Running-water's supervision, Adam loaded the automatic dishwasher, set it to going, fired up the open faced brick ovens. They would hold at least four large roasting pans. He checked the walk-in freezer to make sure it was up and running. As he rummaged around he found several folding tables. He set those up on the back lawn. As loads of dishes were done he carried those out to one of the tables, stacking them. Silverware came out next.

Once Samuel had returned with the necessary supplies Adam soon had a meal in the ovens baking. While the meal was cooking Adam marveled at the owner of the trucking company. He really knew his business. He had included two forklifts, a small tractor, and flatbed carts on one of the trucks. The unloading went faster because of that foresight. Smooth was the operative word. Each item was checked off on the manifest, with a notation of its location. By evening, the caravan of trucks had been unloaded. The security guards, truck drivers, their helpers, Sheriff Vegan, and Chief Warren and the patrol officers chowed down. Afterward, all of them were given hefty cash bonuses. Sheriff Vegan and Chief Warren were each given checks made out to their favorite charities.

The workers, ant-like, eagerly crawled over the compound doing their individual jobs. Adam made an ample supply of hot coffee, sandwiches, and pastries to carry them through the night. While he was stacking the food on one of the counters in the kitchen he felt someone was there. Adam looked around; thinking one of the work crew had come in. He thought he caught a glimpse of a shadow. He stood still, listening. He was sure he heard someone or something breathing. He flicked on all of the kitchen lights. No one was there. He decided his mind was playing tricks on him. Getting tense. Can't afford to get spooked. Yet his feeling lingered.

Running-water checking with the electricians wanted to make sure the double sets of floodlights being installed throughout the property had half of each set as motion activated with their doubles being manually operated from the security base at the Monastery. The chief electrician said they would be fully operable in two days. Next, he checked a series of motion detection sensors to make sure that they automatically triggered infrared video cameras. They were fully operable. He had microphones hidden in various shrubs and bushes leading to the main building and to the guest house. He figured they would need every bit of advanced warning they could get. Satisfied with the light installation, Running-water checked on the progress of the construction of the panic rooms. He had personally designed one for each of the three main floors. Each would have an escape slide similar to those used on commercial jets and would eventually lead into an underground bunker. With the amount of time he and Adam had to be on the road, he wanted to make sure their families were well protected. The bunker was designed to contain a helicopter and an armored stretch SUV. The vehicle built to withstand a roadside blast was currently parked behind the main building and the helicopter hadn't been delivered. An underground entrance to the bunker from the main building was being built with reinforced concrete. Once everything was in place no one would realize it was there. The roof would electronically open so the helicopter could take off and the limo could be brought to ground level by a hydraulic lift. Next, he went down into the basement and took a construction elevator down two more levels. It was used to haul the dirt out and cement in. A single large room was being built as a walk-in vault. Before returning to the main floor and the control panel and its bank of monitors, Running-water stopped at the level just above the vault to check on two other rooms that were being built. These would house the various weapons, ammunition, and emergency supplies. Only he and Adam knew what was being built underground. When the time came the others would be told about the safe rooms and how to use their escape tunnels. He went looking for Adam to discuss security. He felt they were vulnerable until the electronic system was fully operational. Perhaps it was that sense of vulnerability that made him ill at ease. He found Adam and Phillip in the central living room.

Phillip was walking around with a strange device in his hands.

"What are you doing?" Running-water heard Adam say.

"Yeah. What in god's name is that thing?" Running-water said, entering the room.

"It's a Gauss Meter. It's used to check paranormal activity. I've detected nothing unusual at this time. I'd like to get some additional special equipment if you don't have any objections," Phillip said.

"Where'd you find that gizmo?" Running-water asked.

"Had it with me. One of the few things I kept. Don't even know why I did, but I'm glad I did."

"What kind of equipment do you want?" Adam said.

"To begin with, I'd like about a dozen instant-reading infrared digital thermometers, a set of static electricity and ionization detectors, and at least four radiation monitors. Can you get all of this here right away?

"And all of this will tell us what? That we have ghosts? This equipment you're asking for sounds like stuff ghost hunters use," Running-water said.

"Well yes and no. We could possibly pick up ghosts, but if I understand what Adam has said, it's much more than a mere ghost—even more than a poltergeist. Whatever it is, it's a living energy force capable of rational decision. Am I right on that count, Adam?" Phillip said.

"Unfortunately, I think you are. Can this equipment you want be gotten without getting a lot of outsiders involved?" Adam said.

"Yes. Can you arrange for it to be flown here? The sooner the better. It may give you the edge in dealing with this thing," Phillip said.

"Give your list to Running-water. He'll make the arrangements," Adam said.

"Some paranormal forces have an affliction toward mirrors. They might be useful," Paul said, joining the conversation.

Running-water wondered where he had been. He'd not seen him helping to unload the trucks.

"True for ghosts and other minor apparitions. However, I don't think we'll be dealing with them. What we need is a very large EMF," Phillip said.

"What's an EMF?" Running-water said.

"Electromagnetic Field," Phillip said.

"How does that work?" Will Rexford said as he joined the group.

"Wondered where you'd gotten off to," Running-water said.

"On an EMF spectrum, that is, above light, and beginning in ultra-violet frequencies, ionizing radiation has sufficient capacity to break down chemical bonds and actually create an unstable situation in atoms or molecules. Great amounts of energy can destroy or at least, damage genetic material," Phillip said.

"And we are genetic material," Will Rexford said, ignoring Running-water's question.

"Exactly. When the EMF is amplified through resonance, the danger is multiplied a hundred times," Phillip said.

"So what you are saying is if we can set up such a field we can use it to amplify the millions of neurons in the brain?" Rexford said.

"Well yes. Something like that. What we want to do is to amplify certain thought patterns." Phillip said.

"And these can be destructive if that is the inclination of the individual? And since Adam has the ability to use anomalous perturbation, he can influence this entity." Running-water said.

"Yes. These transmitted resonated thought patterns have increasingly larger and larger destructive effects once they are imprinted into the engrams of the individual. For example, an individual could be triggered to commit suicide with a specific thought pattern," Paul said.

"That's what you did to my son, you bastard. You programmed him. You were the one having the affair and wanted your wife out of the way," Phillip screamed as he dove into Paul, knocking him to the floor.

"I thought the issue between the two of you had been settled. If you can't get over the suicide of your son, then you need to reconsider working with Paul. You are under no obligation here. Maybe you ought to move on." Adam said.

"Oh shit! I'm sorry Paul. It just—just hard to let go. I've hated you for so long. I know it would take years to program someone to commit murder let alone self-destruct. This won't happen again, Adam, I'd like to stay," Phillip said.

"One more outburst and you're out of here! Understand?" Adam said.

"Paul, what you were saying is if these neurons can be amplified, Adam can, in theory, turn this thing against itself," Running-water said, bringing the group back to the discussion at hand.

"Neurons?" Samuel said as he sauntered into the room.

"Yes. The human brain is said to contain 10-100 billion neurons, that is, electrically active nerve cells. And ten times as many glial cells—the nutritional support cells surrounding the neurons. The brain normally receives fifteen to twenty percent of the body's total blood supply and uses about twenty percent of the body's total inhaled oxygen. Charge those up, that is, resonate them, they become extremely powerful in generating electromagnetic impulses," Phillip said.

"If what you say is correct, and I'm not suggesting that it isn't, the consumption of ATP must be phenomenal," Paul said.

"ATP? Man, you two are beyond me," Will Rexford said.

"Guess you're not a bodybuilder. Any bodybuilder would tell you that its Adenosine triphosphate, the energy of the cell," Paul said.

"This thing you are expecting has somehow learned to increase all of these and to transfer them from the mental state to the physical state. What I hear you saying, is that it must be neutralized. And maybe the way to do that is to have a stronger electromagnetic field," Phillip said.

"And if I choose not to destroy it, what else can be done?" Adam said.

"Well, first of all, if its location can be pinpointed, we'd need to stabilize it for just a few seconds, and then we could force it into a container where it would be made harmless," Phillip said.

"What kind of container are you talking about?" Running-water said.

"I would guess something made of lead."

"How big a container?" Samuel said.

"Actually I have no idea," Phillip said.

Adam knew that this evil thing, whatever it was, wouldn't be lured into a trap. Had it not reached into a police car and caused it to crash? And had it not reached behind the wall of a prison and killed Joseph? Distance didn't seem to be an issue for it. Material substance didn't hold it back. Adam also knew that those around him needed to be occupied. He decided to add a lead-lined box to the list of materials Running-water would be ordering.

When the equipment Phillip wanted arrived, they began installing what appeared to be lightning rods around the perimeter of the cleared area of the compound. These were steel rods with elongated reversed glass teardrops on their tops. Each rod was connected by a thin copper wire and this was in turn connected to a strange looking voltmeter. Running-water stifled a laugh when a temperature gauge was set up in the middle of the open compound and several in the main building. Both of this fed information to a computer in the house which was the center of the electronic shield that was being set up. A Trifield Electromagnetic Meter was installed along with a harmonic resonator and like the other strange equipment, they provided an endless stream of data to the ravenous stomach of the computer.

"I'd like you to show us the patterns on your computer," Adam said, speaking to Paul and Phillip.

The computer was soon up and running and a fractal pattern began to emerge. The colors displayed were mostly blue but there were a few yellow patterns and numerous red dots that appeared to move rapidly throughout the compound. These were the workers moving about. Their body heat was being recorded.

"Can you translate this pattern into a Medicine Wheel?" Adam said, speaking to Phillip.

"What you got in mind?" Running-water said.

"I'd like the rods to create an electronic Medicine Wheel," Adam said

"We can rearrange the rods into any configuration you want," Paul said.

"How much time do you think we have?" Running-water said.

Before Adam could answer the monitor lit up in a new bright fractal design. The colors were brilliant. "Doppler Radar," Phillip said, making some adjustments on the computer.

"Doppler Radar? I thought that had something to do with weather," Samuel said.

"It does, but there are other implications. Electromagnetic radiation emitted by a moving object also exhibits the Doppler Effect. If the object is coming toward you, in this case, our equipment, the radiation frequency increases. If it's moving away from our equipment, the frequency decreases," Phillip said.

"So, something just set off this equipment. How do you know what set it off?" Running-water said.

"Good question. We know that certain types of objects emit specific radiation levels. We can identify an airplane, for example, as opposed to an incoming thunderstorm. If you'll excuse me, I'll go and rearrange the rods into a Wheel. I'll make another check and then I think we'll have about everything ready," Phillip said.

"I'll go with you. I want to check that the electrical work has been completed," Running-water said.

"What's left?" Samuel said.

"Dowsing Rods for each of us."

"You've got to be kidding. Those are for water detection," Samuel said.

"True, but they are also used to determine electrical current. Let me give you a simple demonstration, Phillip said, handing a straight piece of heavy gauge wire Samuel. "Bend it at the one end to a forty-five-degree angle. Now hold the bent end between your thumb and forefinger. Not too tight. Leave it loose. Now watch."

The dowsing rod began to move, hesitated for a moment, and then settled in the direction of the generator that was in the powerhouse.

"I'll be damned," Samuel said.

"Now go outside and see where it points," Phillip said, heading out.

Outside, the rod bent toward the ground, attracted to the current flowing in the

wires to the lights that had been installed along the driveway.

"Okay. So how does all this help us?" Will Rexford said.

"It will help pinpoint the direction of the energized anomaly. Just another way of locating it. Just remember where the generator and the underground wiring are located," Phillip said.

"I'd still like to see us use concave mirrors as part of the defense system," Paul said.

"And where would you put such mirrors?" Adam said.

"I'd use the outer casings of large searchlights, install low wattage lighting around the edges of the mirrors. I'd keep them covered until this djinni is within range, and then I'd open them up. It's my understanding that if you turn evil upon itself, it will destroy itself," Paul said.

"Hmm. You may be right about that," Phillip said. "It's worth a try."

"I assume you really want to destroy this thing once and for all; that it's not to be captured and studied. I hope you are not intending to make it an object of study, Phillip. If you are you could end up getting us all killed," Paul said.

"We'll not attempt to capture it. It has to be destroyed. Only one of us can survive. Either it will or I will. And again, Phillip and Paul, I warn you that this may cost you your lives," Adam said.

"As I've said before, I've lived too long already," Phillip said.

"Goes for me, too," Paul said.

Adam was pleased with their new cooperation and respect. "At least something is going the way it should," he thought.

[1] Chthonic powers means dark powers from beneath the earth. Taken from Arthur Versluis' *Sacred Earth: The Spiritual Landscape of Native America.* P.60. Inner Traditions International. Rochester VT. 1992. Originally appeared in Tompkins' *Universal Sign Language of the Plains Indians,* 1926.

CHAPTER FIFTY ONE

The delivered searchlights were dismantled, and their concave mirrors made ready. All had been done that could be done. The battle lines had been drawn. It was time for the two warriors to cleanse themselves. Warriors? That's what the two had become—Adam and Running-water—warriors and it took a while for that fact to sink in. Most of their previous battles had been with humans; the exception being Moon-Woman. And that battle had been for Running-water's soul. If their current enemy is Moon-Woman she had become very powerful and had grown in boldness.

Adam leaned back in one of the large red leather chairs he had brought from Esaugetuh's ranch. He felt safe in it; feeling close to his father. Early spring required a fire in the massive fireplace and he needed its comforting warmth to soothe his troubled thoughts. As his thoughts rambled he remembered the personal effects of Moon-Woman that had been delivered. He got up, went into his office, and opened the package and took its contents back into the great room with him.

The obsidian amulet that had once belonged to Howahkan, the Wisdom Keeper, and that now hung around his neck, glowed constantly. Adam felt its power rhythmically flowing through his young body. Habit found him thumbing it. Its sharp edges cut his finger and the blood that dripped onto the shoe he held sizzled. Grabbing its gold chain he tried to rip it off. That was a mistake. The more he pulled, the tighter it became. His head throbbed. He was sure he was going to pass out. Then he heard.

Don't remove the obsidian. It will save your life!

He didn't know where the voice came from but that warning reminded him of the time he was lost in the deep woods in Canada. Then, as now, he had tried to jerk the obsidian and its chain from his neck. And like then, it didn't work. He got up from the chair, sat down on the floor, cross-legged, back straight, shoulders back. He slowly inhaled and exhaled. Gradually his breathing returned to its natural rhythm. He relaxed as the building anxiety subsided. The obsidian loosened.

Running-water walked in and seeing Adam seated on the floor, meditating, waited until Adam recognized his presence.

"Come, sit with me," Adam said.

"What's on your mind?" Running-water said as he sat down beside his friend.

Adam explained his experience with the amulet and how his blood had sizzled when it landed on one of Moon-Woman's shoes. Together they opened the diary. Its pages were filled with strange symbols and writing. One symbol caught their attention; the same as had been on the arms of three of the Brothers.

"Scan one page, put it out on the Internet and see if you can find out what it means," Adam said.

"No problem."

"Good. After that, we have some private preparations to make, just the two of us. Do you remember our trip to the sacred place in Arizona? There you built a sweat lodge for me. We need to do that again, and afterward, I'll tell you of my vision quest. I've never told anyone because

Esaugetuh had disappeared. He would have been the one to whom I should have revealed my vision since he was my spiritual guide," Adam said.

"I am honored, my brother. I'll begin building the sweat lodge as soon as I'm done on the computer," Running-water said, getting up to leave.

"Earlier, I thought I sensed someone else in the building. Have you had any such feelings?" Adam said.

"No. Perhaps someone from the work crew had not left the building?" Running-water said.

"Perhaps."

Early on in their relationship, Running-water had learned to trust Adam's gut instincts. As he walked into the large stairway hall, he thought caught a glimpse of movement, a shadow along the wall. As he walked down the hallway he cautiously checked each room. Ending with the library, Running-water slowly pushed back its large oak sliding doors. No one there. Shrugging his shoulders, he went to the office, scanned one page of Moon-Woman's diary, sent it out on the web, and waited for a reply. Within minutes he had an answer from a professor of esoteric literature. It was an incantation, calling upon the dark powers. There was a time he would have scoffed at such an idea but since his association with Adam, he had learned that anything was possible. He printed out the information and headed back to Adam. Because there was a commotion at the main door, he stopped to see what was going on. When he opened it, he was confronted by a very excited and animated Samuel.

"It's wild! Really wild. My god, you won't believe what's happening."

"What? What are you talking about?" Running-water said trying to calm him down.

"Come see for yourself. There must be a thousand," Samuel said.

"Geese?"

It was not uncommon to have huge flocks of geese in the fields of northwestern Washington;

Sometimes tens of thousands would converge in a large open field devouring everything in sight and leaving a muddy-shitty mess. Flatlands were their normal habitat so it would be unusual for them to be at this elevation. With Samuel's continued urging, Running-water stepped out onto the new portico. And like Samuel, he was astounded. He couldn't believe his eyes. Hundreds of people. Native Americans and First Nation People from Canada had arrived. The tong-tong beat of drums shattered the stillness of the place. Suddenly they were on their feet, all of them, moving with the beat of the drums as they merged into giant two circles. The rhythmic pattern of the 'hu-hu-hu-hu' flooded his senses as he remembered the time he was near death in a Pennsylvania hospital and the People came and they danced, and Adam had fought death to save his soul. And more recently on the mountain where the helicopter crashed, there had been the fire and the drums. Those images brought tears to Running-water's eyes and unashamedly he let them roll down his handsome face.

So much has passed between us.

He felt it, sensed it, and knew it. It was a sudden realization. That's just the way it was. His time had come. He would face his death with dignity. He was a warrior. And that's what warriors did—they died!

Feeling a hand on his shoulder, Running-water turned. It was Adam and for a moment their eyes locked and all his concerns faded away. Almost all of his concerns: Isha and their twin sons weighed heavy on his heart. Inwardly he wondered if the twins would always remember him. He handed Adam the printout.

"We need to destroy that diary. Burn it," Adam said.

The dancers stopped, the chanting stopped, the drums stopped. All was quiet. No bird chirped or fluttered its wings; all night creatures hushed their chatter, and the trees stood elegantly still. The high mountain mist began its descent, a Sandburg moment [1], an Ectoplasmic mist surrounded everything. A soft glow from their central fire created mute specters, shadowy figures. However, one among them, clothed in a long black cloak, moved off into deeper shadows, ever watchful. Adam caught that momentary movement.

The drums began again, the song filled the night air, and the moving feet keep the rhythm. "Hu-ya-hu-a-hu-ya' vibrated as did the hearts of those who chanted. Once again the chanting and dancing stopped. Two men stepped forward, each carrying something.

"Wicasa Wakan [2], I bring you a gift from your spirit guide."

"Welcome, Joseph Cornflower. It's been a long time since our last meeting," Adam said.

"And so it has but now those times live only in memory," Joseph Cornflower said. "I bring you the feathers of your spirit guide, our sacred totem, the eagle. And I bring you the Canupa, the sacred pipe of our people."

"Thank you, brother," Adam said, accepting first the feathers, and then the pipe.

Holding the pipe to the North, Adam said, "Great Spirit overall, fill us with

Your Light. Turning to the East, he said, "Give us the wisdom to understand." Turning to the South, holding the pipe high, Adam said, "Fill our hearts with courage." And turning to the West, and offering the pipe, Adam said, "Teach us to walk tall in your eyes."

Using a lighted stick that had been brought to him, Adam lit the pipe and drew on it, held the smoke, and slowly exhaled. The sweetness of the tobacco mixed with kinnikinic drifted slowly upward and disappeared in the fog. Adam then passed the pipe to Running-water, a statement to all who watched that he was held above all others—chieftains, other medicine men, or seers. Those gathered accepted this; it was not a slight. All had heard of Running-water's great heroism and he had the right to such an honor.

"Ikaee Wicasa."

Adam strained to see who it was that called out his Sioux name.

"Who is it that calls me?" Adam said.

"I am Long Walker. You know me. I bring you a special gift from your father."

Adam's heart pounded wildly. He knew of no gift or anything else that had not been accounted for in the many days of inventory at the ranch as well as at Karuna House.

"Come into the light," Adam said.

Long Walker, stepping out from the crowd, handed Adam a shield and said, "This vision shield was made by your father, the great Esaugetuh, Master of Breath."

Adam looked at the shield. He had never seen anything so beautiful. The tanned leather held taut on its circular wooden birch frame, had in its center, an eagle made of real gold. By its look, it had been hammered by hand. It was held in place by leather thongs. Its eye was a large diamond. The bolt of lightning and a single arrow were made of hammered silver. The arrow's head was made of lapis lazuli. Hanging from the circle were seven eagle feathers attached to the rim of the shield by gold round fasteners.

Wishing that his father had given it to him after he came down from the mountain where he had sought his vision, Adam held it high above his head so those assembled could see. Then turning to Long Walker Adam said, "How is that you are just now giving me my Vision Quest Shield?"

"It was delivered to me just a few weeks ago. It took time to locate you," Long Walker said.

"Who brought it to you?" Adam said.

"It was delivered by UPS. I was not asked to sign for it. Is all this important?" Long Walker said.

"Yes, but only to me. Thank you for your kindness. I would like you and Joseph Cornflower to join us inside," Adam said.

Once again those that had gathered took up the tong-tong beat of the drums. The synchronized dancers moved in four circles, each with a circle of dancers inside. The inner circle of dancers moved in the opposite direction of those on the outside. They would dance all night. The villagers felt the vibrations; some were fearful. Mothers checked their children while men made sure their guns were loaded. It was Moussorgsky's *Night on Bald Mountain* [3] come to life.

As Adam, his two old friends, Running-water, and Samuel turned to go back into the monastery, a young man called out to Adam. He was tall, angular, and broad-shouldered. His black hair, freshly oiled, shone in the firelight.

"I am He Who Walks Alone. I would like to join you. My father says to do so I need to cleanse myself. I ask permission to build a sweat lodge."

But before Adam could answer several dozen other young men came forward and were soon joined by all those who had gathered. Everyone sat down and waited. All wished to participate. All desired the sweat lodge. The wanted the eneepe [4] to engulf them so they would be purified, made ready for battle. That's why they had come—to do battle in the way of tradition.

Adam agreed to the construction of a sweat lodge, asked that the Grandfathers among them appoint guardians, keepers of the fire.

Addressing the crowd, Adam said, "I note women are here also. And since many are tribal chiefs I believe it is appropriate that women should enter the sweat lodge if they wish." [5]

Applause gave him an answer. And accepting that as a cue, the group stood up, split and began the unloading of trucks, SUV's, trailers, and cars. The fog, becoming denser, set out to impede their work. The grounds were lighted; some turned their vehicles around and turned on their headlights. In protest, the fog lifted, but by early morning it had come back with a vengeance. It was impossible to see two feet in front of you. Yet stubborn perseverance would not be dissuaded. The workers completed the sides of the pole building by midday. And since they were preparing for a Hanblecheyapi, [6] food was not taken.

By nightfall, a canvas patchwork roof had been put in place. The sides were covered by dozens and dozens of blue tarps. The entrance to the large circular building was covered with heavy handwoven blankets. Inside, a large fire pit had been dug and its bed laid in. Cedar boughs were cut and put on the earth to make a soft pleasant scented flooring. Some of the women took it upon themselves to make tobacco prayer ties. These were two-inch squares of red and yellow cotton cloth. Each square filled with a pinch of tobacco and then tied in a continuous string. Their nimble fingers had made a thousand. The prayer ties were fastened around the outside of the sweat lodge. Four maple poles were cut. To these were attached strips of blue and white silk, and to each of these were attached an eagle feather. These were posted at each side of the entrance to the sweat lodge, seven feet apart in keeping with their belief that the number seven was sacred.

Inside, Adam and Running-water watched Moon-Woman's diary burn; its flames shooting up through the massive fireplace chimney—a protest as sparks flew out over the roof. Then Adam went back outside and busied himself looking for seven sacred stones or Tunkan. He would know them by their warmth; something Esaugetuh had taught him while preparing for his vision quest. After checking several, sensing their inner strength, he selected those he considered worthy. These he placed seven inches apart within the inner circle of the fire pit. Once he was satisfied with their placement he returned to the monastery.

[1] Carl Sandburg. *Fog* in *Chicago Poems*. New York: Henry Holt and Company, 1916, p. 71.
[2] Sacred seer or holy man, a guide. Pronounced as 'wih CHAH shah wah KAHN'.
[3] Modest Moussorgsky. 1867. A fantasy for orchestra.
[4] Purifying vapors made from fir, sweet grass, tobacco and other natural ingredients.
[5] Menstruating women were not allowed.
[6] From the Sioux, meaning a lamenting for a vision.

CHAPTER FIFTY-TWO

"Certainly a touch of irony here," Adam said.

"Irony?" Running-water said.

"Yes. A Christian Monastery is to be the battleground of a bunch of heathens."

"You've forgotten I'm a baptized Christian. I assumed you were. But what difference does it make, Adam? I mean what difference does it make what we call that which created all?" Running-water said. "Isn't what's important the recognition of our spirituality?

"As far as I am concerned, it makes no difference. It's the acknowledgment of the divine and of that divinity in each of us that is important. Too bad our early ancestors, the Anasazi could not see that and stop their religious war," Adam said.

"Seems to me that man's history is full of religious wars. We just don't seem to get it," Running-water said.

"Yeah, you are so right. Want to give me a hand?"

"Sure. What do you want me to do?" Running-water replied.

"We need to make wasna."

They went to the kitchen and began making wasna, a mixture of dried meat, berries, and fat. This was put in a large wooden bowl which was to be placed at the top of a tall pole. It was an offering to the eagles, Adam's sacred totem. A gift of meat formed into a ball was prepared for the cougar, the sacred totem of Running-water. Come morning, they would set out their special offerings. And each would pray in his own way.

Elsewhere, Samuel, Will, Phillip, and Paul kept themselves busy tweaking the security system. In the time they had been together at Karuna House, Samuel had never seen Phillip and Paul show so much cooperation. They had always been distant. He now understood that distance was suspicion.

Guess people can change. I did.

Yet their sudden brotherliness struck him as too sudden.

The time had come for those who would cleanse themselves to enter the sweat lodge. Each had made his prayers and each removed his clothes and placed them in a bundle at the entrance to the sweat lodge. Several hundred filed in, no one spoke, and each seated himself according to position and tribe. The last did not indicate a lesser tribe or personage. They had been selected by the draw of the straw. Running-water came to the entrance, removed his clothing, entered, and went to the front where he seated himself, legs crossed. His back straight, head erect, and eyes open. He surveyed the mass of people in front of him, searching, checking every movement. He had secreted his set of twin Glocks in what appeared to be a prayer bundle. Under no circumstance would he allow himself not to be armed while Adam's security was essential. He had let that happened once and had made a sacred vow not to let it happen again.

Adam came to the opening, stripped off his clothes and entered. No one looked up as Ikaee Wicasa, the Wicasa Wakan walked to the front. There, next to Running-water, on his right, Adam seated himself. As he did, a shadowy figure squatted just inside the entrance. His long black cape helped conceal him from the ever watchful Running-water. Sensing its presence, Adam opened his eyes.

Did you see something move at the entryway? He said to Running-water.

No, my brother. You want me to go and check?
No. Just stay alert.

CHAPTER FIFTY-THREE

Samuel positioned himself outside the sweat lodge, a few feet from its entrance so he would have a broader view of the area. He carried a pair of Uzis and had automatics strapped to his hips. He looked Rambo-ish, standing sentinel. He remembered how the 'old one' as Esaugetuh was called, had rescued him from a severe beating by a gang of thugs. He had wandered into one of the darker areas of Toronto and nearly didn't live to regret it. Esaugetuh's chauffer slammed his fists into the leader of the gang, breaking his neck. The others took off on a run. He had been nearly unconscious when he felt the most wonderful warmth flow through his body. When he could finally see, he saw the most wondrous azure blue eyes peering at him from beneath a wide-brimmed black hat. Unlike the other members of The Brothers, he had chatted with Esaugetuh on several occasions.

I wonder why Adam has never asked me how I met his father.

The whirr of a helicopter approaching set him in motion. A quick call to Will Rexford set him on the run. Jumping into his ATV Samuel sped toward the helipad. The lights came on as the chopper sat down. Will Rexford arrived on a second ATV just as a second helicopter began its approach for landing. Those on board were loaded into the two ATVs and whisked at break-neck speed back to the sweat lodge.

With a flourish, the canvas door to the sweat lodge was flung open and three dazzling women entered. They were dressed in white leather; Miigis shell belts hung from their waists and around their necks were lapis lazuli, turquoise, and sterling necklaces. Their black hair, pulled back and tied in a single braid, glistened in the soft firelight. First to walk through the center of the circle was Daphne with two of her sons; she was followed by Cornelia, her mother, who carried the other two of the quads. Next, Isha came with her twin sons. With deliberate show of authority, the women uncovered their children, laid them upon the scented boughs in front of their fathers. And they, like their fathers, were naked. Without a word, the three women dropped their clothing, walked to the right of their husbands, and squatted. The naked grandmother of the offered children, sat down between her grandchildren, keeping her head bowed.

The women had come and they had brought the ultimate sacrifice, their children—special children—Indigo children. They had taken a sacred vow that if their men should die, they would die with them. Unable to dissuade them, the grandmother decided that if her only son and daughter were to die and if her grandsons were to die, she too would die, knowing that they would join together once again in the afterlife.

Neither Adam nor Running-water moved to greet their families. Only the keepers of the fires and the one in the shadows saw these women. All others had their eyes closed as they sought their peace through hambeday; solitary prayer.

CHAPTER FIFTY-FOUR

At the helicopters, old friends greeted one another. Dutch and Brett took up their positions with Samuel and Will Rexford. Samuel noticed a slight coolness between Brett and Will Rexford.

And unlike their two comrades, he noticed that neither Dutch nor Brett seemed to be armed. Samuel thinking this was unusual asked them where their guns were. He had never seen them without their weapons. Within minutes he had his answer. Dutch and Brett, thanks to the research of Running-water's uncle Gordon Rapport, had come armed with a different kind of weapon. They had set up miniature Gatling Guns with unusual shell chambers. Instead of the standard shell, a round ball was required for each of the ten barrels of each gun. The gun could be elevated as high as 95 degrees or lowered to 25 degrees. Each gun could rotate 360 degrees.

Samuel was nearly beside himself. Curiosity claimed him. He blurted, "What kind of guns are these?"

So absorbed with the assembly of the two machine guns, Samuel had not noticed two figures had slipped out of one of the helicopters. As he bent over to get a closer look at these guns and their strange shells, his butt was pinched. He stood up with such force that he nearly knocked over one of the guns.

"You do have such a cute ass, you know," Julie smirked as she grabbed her husband around his neck, and kissed him.

Samuel could barely utter her name. He was elated and just as quickly that elation turned to fear and concern.

"You should not be here. It's very dangerous. Leave immediately."

"Not in this life, kiddo. You're stuck with me. I'm not going to be left alone to go back on the streets as a drunken bitch of a whore."

That caught Dutch by surprise. Brett gave him a nudge. They knew that Adam had brought her from a life of prostitution, but to hear a woman refer to herself as a whore was a different kind of statement.

"Damn! That Samuel must be something else," Dutch said.

"What do you mean by that?" Brett said.

"You know. To be able to satisfy a whore."

"Who's a whore?" Patricia Livingston said.

"Eavesdropping are you Mrs. Montana?" Brett said.

"Couldn't help but overhear you, two loudmouths. And if I were you I'd be careful about talking about whores. I want to get inside that sweat lodge. Can you get me in without a ruckus? I wanted to slip in with Daphne, Cornelia, and Isha but I had trouble with my damn video camera."

"Guess you can just walk in. They are all naked in there, so keep the video clean," Dutch warned.

"Always the tease," Patricia Livingston Montana said. "Now if you were in there."

She knew she had to be very careful. It wasn't necessary for Dutch to warn her like that. Jesus, the way he carries on, you'd think I was a green kid on my first assignment. If I can get in and close enough I'll be able to capture a very special spiritual ceremony—something that has not been done before.

And she knew if her luck held, and that's what she had to call it, luck, she'd get to video Adam doing one of his shaman things. She hurried to the sweat lodge. As she slipped in between the canvas tarps that hung down over the opening, an unusually pleasant aroma, slightly sweet seemed to bathe her whole being. Its subtleness melded into her consciousness as she slowly inched her way along the outer wall, trying to adjust to the darkness. She stifled a scream when she felt a hand pulling her down.

It took a couple of minutes for her to realize that the person who had pulled her down was fully clothed as she was. It was just an image. Nothing definable. Any sense of fear left her as she concentrated on managing her camera, getting it at an angle where she could film the shadowy figure next to her. At that moment, the figure turned to her. Azure blue eyes flashed at her as he folded her within his black cape. Her heart pounded wildly. And for a brief moment, fear returned. But before she could react, she heard him.

"Even though you are one of the women in *his* group, it would not be wise to be caught filming this sacred ceremony. My cape will shield you from the ever watchful eyes of his protector."

Patricia Livingston opened her mouth to speak but he placed a finger on her lips.

"Come. Move with me. We'll get you closer to the front. If I stop, you stop. You understand? If you do, say nothing, just touch me."

Slowly, working their way around the circular side of the sweat lodge, they came to the left side of Running-water and Adam. Patricia Livingston's camera softly whirred as she panned the group, zeroed in on Adam and back to Running-water. Once she thought he had caught her.

Got to be more careful. That was too close.

She wasn't quite sure at what point she became aware of the change. Her escort, whoever he was, pulled her back down to the ground as he sat down. She finally heard the sound as it increased in pitch. She looked at Adam and he had become a blue transparency and the small ones at his feet began to glow. The humming sound was joined by a slow beat of drums. Yet there were no drums or drummers present. Awestruck, the keepers of the fire, froze in their places.

The pitch of the humming leveled and the sweat lodge filled with strange apparitions that floated in and out of the large room. Moaning rose up from some of those present; some keeled over in a swoon.

"Who is it that dares call us from our rest?"

"I am Adam Kadmon, [1] I am Adam Kasia, [2] I am Ikaee Wicasa [3]

"And so you are!" Boomed the voice. "Why have you called us from our rest?"

"Your people seek your wisdom." Adam said.

"And why do they do that?"

"One of our members has fallen; one who has gone to the other side and who now desires to bring great harm to your people," Adam said.

"And why should we help you?"

"Because we are your children because we honor you. Your spirit is our spirit, we are one with you," Adam said.

"Ananda."

"Ananda," Adam said, " And may you also experience the continued blessing of spiritual love."

The humming stopped. The blue aura surrounding Adam diminished. The fire keepers moved to replenish the fire but stopped. Adam had indicated that the flap of the lodge should be opened. Patricia Livingston turned to thank her unseen escort, but she was alone, but not unnoticed.

Unashamed of his nudity, Adam strolled up to Patricia Livingston. She blushed and that surprised her.

"Don't be embarrassed. I see you have been filming our ceremony. I would like to see it, all of it. When you have time would you and Brett join us at the house?"

All she managed to do was nod her head in agreement.

My God! You are such a hunk! There's isn't a woman here who wouldn't --- She caught herself, remembering Adam could mind read.

Outside, Adam started to walk back to the house. Daphne caught up with him, handed him his clothes.

"Show off," Daphne said, laughing.

He slipped his arm around her. He felt her firm breast rub against him. He was glad she had returned.

"Oh, what's that?" Patricia Livingston said, pointing at the night sky.

Fireballs were flying across the sky. Everyone was awed by the display. Running-water, Isha, and Cornelia joined them as they walked along. Isha was carrying their twins and with each flash, she felt them vibrate.

"Sure is unusual for this time of year. I was sure the Taurid meteor showers [4] weren't until fall," Running-water said.

"Adam, the quads are behaving in a strange manner," Daphne said taking the other two of them from her mother.

Adam took the four boys. Holding them, he felt their vibrations. Then he heard them.

The time is fast approaching, father. We are ready.

"We should go in now," Adam said, indicating that they should hurry.

"I'll be right with you I want to check something," Running-water said.

"No! Come!" Adam said. "Tell Samuel that he and Julie are to come into the house immediately."

"How'd you know Julie is here?" Patricia Livingston said.

"Remember he's psychic," Daphne said.

Samuel and Julie joined the group at the house. Adam, taking Samuel aside, spoke to him in whispered tones. He left immediately. On a fast run, he stopped long enough to deliver a message to Dutch and Brett. From there he went to the sweat lodge. Taking a deep breath, sucking in his gut, and throwing back his shoulders, Samuel entered the lodge. Posturing in his best military stance to cover his nervousness, he turned on the million candlepower halogen spotlight he carried. Carefully, sweeping the areas from side to side as he walked along, Samuel found no one still inside. He went outside, walked the perimeter of the sweat lodge, dousing its sides with gasoline as he went. As soon as he had completed the circle, he lit a match, tossed it on the tent. With a loud poof, the entire structure burst into flames.

Those who had come to join Adam in his fight rushed to put out the fire. Samuel, with double Uzis, stopped them.

"Adam has asked me to tell you that your prayers have been sent on the tongues of the flames. He thanks you and asks that you meet on the lawn in front of the portico."

He lowered his guns and walked back toward the house. As he approached a small grotto of trees, he heard someone giggling. Cautiously, he crept closer to the trees. This time the giggles were more pronounced and he was able to identify the exact location. He turned on the spotlight. The young man who first asked to join Adam, He Who Walks Alone, was naked with a fully erect large penis, and lying beneath him, waiting for him, was a naked young girl. Samuel held his spotlight on her, admiring her firm conical breast. Like his Julie, she was stacked. Turing the spotlight back to the young man.

"I think I ought to take you to—,"

A tug at his arm silenced him.

"Turn off that light and leave them to their pleasure. There's more for you to do before this night is over."

Samuel was sure he had heard that voice before. He turned the spotlight back on. No one was there. He did a 360. No one. He thought he'd ask the young couple if they heard anyone but thought better of it.

Turning to them he said, "As you were."

He waited for a moment. He heard the familiar grunt as the young man made contact Then he left.

[1] Hebrew. Means 'primordial man'.
[2] Iranian Mythology. Means 'soul of the first man'.
[3] Sioux. Means 'original man'.
[4] These fireballs were witnessed during October and November of 2005 in Germany, Japan, Canada, The Netherlands, and the United States. They come from the constellation, Taurus.

CHAPTER FIFTY-FIVE

In the large great room of the monastery, Adam brought his immediate and extended family together. In the old days, it had been the room where hotel guests hobnobbed with one another and before that where young ladies sat crocheting. The carpenters had done a beautiful job in restoring its past beauty. The rich tones of the mahogany wood reflected the light from the fireplace. The marble floor, shiny clean now, revealed its subtle blue borders. The high ceiling with its scrolled squares and centered rosettes sparkled with its long chained crystal chandeliers. When Dutch and Brett entered with Patricia Livingston and Julie they were struck by its beauty. Phillip and Paul, who were now considered part of the extended family, came in next. Running-water was busy connecting a video cam to a large screen television that had been installed above the fireplace mantel. Samuel and Will Rexford were not present. Patricia handed her video cam to Running-water.

"Where's Samuel?" Julie said.

"He and Will Rexford are on an errand for me. They'll be back after a bit. Patricia's video may give us a clue as to who our mystery guest is. I've sensed him for some time, even back on the train. Running-water has told me that he has seen someone lurking about. I think our security system has failed. Phillip and Paul your system has failed to pick up this individual. I believe you said the dowsing rods would indicate the presence of an apparition. Yet they have not. That tells me that our mystery guest is human," Adam said.

"The video is ready to roll anytime you are," Running-water said.

Patricia Livingston liked what she saw. She had captured many faces showing various prayerful expressions—beautiful peaceful faces. She was delighted that she had caught the blue glow that had surrounded the six babies as they lay upon the cedar boughs. But what brought a gasp from her was when her lens was turned on Adam. She not only caught the blue glowing aura that surrounded him but caught his transition into blue light making him nearly transparent. She had caught his outline and at the same time, you could see right through him to the back wall of the sweat lodge. The viewers had held their breaths as they watched this phenomenon and they expelled it simultaneously.

"Damn! You didn't get him," Adam said.

"I'm sorry, Adam," Patricia Livingston said, sensing Adam's disappointment. "I was sure I got a couple of shots of whoever it was. Running-water can you reverse that video and then slow it down?"

The video was rewound and slowed down.

"I don't think I can slow it anymore. We may not have the necessary editing equipment unpacked," Running-water said.

"Hold it! There! That's your man," Patricia Livingston said, jumping up and down. "I didn't think I'd lost my touch."

"It can't be! My god, it just can't be. It's not possible. He's dead! I have his ashes to prove it," Adam said.

"Back it up, focus the frame, see if you can capture it, and then enlarge it. I know I got his eyes. They glowed," Patricia Livingston said.

"I'll try. The editing program on my laptop is not the most sophisticated," Running-water said, rerouting the video.

"I saw his decomposed body. I know that as a fact," Adam said.

"You can't be sure. You saw the remains of a body with some strands of long white hair," Running-water said.

"I got the ring he had clutched in his hand, the ring inscribed with my mother's name," Adam said.

"But that ring could have been planted. If you really saw him in that room at Karuna House, then someone is now playing a very dangerous game," Running-water said.

Echoing thunderously throughout the monastery, rattling the beautiful cut crystal chandeliers, and thumping against Adam's heart came the resounding, "You haven't learned much have you?"

"Where are you? Damn it! Come out! Show yourself whoever you are. Only cowards hide," Adam said.

"How soon you forget. I told you I am wherever you are. Change your perspective."

The group was stunned into silence by this voice that seemed to rush like howling wind throughout the building. For once in her life, Patricia Livingston was unable to utter a sound. She felt her husband's hand clutch hers. She was grateful that Brett was there. Julie had sunk into one of the chairs and buried her face in her hands. Daphne, trying to comfort Julie, whispered to her that Samuel would soon be returning.

"Come out and do it now!" Adam's voice boomed.

"You really haven't learned much, have you?"

It was then that Adam noticed that there was something different in the room. Squatting down, Indian style, he looked around. He noticed a dark object in the far corner of the room.

"Ah, so you have changed your perspective. But you failed to change your perception," the voice said, quieter now

As the figure unfurled itself in the corner, Adam heard a groan as it stood up. For a moment, the figure seemed to struggle to steady itself and then it stepped into the light.

"Esaugetuh!" Adam yelled.

CHAPTER FIFTY-SIX

Adam's mind was at war; fighting with what he knew and what he was seeing. His long search for his missing father had ended at Karuna House in Toronto when he had found decaying
human remains bricked up in a small room. Then, as now, his stomach did a flip-flop. He still remembered the terrible sickening smell. He felt his soul had been wrenched from him. The wedding ring with his mother's name inscribed inside was clutched by the skinless bony hand of the corpse. And here— now— standing before him was his father.

How can this be? What cruelty is this?

"Ah, still full of questions are you? But before I get to those there is something I need to tell you and then I'll give you my full attention," Esaugetuh said.

"You have got a hell of a lot of explaining to do. Do you realize what you've—,"

Adam didn't have a chance to finish his sentence. Esaugetuh raised his hand, held it palm outward, and drew a circle in the air. All time stopped. No one moved. And for a moment, they experienced eternity, a never-ending flow of non-beingness.

"I love you. I've always wanted to tell you that but I avoided it because I really thought you would reject me. I was willing to settle for just having you around for a few months, seeing you once in a while, or coming to you through time. That has never been enough. I want you to know that I love you more than life itself. Forgive me," Esaugetuh said, struggling to control the quiver in his voice.

Adam grabbed his father, hugged him, cried, laughed and began to dance and whoop around the room. Realizing he still held his father, Adam stopped.

"I'm sorry, Old One. Are you okay?" Adam said.

"Yes quite all right. Just a bit out of breath. A glass of brandy would be nice about now,' Esaugetuh said, sitting down.

Adam served his father a glass of the favored aged brandy and then offered a drink to the others. And as in days gone by, Esaugetuh took out his clay pipe, carefully filled it, lit it, and relaxed in the familiar large red leather chair. The rings of smoke slowly floated upward as he exhaled. The smell of aromatic red willow bark soon filled the room. Nothing was said between them as Adam sat looking at his father, memorizing every wrinkle, noticing the slight flare of his nostrils, and the set of his azure blue eyes. These would be permanently etched into his psyche.

Finally, Esaugetuh passed the pipe, a sign of social acceptance and hospitality. Adam took a hit and slowly exhaled. He then passed the pipe to Running-water and from him to the rest of those present. For a moment, as they sipped their brandy, savored its flavor, and enjoyed the smoke of the pipe, the world vanished from their view.

"Adam, you said you would tell me of your vision quest. Esaugetuh is here now. Perhaps you would share it with all of us," Running-water said.

"It is extremely difficult for me to describe what happened while on my Vision Quest. It was at once painful, joyful, unreal, real, fearful, and awesome. I was flattened to the ground by a force so fierce that I was driven deep into the very bowels of the earth. Dirt and stone bruised me. I felt my lungs being filled with dirt and I was sure I was suffocating. I was traveling so fast the heat seared my skin. And then I was flung out of the earth into outer space. I traveled around the world, looking down upon this fabulous blue planet. I saw a tornado sweep across the plains, a hurricane off the coast of Africa, and an eruption of a volcano.

Suddenly I was hurled into deep space at such a speed I felt my lungs collapse. My eyes bulged. I was sure they were going to explode. And just as suddenly I stopped moving, floated slowly, upright. Before me was the most spectacular sight imaginable. I was seeing what Hubble saw and recorded. Beauty indescribable in its breadth and depth. As I rotated slowly I saw new stars being born, planets being formed. Others being destroyed. Massive explosions and yet I didn't feel them. I was witness to what Esaugetuh calls *fecundity*.

Just as I was really getting into my panoramic mode, strange shapeless beings floated into my view. Some seemed peaceful, others were aggressive. Their faces were large wide-open eyes and gaping mouths, lifeless and empty of all feeling. As I focused on particular shapes they gradually changed to an expression of great sorrow. I was overcome with an uncontrollable urge to weep. I tried calling out to them, a useless effort. Vacuumed silence froze my voice.

I was shot straight up, leveled off, and then hung there. As I looked down I realized I was looking into a swirling vortex. Its outer ring was an Ouroboros. As I continued looking into the vortex I realized I was looking through a fabulous Komodo dragon's eye. The colors were brilliant blues and gold. There seemed to be no end to the depth of the vortex. Slowly out of this marvelous celestial eye floated transparent spheres containing naked bodies— Small humans; miniature adults. I now know the ancients called such beings Homunculi. One particular sphere floated very close to me and hovered, slowly turning so I could see. It shook me to the quick. I saw myself. My I of me. My soul. And we winked at each other; a mutual recognition.

I was again propelled at breakneck speeds throughout the vast expanse of outer space. I was so absorbed by the colors that I almost didn't hear a deep baritone voice slowly filling all space, eroding all time. "Tat tvam Asi!"

I replied, "I am what?" The answer blew me away.

"What was the answer?" Running-water said.

"You are the Self of the Universe, the conscious and the unconscious, the Aham [1].

And what did you say to that?" Esaugetuh said.

"So I am."

"And so you are," Esaugetuh said. A smile penetrated his deep wrinkles.

"But, Old One, what does it all mean?" Adam said.

"Let me begin with the first and most obvious symbol or metaphor. Your plunge into the earth is a reminder that we are made of earth. When you were shot into the air it was to remind you that you are made of air and when you saw the exploding stars it was to remind you that fire was added to your creation."

"Fire?" Running-water said.

"The breath of the Creator. You said you saw shapeless beings floating and that you felt sad and tried to call out to them. Some among us can't be helped because of the choices they have made. Moon-Woman is as good an example I can think of. She burned up the positive energy of her soul. Any advice or help you offer to those who have no positive energy fall upon deaf ears; thus your frozen voice."

"I realize the Ouroboros symbolizes nature's cyclic pattern, but what about those little adults in the spheres?" Adam said.

"You said they came up out of an endless vortex. The vortex suggests eternity and when you saw your Self, that is your soul; it suggests that it is eternal. I suspect all of the Homunculi were your transitory souls. And since you did not indicate any of them were offensive I believe that means your Soul in all its transcendence is safe from corruption."

"Okay," Adam said thoughtfully, "what about those strange words; 'Tat tvam Asi' and 'Aham'?" Adam said.

"A new age is unfolding and you are at its center," Esaugetuh said. "I thought the men I had found were to be the founders of a new age. I have been so terribly mistaken."

The room was so quiet, so totally still, nothing was heard, not even their breathing Finally, Adam spoke.

"Daphne, I want you to present our sons to their grandfather. These children, father, you shall know and not from a distance."

Each of the four boys was handed to Esaugetuh, one at a time. He held each, noting its blue eyes, muted complexion, and he sensed their developing special gift.

"They have not been named. Why is that? And you have not sung their names," Esaugetuh said.

"Adam was under attack when they were born. He has given them borrowed names and because *we* are still under attack, they have not had their names sung," Daphne said.

"And what are their borrowed names?" Esaugetuh said.

"Paul, Jedediah, Gordon, and Zachariah," Adam said.

"All Christian names. What Indian names have they been given?"

"None," Daphne said.

"Uh huh. I see, and do you know if they have chosen their own names?" Esaugetuh said.

"They have. We simply have not sung them. Would you like to have a naming ceremony?" Adam said.

Esaugetuh stood up, pulled a sage bundle from his cloak, lit it, and smudged it over each of the quads. In a quiet baritone, he began to sing a prayer.

Oh, Great Spirit open the Hearts of these Souls.
Oh, Great spirit open—

Open the Hearts of these Souls so they may receive you
Oh, Great Spirit awaken—
Awaken so we may sing you their names
Awaken so their names may be blessed
Oh, Great Spirit open—
Open the Hearts of these Souls so they may know you.

In her heart, Daphne heard the name of her first born. At first, she thought she was hearing things but when his name was said a second time she knew. He is Mahpee which means sky. Then she heard the name of her second born, Mahkah which means earth. The third son called out Miri which means water, and finally the fourth called out his name, Paytah which means fire.

She heard them, in unison, actually more of an undulation, "We are the four elements. We compose all things living and nonliving. We sing of the beauty of our world; we sing of the love that is for all living things, we are because we are."

"And so you are," Esaugetuh said, giving each of the boys to their father. "I believe, he said to Running-water, "that you and your woman have twins boys. And I understand they have had their names sung. And that is good. I would like to meet them."

Isha brought in her sons and introduced them: first in their Christian names of Lance and Colt. Then she spoke their Indian names: Lance is called Moojog [2] and Colt is called Kiim [3] Esaugetuh took each, in turn, smudged them with sage then he sat down on the floor and picking up a small drum, he began to chant.

"Ho-a-a! Ho-a-a! Hu-hu-hu-hu."

Adam and Running-water joined in the chant. The quads and twins glowed as they basked in the manly recognition of their elders. Even though they were but infants, they felt the rhythmic flow of past times that had been transferred to them. And they knew they were unique! Especially the twins since they were older than their cousins. And had they not saved their fathers.

The pleasantness of the moment, that sweet time when parents are filled with love and pride, was interrupted by the clanging of the bell at the main entrance. The security cameras picked up the image of a hulk of a man, a second man, and two smaller figures. With an adjustment of the focus, Phillip brought the images into clear view. Daphne caught the mischievous twinkle in her husband's eyes.

"Ah, Samuel has returned from his errand. Brett, will you let them in, please?" Adam said.

When Samuel and his charges entered Dutch shot up out of his chair. His mouth agape, and like Adam when Esaugetuh made his presence known, stood dumbfounded, incapable of speech. His face flushed red.

"You must be Lilli," Adam said, extending his hand in greeting.

"Yes I am Lilli and this is my daughter, Stephanie."

She felt ill at ease. Uncomfortable in front of the man she divorced within two weeks after their marriage. She would not have come here and allowed herself to be presented to this crowd, had she not been offered a large sum of money if Will hadn't been so insistent. She didn't care who you were, five thousand dollars is a lot of money. And so she stood there waiting for someone to say something.

"I'm sure you and Dutch have much to talk about. Samuel, please show them one of the sitting rooms so they may have some privacy," Daphne said.

"So now all have been accounted for," Running-water said.

"Not quite," Adam said, "there's still one."

"You're right. Wonder where he is," Running-water said, "Maybe Samuel knows."

When Samuel returned from showing Dutch, Lilli and Stephanie a sitting room, Running-water asked him where Will Rexford had gotten off to. He had not come in when Brett opened the door.

"Samuel, you and Brett go and see where Will Rexford is. Take Phillip and Paul with you. I want to talk with Adam," Running-water said.

As they left, Esaugetuh got up to leave but was stopped by Running-water.

"There is no need for you to leave, Old One."

"What's on your mind, my brother?" Adam said.

"We need to decide on a plan of attack. I don't think we should just sit around and wait to be reactive. What can we do against this vermin that constantly threatens our lives? Yes, our lives. Or have you forgotten she tried to kill me in the hospital? Have you forgotten that she drugged me at my grandfather's cabin?" Running-water said.

"You think it's Moon-Woman also. Yet she died in the Pennsylvania jail. So how can it be?" Adam said.

"Look, if your father could fake his death, why isn't it possible that Moon-Woman did the same? Now Joseph seems to have experienced this spontaneous combustion. What if Joseph and Moon-Woman are one and the same?"

"Good god, you're worse with your questions than I am," Adam said.

"Running-water has a point," Esaugetuh said. "Do you have something in mind? Or are we just going to sit around and wait?"

"We've put in all kinds of security systems, called upon our ancestors and our spirit fathers; we've called upon our spirit guides, and we have prayed. What else is there?" Adam said. He was perplexed that his father thought there should be something more. "Why doesn't he suggest something?" Adam thought.

"Why not use your powers to locate her. Take the battle to her. Don't let her choose. The longer you delay the more she learns about you, the stronger and viler she becomes," Esaugetuh said.

"Your father is right. You need to draw her out. You put out a bowl with wasna as an offering for the eagle and a round of meat for the cougar. Why not put out bait for this bitch that torments us?" Running-water said.

"Any suggestions as to what would make good bait?" Adam said.

"Samuel has been a natural conduit, has he not? Use him," Running-water said.

"Use me. What do you want me to do?" Samuel said, entering the living room with Brett.

"No. I won't put him at risk like that. It's just too dangerous," Adam said.

"What is too dangerous?" Samuel asked, "Clue me in."

"I've suggested that Adam use you as bait to draw out the demon since you have been a natural conduit for her," Running-water said.

"I'll do it. Maybe it will put an end to all the killing," Samuel said.

"No. She could destroy you physically or destroy your mind leaving you incapable of even feeding yourself. It's just too risky," Adam said.

"I agree with Adam. It's much too dangerous for you, Samuel. I'll do it. I'm old. Anyway, I've lived long enough," Esaugetuh said.

"Absolutely not! My sons will not be denied knowing their grandfather. I'll do it myself," Adam said.

"That won't work. She'll know you are up to something," Running-water said, turning to Esaugetuh he continued, "Old One, father of my friend, is there nothing we can do to protect Samuel ?"

"There may be a way. Adam if you and I mind meld with Samuel beforehand. If she connects with him we'll know it and have a chance at her. Then she can be destroyed once and for all. If you agree to this, we should begin right now. I'm afraid there's not a whole lot of time left before she makes her move," Esaugetuh said.

"I don't want to destroy her. There's been enough killing. It's got to stop! My sons are the next step in the evolution of higher human consciousness in our people—No! All people. The same holds true of Running-water's twins. What kind of example are we setting for them if we go on with this endless killing?" Adam said.

"What do you propose to do? Just let her kill you? Hell, that won't stop her and you know it. Next, she'll come after our sons and I'll be damned if I'm going to let that happen. She dies! That's that!" Running-water said.

"I know you are concerned as I am, but I ask you to trust me. I will mind-meld with your father and with Samuel. I want Running-water to be part of this meld. He's been through all of this before. His gift is his spiritual strength. I'll plant a subliminal suggestion in each of you with a specific trigger. That's where you'll have to trust me," Adam said.

Curious as to what Adam viewed as his strength Samuel asked, "And what is my strength?"

"Your strength is your loyalty. You have never erred or wavered," Adam said. "For that I am grateful and because of that, I am not willing to make you the lamb.

Curious as to how his son viewed him, Esaugetuh said, "And since we are listing strengths, what do you consider mine to be?"

"Yours, father, is your wisdom. It will be most valuable when we meet Moon-Woman's vile nature. You will see things in her character that the rest of us may miss."

"To change the subject, we didn't find Will Rexford. Not a sign of him. Even his backpack is gone. Where's Dutch? Maybe he can explain," Brett said, joining the group.

"Excuse me. Is it okay if I come in and pick up my tape?" Patricia Livingston said, entering the living room.

"Of course, there's no reason for you to have left. You are family," Adam said.

"The tape? Do you have it?" Patricia Livingston said.

"It's still in the camera," Running-water said.

"The camera's not here. Where's the camera? Damn!" Patricia Livingston said.

"Too much of a coincidence, don't you think? Will is gone and the camera's gone," Samuel said.

"Rewind the security tapes. That should give us an answer," 'Running-water said.

"Brett, while the surveillance tapes are being rewound, ask Dutch to join us. Lilli and Stephanie are to come back in. No use for them to be off by themselves any longer," Running-water said.

The surveillance tapes showed Will Rexford picking up the camera during the excitement of Esaugetuh's emergence.

"You want to see me?" Dutch said, entering the room with unhappy Lilli and Stephanie following close behind.

"What's the story on Will Rexford? We have him stealing Patricia Livingston video camera and he's disappeared. Sure hope you've got some insights and they better be good," Running-water said, adjusting his twin Glocks.

Understanding the implications, Dutch looked directly at Running-water and said, "I don't know where he is and I haven't a clue as to why he would take Patricia's camera. It's not like him. I've known this guy since grade school for Christ's sake. We went through college together as well as training for the Seals. He was picked by the CIA and I just floated around doing fly jobs here and there. I can make a call to see if he's returned to Washington."

"Do that. Phillip and Paul should have come back in by now. Brett, you mind going out to check on them?" Running-water said.

Outside, Brett felt the late night air was heavier than usual. As he began his search for the missing Brothers, he felt the air burning his lungs. It was hard for him to breathe. "Oh shit! Swamp gas," he thought, breaking into a run toward the house.

Gasping and barely able to speak Brett collapsed on the living room floor. Coughing and sputtering he managed to say, "Swamp gas."

"Impossible. There are no swamps up here," Running-water said.

"True, but there is that pond in front of the house. Maybe that's why the place always closed in early spring and didn't reopen until summer," Adam said.

"So what's the big deal. It just stinks, right?" Samuel said.

"Actually there is no odor. It's anaerobic bacterial decomposition. It's highly combustible and very explosive. It's deadly because it causes suffocation," Brett said, still clearing his lungs.

"Suffocation?" Samuel said.

"Yes. It reduces the concentration of oxygen inhaled. Your lungs fill up with the methane and you die," Brett replied, coughing.

"That makes it all the more important for us to find Will, Phillip, and Paul. They may be in serious trouble. There should be some gas masks in one of the boxes we brought from the train. Running-water, check those manifests and find them. Meet me outside," Adam said.

As he left the house, he turned on all the floodlights and then rushed to the camps of those who had come to help him. Most were asleep. He grabbed a drum he found by one of their tents and began beating it. The light sleepers came out of their campers and tents. Shaking their heads, stretching, and yawning. They began to cough. Panic seized some of them because they couldn't breathe.

Adam spotted a couple of cans of kerosene, grabbed both as he continued to look for something he could use as a torch. He found some leftover construction material, soaked it with the kerosene, lit it, and tossed it into the pond. The explosion rattled windows, toppled a couple of tents, and sent everyone scrambling.

"Man you just about singed off my hair. You could have let me know," Running-water said.

"Close call," Adam said, getting up from the ground. "We need to check to see if all are safe. Have Brett and Samuel do that. Have Dutch join us. We've got to find Will Rexford and the last two of The Brothers."

"Close call is right. I see the old girl is testing you again. Take care. Don't assume anything," Esaugetuh said, joining them.

"I know, change my perspective and that will change my perception," Adam said, smiling at his father. "Join us in our search."

"No, it's best I look to our people who have come to help you. It's fitting that I do this," Esaugetuh said.

"Why more so than it is for me to do it? Actually, is it not my place to do so?" Adam said.

"No, you are a warrior. They will find shame if you were to do a woman's work," Esaugetuh said.

"And there is no shame if you do what you call a *woman's work*?" Adam said.

"It's acceptable for an old man to do such things."

"Father, *you* will join Running-water and me. At no time are we to be separated," Adam said.

Placing his hand on his father's heart, looking into his azure blue eyes, Adam allowed his father to see his personal sadness. The Old One shuddered as he felt the terrible heaviness consuming his son. He agreed to join the search.

The whole encampment was now fully aroused. And upon an unseen signal, the drumming began. This time it was slow, evenly paced, strong in resonance and vibrancy. The drummers were changing the harmonics of the place. Isha, Daphne, and Cornelia Dakota came out to minister to those in the camps. Julie and Patricia became baby sitters. Dutch, fully armed, joined the searchers.

Since the main compound had been made into a Medicine Wheel by the electronic surveillance equipment set up by Phillip, Adam, using the monastery as the hub of the wheel made a natural division along those lines. The search would be more thorough and quicker. Running-water, using his high beam spotlight, soon spotted a heap on the ground. Using the walkie-talkie, he called Adam.

Will Rexford had been found. He was barely alive. Adam placed an oxygen mask over Will's face, turned on the portable oxygen tank one-quarter turn, and then he began to push up and down with the flat of his hands on Will's chest. Unlike the standard CPR, his thrusts were rapid and nonstop.

Will opened his eyes, tried to sit up, but could not. He felt a terrible weight holding him down. He began to cough, gasping for the breath of life. Adam quickly removed the mask, put his arms behind Will's back, and pulled him forward until he was leaning over his shoulder. He thumped him on the back as if he were a baby being burped. The coughing and wheezing spasm stopped. Color returned to his face.

"You've got some serious explaining to do," Adam said.

"How do we know he's really Will Rexford?" Running-water said.

"Easy. Pull his pants down," Dutch said, approaching them.

"What?" Adam said.

"Pull his damn pants off. I'll know if he's the real Will Rexford or not," Dutch said.

Under much protest, they finally got Will's pants off. Lashing out at Dutch and cussing up a storm he said, "I won't forget this, you son-of-a-bitch!"

Unabashed by Will's threats, Dutch, pulled out a knife and with a flick of his wrist, cut Will's shorts up one side, flipped it over, exposing Will's penis.

"Turn the light on him so I can see," Dutch said.

"Yeah, this is the real Will Rexford. No question about it. You can turn off that light now," Dutch said.

"And just how has this proven who this guy is?" Running-water said.

"Simple. Will Rexford had the number nine tattooed on his prick," Dutch said.

"Care to explain?" Esaugetuh said.

"Sure. I was with Will when he had that damn hang-down thing of his tattooed. We were both drunk."

"And where did all of this take place?" Running-water said, still suspicious.

"Can't tell you that. Sorry," Dutch said.

At that point, Will managed to stand up, pulled his pants back up, and still angry said, "I'm gonna fix your wagon but good, just wait."

"Just knock it off. I don't want any more of this crap out of either one of you. It stops here. Now! Why did you steal Patricia Livingston's camera?" Adam said.

"She photographed me. She's an international news reporter celebrity. I couldn't have my picture spread halfway around the world. It would compromise too much," Will said.

"If that's true, why didn't you just ask her for the tape?" Running-water said.

"She would not have let me erase it."

"Where are the camera and film now?" Adam said.

"In the basement of the monastery. I was using one of the computers down there to wipe out photos of me. Nothing more," Will said.

"Okay let's assume you're telling the truth for the moment. Explain why you are out here." Running-water said.

"I thought I heard someone yell for help. That's the truth. And here we are. That's all I remember," Will said.

"Okay. We still need to find Phillip and Paul," Adam said. "And, Will, you still have much to prove before you are off the hook."

Running-water's lawyer's mind always zeroed in on issues that didn't seem to hang together. Adam had tuned into those suspicions. He, like Running-water, wondered how Will knew there were computers in the secure room in the basement. More importantly, how did he know where it was and how to access it? From there it would have been impossible to hear anyone call for help unless he had activated the interior communication system. If he had done that, then he would have known in advance that they were out looking for him. He decided to keep this to himself for the time being. Wait and watch.

And learn.

Eavesdropping again, are you, my brother? It is good that we move cautiously with Will Rexford, Adam replied telepathically.

Within a short distance from the back of the monastery, they found their answer to the whereabouts of Phillip and Paul. Phillip was found first and a few feet from him lay Paul. Both dead. Adam was about to attribute their deaths to the methane, but while taking a closer look, he found each with a small hole behind the right ear.

Sending a mind-message to Running-water, Adam said, *Look at this? We have seen this before, you and I. What do you make of this?*

Bending down to get a closer look, Running-water nodded his head. He had seen this before. The two men in the car outside Marie Copa's apartment in Arizona, and on the two men who had nearly beaten Running-water to death. They were found dead in the Pennsylvania jail. All had a small hole behind the right ear.

"Looks like you've got an invisible protector," Esaugetuh said.

"What do you mean?" Will Rexford said.

"The methane didn't kill these two. They were killed by someone or something," Adam said.

"I don't understand. How can you say that they were killed?" Will said.

"There's a small hole behind each man's right ear," Running-water said.

Will Rexford knelt down and looked first at Phillip and then at Paul. There were no traces of blood, no blood on the ground, and the wounds were not jagged. The wounds were the size and shape of a hole created by a small hand-held paper punch. Even with his experience in the jungles of South America and his time along the Amazon River, Will had never seen anything like this. If an Amazonian blowgun had been used there should have been a small prick and the dart would have remained. Even if such a dart had been removed by the killer, there would have been a small amount of blood at the point of impact.

"Man, I'm telling you now, I've never seen anything like this. Never! How about you, Dutch? You ever see anything like this?" Will said.

After taking a closer look, Dutch stood up, shook his head and said, "Damndest thing I've ever seen. Sure is a puzzle as to why there's no blood. Wish I had a blue light and some luminal."

"What for?" Adam said.

"Blood would show up."

"There is an ancient weapon used by some shaman in South America to execute those who failed to make payment for their favors. Certain Voodoo practitioners use the same thing in some of the islands," Esaugetuh said.

Adam looked at this father, indicated that he should mind-talk. But the Old One ignoring that said, "It's alright, Adam. Notify the local authorities. It would be prudent not to bring up the nature of the wounds. If the coroner is busy he may not notice those marks especially if you indicate the methane gas problem. He'll go for the lungs."

"You sure about all this?" Running-water said.

"Yes. More so than you when you recommended Dutch and Brett to Adam. You never checked on their references. And when Dutch brought Will on board, you never checked on his background," Esaugetuh said.

Adam caught the twinkle in his father's eyes. He used to do that when he was pleased with a little trap he had set during one of their many earlier conversations. Esaugetuh noticed the bemused smile on his son's lips.

"What? Well, I—my uncle made the suggestion. Why should I question him?" Running-water said.

"You should always check your sources. Gordon surely expected you to do that," Esaugetuh said.

Catching on, Running-water said, "So you are the source. Hold on. How do you know my Uncle Gordon?"

"Simple. He's been my attorney for a number of years," Esaugetuh said, laughing.

"I'll be damned," Running-water said.

"Leave all of this for the local authorities. Call them and simply tell them you found two dead men," Adam said. "We've got other issues."

As they hurried along the narrow winding path back to the monastery a flash of lightning scored the darkening sky. For a brief moment, Adam was sure he had seen that all too familiar green that indicates the vile energy surrounding Moon-Woman. A second burst of lightening plummeting downward stopped in midair, spiraled, and then making a ninety-degree turn, shot back up into the night sky. The challenge had been made. Time was running out. Adam felt Moon-Woman knew his plans and a new urgency spread its pangs over him.

Reaching the entryway to the monastery, Adam and Esaugetuh turned and looked back. A massive black cloud was building, blocking out the stars. Another flash showed the fast developing energy charge that Moon-Woman was building.

Inside, Adam ordered everyone to a safe room, ordered them to stay put until he told them they could come out. Daphne with the help of her mother, Cornelia, grabbed the quads and rushed to the first floor safe room. They were followed by Isha with her twins, Julie, Lilli, and Stephanie. One from the household slipped out unseen through another door.

Adam ushered his father, Running-water, and Samuel into another of the safe rooms in the basement. It had been reinforced to make it impervious to electromagnetic energy blasts. He had them sit in a semicircle in front of him, each holding a hand of the other. Adam began to hum, and as he increased the pitch he changed into a pale blue aura, making him nearly transparent.

Esaugetuh was in awe of his son's powers, a proud father, yet fearful for his son's safety. He remembered the time when he first saw his—,"

The humming stopped.

"Please, father, empty your mind of past memories. We haven't much time," Adam said.

"I'm sorry. Can you begin again?"

Adam nodded, smiled briefly at his father, and began to hum again. This time he held the pitch a bit lower, holding it there allowing it its own life. It grew until it shattered a light bulb. The subliminal trigger had been planted. The meld had taken. The three men felt their bodies vibrate and then a wonderful peaceful sleep enveloped them. They remained that way for several minutes. When they opened their eyes, Adam was gone.

Running-water bolted for the door, flung it open, and raced to an elevator. After reaching the first floor, he ran into the living room. Adam was not there. His heart was pounding as a realization struck him.

"My god! He's given himself so that the rest of us may live," Running-water said aloud.

"No, my brother, I am here and very much among the living. Are you ready to face the she-devil?"

Adam walked in. He was magnificently dressed in traditional Indian regalia. White leather britches and moccasins. An open white leather vest, revealing his naked broad chest, was decorated in silver eagles on each side with beads of porcupine quills hanging down from each. Around his neck hung the Wisdom Keeper's obsidian amulet. Its glow was brighter than usual. Esaugetuh's Nimapan on its leather string and sculptured gold eagle with a diamond for its eye completed his neck adornments. The eagle seemed to wink at the obsidian some secret communication. And in keeping with warrior ways, Adam's hair hung loose and tumbled down to his broad shoulders. A white headdress made of white plumes bound in white horsehair adorned his head. Each side was jeweled with rosettes with golden eagles in their centers. Hanging down from these were thin strips of white rabbit fur.

"I want to dress. Give me a few minutes," Running-water said.

"And I will do the same," Esaugetuh said, entering the room with Samuel.

"What about me? I'm not an Indian. What should I wear?" Samuel said.

"You are as you are, my friend. Remember you are the bait. I'll tell you what you are to do as soon as we are in position," Adam said.

Within a few minutes, Running-water returned. He was dressed in full Indian regalia. His tan leather britches and matching open vest with the head of a cougar burned into it. His tight britches hung low, showing a thin line of black hair cropping up from their top to the middle of his bare chest. His moccasins, also of tan leather, were decorated with a strand of red beads across their tops. His headdress was an undecorated band of tan leather with two feathers in the back. These were pointed downward. Around his neck, he wore a cougar's tooth strung on a gold chain. His blue-black hair spilled over onto his broad shoulders.

When Esaugetuh stepped into the room, Running-water and Adam were amazed at the transformation. His white leather britches and matching shirt fit snug enough to outline a body that was still muscular, lean, yet somewhat bent with age, nevertheless, one that was to be admired. Esaugetuh stood tall, elegantly sophisticated with his full headdress. It was made of a black beaded headband containing geometric designs, long white feathers, blackened in the middle and ending with white tips fanned out from the band. Hanging down each side were strips of white and black rabbit fur held in place by silver rosettes. Fringe played along the sleeves of his shirt. A belt of Miigis shells and lapis lazuli hung around his waist. An amulet made of a single bear claw hung around his neck. His long white hair flowed over his shoulders that were not quite as straight as they once were. He was still the grand old man. Using his cane he steadied his walk.

The four of them left the monastery and went to the center of the compound. There Adam placed a blanket upon the ground and asked Samuel to sit on it. A small prayer bundle containing Miigis shells, an eagle's talon, and a pinch of tobacco were placed at Samuel's feet. Adam and his two companions stepped back a few feet behind some statuary to wait. Someone began the tong-tong beat of the drums. Slowly the crescendo increased. A fire was lit and once again the dancers took up their positions. An outer and inner circle was formed and the dancers moved in perfect step with the rhythm of the tong-tong beat. The familiar chant in a rondo met the vibrations of the drum. Then the inner circle of dancers changed directions, going counter-clockwise. If you looked down upon the dancers you could see a vortex forming. And that was the view seen by the unseen seeing eyes.

Rumbling in the dark clouds increased. Adam noted they took less time to be heard and that meant the Ifrit [4] was well on its way. The chthonic powers were fierce as the clouds churned and swirled into an ever more fearsome size. The mountain top monastery was encased in an Ectoplasmic mist of such proportions that nothing could be seen for miles. It was so huge it spilled over into Canada and covered parts of Idaho and Montana. Fortunately, most people were unaware of the approaching monster, asleep in their false security.

Lightning strikes, random at first, intensified in locations as the demon searched for its target. To counterbalance these strikes, the firekeepers piled more wood on their fire, heating the heavy air, forcing it upward. The security system set up by Phillip and Paul was humming. The clouds split apart and reformed into a hideous face with blood red eyes and gaping mouth. Angry at the audacity of these puny humans, she came closer, swung low over the fire scattering sparks on to the dancers. But this did not stop them. They had come to dance her death and they would continue until the last of them were dead.

It was during the low sweep that she spotted Samuel, a beacon directing her in. As she approached him, the firekeepers doused the remaining burning embers with gasoline and it exploded high into the air. It was just enough of a distraction. Adam spoke the trigger word and Samuel began to speak to her.

"Look at you. A nightmare created by your own hatred—a pitiful wreck who has forgotten the wisdom of your own soul—forgotten why your soul was sent into this world; forgotten the very essence of your soul, the purpose of your soul. And because you have, you have lost yourself. I give you my pity! What a shame you never took the time to accept the love of your nephew and niece. Never to know the joy of holding them in your arms, looking into their adoring eyes, and hearing them call your name. Pity on you that you have not known your great-nephews and the love they could give you. You have lost so much just because you chose to wallow in self-pity, degrading and vile. Shame is yours for not accepting the love of others. You have missed a world."

The she-devil gathered herself up in such a rage that the sky seemed to catch fire. Hissing at him she said, "How dare you? You worm! You will pay!"

Samuel was sure he was about to die. As she swooped down to destroy him, a huge burst of gunfire shattered the night. Dutch and Brett had set the Gatling guns going. Their special shells, exploding in the air, filling her with radiating energy. Round after round was fired until all the shells had been spent. The sky glowed with a chatoyant sheet. Quiet reigned.

The sky seemed to come apart, unfurling as Moon-Woman came back even more powerful. Her descent to the compound was fierce, unrelenting as she unleashed strike after strike of violent lightning. One burst knocked Samuel unconscious and cat-like she circled her prey, savoring the moment of play before she sucked out his soul. As she closed in for the kill, Adam's voice thundered in her ears sending her reeling. Gaining her composure, she screamed at Adam.

"Come out! You are nothing but a son of a worthless dog."

"I am here. Give up your hate. Free yourself," Adam said, looming gigantic in front of her.

"You think your little illusion is going to fool me. You are indeed stupid. Come out so I can destroy you. Why prolong the inevitable? You are really very foolish. Did you think those silly mosquito pellets you fired at me would harm me? All they did was to increase my energy, giving me more power with which to destroy you."

"No, old hag. You are the one who is finished. You are so unworthy you could not conceive a child of your own. You are no threat to us," Esaugetuh said.

"Ah ha, the Old One himself. Well, well. I wondered where you were. Think you're clever, do you? I'll show you clever," Moon-Woman screamed.

"How can nothing do anything? And you are nothing. You were allowed to live the last time around. This time you will not be so lucky," Running-water said, stepping into the glow of the fire.

"Ha! Now I've got the three of you and will dispense with you at the same time. Such pleasure." Drool seeped from her gaping mouth.

In a terrible rage, she flung herself at Adam. He shot out the palm of his right hand, drew a circle in the night air, engulfing both of them in a blue sphere. For a brief moment, the circle encompassed her; she stopped but only for the moment, and then lunged at him with greater force, shattering the sphere and sending green lightning across the sky.

Knocking him to the ground, Moon-Woman screamed, "I'm going to rip your heart out, squeeze it like a sponge letting its blood drip slowly as you watch your life end."

She had him, sinking her fingers deep into his chest, ready to deal the death blow as Adam struggled to free himself from her strangling grip. Running-water dove into her massive shapeless body. She screamed in agony as he ripped into her with his bare hands, tearing at her every way, kicking and clawing at her, and like his alter self, the cougar, he looked to rip her jugular vein. With a backhand, she slapped him to the ground while still clutching onto Adam.

Desperate now, Adam summoned all his strength to free himself, but it was already too late. He felt his strength ebb. It was then that Esaugetuh jumped in to try and save his son. He emptied the contents of his medicine bag, flung it into her hideous face. It burned deep, eating away at her. Writhing in agony, she still held her grip on Adam.

"Use the obsidian. Stuff it in her mouth," Esaugetuh yelled.

With frantic effort, Adam grabbed the obsidian amulet hanging around his neck. With a jerk, it came loose and he flung it into her drooling mouth. A horrific scream filled the air. The sky caught fire and the clouds rolled into a funnel, shot straight up, and filled the void it left with stinging ozone. It turned and plunged back toward the battling men. A flaming golden arrow shot out of the darkness, found its mark. The funnel shrank to a mere speck and then it was gone. And from somewhere, and at the same time everywhere, they heard, "There! Take that!"

All was quiet. No bird, no animal, no tree, not even the wind made a sound. The Master of Breath, the great Esaugetuh, bent over his wounded son. Tears splashed down his weathered face. In quiet desperation, he laid his head down on Adam's bare chest and sobbed.

"I am that I am," Adam said, stroking his father's head.

Running-water staggered to his feet and yelled, "Yes!

Helping Adam up, Esaugetuh saw the marks of clinched fingers over his son's heart. Gently he touched the spot with the palm of his and, the ugly mark faded. But in his soul, Esaugetuh knew this was not really the end of it.

Elated over their survival, Running-water said, "This calls for a celebration. It's time for a pow-wow."

In agreement with that suggestion, the sun spread his morning call across the once dark ominous sky, breaking it into a multicolored splendor for all those who had gathered. It was an eternal promise of a new beginning—a genesis. And not to be outdone by those around them, the birds began a chorus of praise lifting their voices to the heavens; those that heard were filled with joy.

Some, however, did not hear this melody of life. They were too busy. Two of these, both furtive, watched from their hiding place as another figure shimmied down a large tree from where it had been perched, witness to all that had transpired. The eyes that saw all had been seen and two wondered what she wanted. Her presence made them nervous. They wondered if she should be allowed to exist. They would wait.

Realizing the drums had stopped, she with the eyes that saw all stopped all movement. The songbirds quieted. And those who had gathered moved toward the three warriors, and like small school children, sat down in front of them, trying to get closer, anxiously waiting to hear the story that had to be told. They tried to be patient, something she had learned how to be years ago. Her eyes followed them as they seated themselves. She looked at Adam. Wan as he was, he was still spectacular. Like those who watched her, she watched for further signs of the toll the terrible struggle had taken. She noticed he seemed to be preoccupied. His protector was as cocky as ever, and the Old One seemed years younger. She shook her head in disbelief giving her trained eyes time to refocus. He was indeed younger.

While the crowd watched Adam, he felt a new surge of energy coming from his sons and from the sons of Running-water. He listened and waited. Some in the crowd coughed, others stood up and sat back down again. Then they had their answer. The door of the old monastery flew open and four women came running down the steps of the portico. Daphne reached her husband before the others and jumped into his arms. She wanted him to feel the love she had for him. He returned her kiss, held it, and released her as their sons were brought to them by Cornelia. Isha, with their twins, was in Running-waters' arms, secure in the knowledge of their union. Julie sought her husband, but he was not there. Panic seized her. She began calling his name as she ran along the narrow path leading from the house.

She heard voices. Recognizing Dutch and Will's voices. She ran to them, hoping to find Samuel with them. He was. They were totally immersed in their examination of part of the warning system installed by Phillip and Paul.

"I've been looking everywhere for you, Samuel. You've had me worried sick," Julie said, wiping back tears of happiness and anger. "You could have let me know you were okay."

"I didn't mean to cause you to worry. I'm sorry about that, but I had another concern. It appears that the system installed by Phillip and Paul was actually a honing device to ensure Moon-Woman would home in on Adam," Samuel said.

"Oh, lord. Have you let Adam know?" Julie said, taking her husband by the hand.

"We will," Dutch said. "Have you seen my ex-wife and daughter?"

"No. I don't think they came out of the shelter," Julie said.

"We need to go back to the monastery. The sheriff should be arriving anytime. Two deputies are on their way up from the village," Dutch said.

As they approached the front of the monastery they heard Adam speaking to the gathered crowd.

"Some may view today as a victory. Any death is a time for mourning. The devil-woman was the aunt of my very best friend and soul brother Running-water, and his sister, my wife, Daphne. Bitterness can destroy a person, festering until it eats away at the normal compassionate soul—the soul given to us upon our conception. I ask each of you to join us as we remember the sorrow of a lost one. My father, Esaugetuh, Master of Breath, will begin the ceremony of the pipe."

In spite of the solemnity of Adam's words, the mass of seated people cheered. One from those seated rose up. Even though it was painful for her she managed to steady herself. With august authority she stretched out her arm, moving her hand across the crowd. It stilled itself. Those close in recognized the elderly figure as Matron Sun Bearer of the Sioux. Her silvered hair reflected the firelight as she slowly turned toward the standing Adam, Running-water, and Esaugetuh. As becoming his position, she spoke first to the elder shaman.

"Shaman," she paused, "There needs to be a cleansing. Especially the three of you," she said, nodding toward Adam and Running-water. "The evil taint must be removed."

Matron Sun Bearer looked out over the crowd. It would be a difficult task—cleansing everyone. Yet she knew, no matter how difficult, it had to be done. With a labored sigh, she agreed to help. They would cleanse themselves. Many of the younger members of the tribes weren't sure what was going to take place. They had done the sweat lodge gig; even though it was cool especially when Adam had become nearly transparent. If you asked them what they had just witnessed they wouldn't know. "No regard for the traditions," she thought shaking her head. "Children are no longer taught the prayers; no longer taught to believe. Just look at the hoopla that goes on in this country over the mention of Christmas in public. Heaven forbid if one should say Merry Christmas! Or show a Christian display in a public building. Wonder what would happen if people realized the Christmas Tree was really a pagan symbol? Even though the young shaman may be right that we can't live as we used to, but somewhere there ought to be a place for tradition. Maybe, just maybe the old witch did us a favor. Tradition lives!"

The elder and the old shaman spent the day tying bunches of sage, lavender, and juniper into smudge sticks. Once everyone's clothes were burned, the bundles of herbs would be lighted and their smoke wafted over each person's body. After that, they would scrub themselves with sweet bayberry oil.

Once the bundles were distributed, Adam was the first to strip down and throw his clothes into the still smoldering fire. Flames shot up; their light bounced off his broad chest highlighting his muscled arms. Next Running-water stripped down. He was followed by the women: Isha, Daphne, Cornelia, Patricia Livingston, and Julie. No one looked at them. They were too busy removing their own clothing. As Samuel dropped his shorts, Julie stole a quick look at him. A sensual smile spread across her heavily painted lips. Dutch and Brett were the last of the household to strip; both sputtering in protest.

Hundreds of smudge sticks were lighted and their smoke-smudged over the eager participants. The wash down, including private body parts, created a good deal of grumbling by some of the pubescent who were still shy about their anatomy. Some would have assumed an orgy was about to take place, however the set of unseen eyes knew better. They focused on the Matron as she slowly moved from group to group, making sure that everyone cleansed themselves. Satisfied, Matron Sun Bearer edged her way to Adam. Her whole body ached. "Ikaee Wicasa," she said using Adam's Sioux name, "You must place anise leaves in every room of your house. They will drive off any remaining evil."

"Isna-la-wica has said, 'I have seen that in any great undertaking it is not enough for a man to depend simply upon himself,'" [5] Adam replied. "I thank you and everyone else here for the unselfish help they have given." In keeping with the ancient tradition of not mentioning the deceased name, Adam referred to Moon-Woman as the djinni. "The djinni was a nightmare created by the self-debasing desire for self-suffering. May the gods take pity on her lost soul!" With that, Adam threw her dress and shoes into the fire.

While Esaugetuh prepared for the ceremony of the pipe, Samuel spoke to Adam of his suspicions that the system Phillip and Paul had installed. Interrupting them, Dutch asked if they had seen Lilli and Stephanie. They had not. Dutch excused himself to go in search of his ex-wife and daughter. Brett, now dressed in fresh clothes and packing side arms joined Adam and Samuel, asking about Patricia Livingston. He had barely spoken her name when she walked up.

"Wondered where you got off to," Brett said handing her a blanket.

"I always follow the rule, 'a girl's gotta do what a girl's gotta do,'" Patricia said, giving her husband a kiss on the cheek. She didn't resist his hands brushing across her breasts. Turning to Adam she continued, "That was one hell of a battle. Many stories will be told of this night and day. A new tradition has been established, a new legend. Here, this is for you. I got the whole thing on tape. It's spectacular. Maybe someday you'll let me have it back. Maybe, I'll write a book about it."

"You took an awful chance, but I thank you and *you will* get your tape back, unaltered," Adam said.

"By the way, Adam, I picked up a couple of lurking shadows several times. Their images may be on the tape. I think they spotted me at least once. Maybe you had better look into it," Patricia Livingston said, as Esaugetuh approached with a ceremonial pipe.

Esaugetuh held up the pipe for all to see. He raised it to each of the Four Directions. After he had taken a drag, Esaugetuh passed it to his son, and he, in turn, passed it to Running-water, and so it went to each in his turn. From the inner circle, the pipe was refilled. The aroma of red will bark filled the air.

"There is one here who has proven himself a great fearless warrior, a man of exceptional courage. To him, I offer the pipe," Adam said, passing the pipe to Samuel.

The crowd applauded its approval. Samuel's eyes watered as he took the pipe. When he had taken a hit and slowly exhaled it, he sent it out to those gathered.

Running-water's edginess increased when he realized that Will Rexford was not among the group. He couldn't rid himself of the nagging question about who Will Rexford was. He sent a telepathic message to Adam that he was going to go look for him.

"I'll go with you," Samuel said, surprising Running-water with his increased telepathic abilities.

"Wait a minute and I'll go with you," Adam said. "I want to tell everyone that there will be a pow-wow of thanksgiving."

The large crowd gave a roar of approval when they heard the news. People immediately got up and left to prepare the vast amounts of food needed to feed the crowd. The huge kitchen in the monastery would be given a good work out. Roasting pits were dug and filled with various meats. A new spiritual fire was built and blessed by the tribal chieftains. Great care was taken to include just the right amount of sage, lemon and sweet grass, and tobacco. Adam asked that it be maintained for seven days and seven nights. The drums began again, a faster pace this time, and dancers formed a single line, moving through the crowd, snaking their way around the spiritual fire pit, inviting those who wished, to join in the long dancing line. Joy filled their hearts. But not everyone's heart celebrated.

Inside Dutch and Will were seated in front of the massive fireplace in the great room. A rain cloud hung over them, dark and gloomy. Neither spoke as Adam and Running-water entered the room. Lilli and her daughter, Stephanie stood at the other end of the room, detached and emoting sullenness. Everyone was in a pout. Adam, standing with his back to the fire, faced the two men and waited.

"It didn't work out, Adam. Thanks for trying," Dutch said. "I guess it's about time I shoved off. Miles to go, roads to travel as they say."

"Me too. I've been given a new assignment," Will Rexford said.

"That's not true! You should have learned by now that one lie always leads to another," Esaugetuh said. "Tell Adam who you really are."

"I don't see what difference that will make. Lilli's not interested," Dutch said.

"I'm Lilli's brother. She blames me. Not that I shouldn't be. No need to take it out on Dutch," Will Rexford said.

"And since this discussion involves you and your daughter, Mrs. Masters, would you join us?" Esaugetuh said. "Perhaps there is some truth you'd care to share?"

"Well, Old One, I see you know something I don't," Adam said, smiling at his father.

"Yes, but I would prefer those involved come clean."

Joining the group in front of the fireplace, Lilli said, "Oh, all right! It won't make any difference anyway. Dutch is not Stephanie's father. I've wrestled with this long enough. It was easy to marry a drunken sailor. We stood up in front of a fake preacher. You know the street corner kind. I never dreamed he'd really take it all serious. I needed an excuse for my pregnancy and he was it. My kid needed a last name."

"I guess you didn't realize that in the state of Nevada, those 'street preachers' as you called them, are licensed. You and Dutch are legally married," Running-water said, joining the discussion for the first time.

"No. You're just saying that. I don't love Dutch, never have. He might be a nice man for all I know, but I'm not in love with him," Lilli said.

"And this business of Dutch and Will getting it on was just the excuse you needed to split," Running-water said.

"Jesus! You used me, totally. You are a real piece of work," Dutch said.

"Well, you got what you wanted. So, who's using who?" Lilli said.

"I have a question for you, Dutch," Adam said.

"Shoot."

"You no longer want to work for me? Too dangerous?" Adam said.

"Hell no! I'm used to danger. I just thought—,"

"That since Brett has married leaving you the only unmarried one in the group, you'd be better off moving on. That's kind of dumb reasoning if you ask me," Esaugetuh said.

"I'd like you to stay on as my pilot," Adam said. "You and Brett make a good team. I don't see any reason to break that up."

"Yeah, man. I don't want to break in a new pilot. It was tough enough with you," Brett said, laughing.

"It's settled then. You will stay. Lilli, please accept my best wishes for you and Stephanie. Since you never thought you were really married and only pretended to get a divorce, you now need to do that. Samuel will drive you back into the city. You can hitch a ride with them Will, if you're ready to leave," Adam said. "Now if you will excuse me, I need to go and mingle with our guests."

Preparations were in full swing for the pow-wow. As soon as the food was brought out, the chatter quieted down. Entertainment went on the rest of the night. Finally, the last retired, security was checked and Adam and Daphne returned to the house. She excused herself to check on her children.

"Can we talk, my brother?" Running-water said.

"Of course. Can you explain the slip up with Will Rexford? I would have thought Brett would have been in all of this other business. But he seemed surprised, almost hurt having been left out," Adam said.

"Sometimes close friends, really close friends, keep some things to themselves," Running-water said.

"I don't understand," Adam said.

"Well, Dutch, Brett, Daphne, nor Isha know about you riding around with me in your underwear, checking into a motel together. Some things are just not said."

"Hmm. Guess you're right about that," Adam said, giving Running-water an affectionate slap on his butt. "Looks like a new beginning, wouldn't you say? Finally, a stay-put place!"

"Yeah, a Genesis alright."

[1] Sanskrit meaning 'becoming'.
[2] Ojibwa Language meaning 'never silent'.
[3] Algonquin Language meaning 'secret'.
[4] A powerful demon; a Jinni; a winged creature that is snake like in appearance.
[5] Lone Man, Teton Sioux. Quoted on
http://www.FirstPeople.US.com

ALSO BY NORMAN W. WILSON

Textbooks

How to Analyze the Short Story with Arthur W. Savage
The Humanities: Contemporary Images
Butterflies and All That Jazz with Drs. James G. Massey and Arthur J. Powell
Windows and Images: An Introduction to the Humanities with Drs. James G. Massey and Arthur J. Powell
How to Make Moral and Ethical Decisions A Guide

Novels

The Shaman's Quest
The Shaman's Transformation
The Shaman's War

Nonfiction

Shamanism What It's All About
DUH! The American Educational Disaster
So You THINK You Want to be A Buddhist?
Promethean Necessity & Its Implications for Humanity
Activating Your Spirit Guides
Shamanic Manifesting
The Shaman's Journey through Poetry with Gavriel Navarro.
Healing The Shaman's Way
How to GET What You Really WANT
Reiki The Instructors' Manual
The Sayings of Esaugetuh

www.ingramcontent.com/pod-product-compliance
Lightning Source LLC
Chambersburg PA
CBHW060452090426
42735CB00011B/1969